THE DOCTRINE
OF
REVELATION

EDINBURGH STUDIES IN CONSTRUCTIVE THEOLOGY

FORTHCOMING TITLES IN THE SERIES

The Doctrine of Creation
Colin Gunton

Theism
Philip D. Clayton

Constructive Christology
Alister McGrath

Divine Action and Providence
Kevin J. Vanhoozer

The Holy Spirit
Bruce Marshall

Salvation
Paul Fiddes

The Shape of the Self
John Webster

THE DOCTRINE
OF
REVELATION

A Narrative Interpretation

—⁓⁓ЯЯⓞЯЯ⁓⁓—

GABRIEL FACKRE

WM. B. EERDMANS PUBLISHING COMPANY
GRAND RAPIDS, MICHIGAN

© Gabriel Fackre, 1997

Edinburgh University Press
22 George Square, Edinburgh

Typeset in Bembo
by Pioneer Associates Ltd, Perthshire
Printed and bound in Great Britain

ISBN 0–8028–4336–0

This edition published in the United States of America 1997
through special arrangement with Edinburgh University Press by
Wm. B. Eerdmans Publishing Co.
255 Jefferson Ave. S.E., Grand Rapids, Michigan 49503
All rights reserved

CONTENTS

⸻⸺⸻

COPYRIGHT ACKNOWLEDGEMENTS

The writer, who has made every effort to trace the copyright holders of all material quoted, expresses thanks to the following publishers and authors for permission given to quote passages from their works: *Systematic Theology, Vol. I* by Paul Tillich, Copyright 1951 by The University of Chicago Press. Used by permission; *Church Dogmatics, Vol. IV, Part Three, First Half* by Karl Barth, translated by G. W. Bromiley. Copyright 1961 by T. & T. Clark. Used by permission; *God, Revelation and Authority, Vol. IV* by Carl F. H. Henry. Copyright 1979 by Carl F. H. Henry. Used by permission; *Foundations of Christian Faith: An Introduction to the Idea of Christianity* by Karl Rahner, translated by William V. Dych. North American copyright 1978 by Crossroad Publishing Company and UK/ Commonwealth copyright 1978 by Darton, Longman and Todd. Used by permission; *The Spirit and the Church* by Karl Rahner, translated by W. J. O'Hara. Charles Henkey and Richard Strachan. North American copyright 1979 by Crossroad Publishing Company and UK/Commonwealth copyright 1979 by Search Press, Ltd. Used by permission; *The Acts of God: What Do We Mean by Revelation?* by William Placher. Copyright 1996 by Christian Century Foundation. Reprinted by permission from the March 20–27, 1996 issue of *The Christian Century*; *Revelation and Theology: The Gospel as Narrated Promise* by Ronald Thiemann. Copyright 1985 by University of Notre Dame Press. Used by permission; *The Trinity* by St. Augustine, translated by Stephen McKenna. Copyright 1963 by The Catholic University of America Press. Used by permission; *The City of God* by St. Augustine, translated by Gerald G. Walsh and Grace Manahan. Copyright 1952 by The Catholic University of America Press. Used by permission; *Biblical Interpretation in the Philosophy of Paul Ricoeur: A Study in Hermeneutics and Theology* by Kevin J. Vanhoozer. Copyright 1990 by Cambridge University Press. Used by permission; *The Broken Wall: A Study of the Epistle to the Ephesians* by Markus Barth. Copyright 1959 by Judson Press. Used by permission; *Theories of Revelation* by H. D. McDonald. Copyright 1979 by Baker Book House. Used by permission; *Biblical Theology of the Old and New Testaments* by Brevard S. Childs. Copyright 1992 by Augsburg Fortress. Reprinted by permission; *Scriptural Theology and Narrative Interpretation* edited by Garrett Green. Copyright 1987 by Fortress Press. Used by permission of Augsburg Fortress; *New Horizons in Hermeneutics* by Anthony C. Thiselton. Copyright © 1992 by Anthony C. Thiselton. Used by permission of Zondervan Publishing House; *General Revelation* by Bruce Demarest. Copyright © 1982 by the Zondervan Corporation. Used by permission of Zondervan Publishing House; *Models of Revelation* by Avery Dulles. Copyright 1992 by Orbis Press. Used by permission; *Salvations: Truth and Difference in Religion* by S. Mark Heim. Copyright 1995 by Orbis Press. Used by permission; Thomas Torrance, *Reality and Evangelical Theology*. Copyright 1982 by Thomas Torrance. Used by permission; *The Eclipse of Biblical Narrative* by Hans Frei. Copyright 1974 by Yale University Press. Used by permission; *The Light of the World* by Jaroslav Pelikan. Copyright by Jaroslav Pelikan. Copyright renewed 1990 by Jaroslav Pelikan. Used by permission; *Women–Church: Theology and Practice of Feminist Liturgical Communities* by Rosemary Radford Ruether. Copyright 1985 by Rosemary Radford Ruether. Used by permission; *Christ and Culture* by H. Richard Niebuhr. Copyright 1951 by Harper & Row, Publishers, Inc. Used by permission; *Early Christian Doctrines, Revised Edition* by J. N. D. Kelly. Copyright 1960, 1965, 1968, 1978 by John Norman Davidson Kelly. Copyright renewed. Used by permission; *Divine Revelation and the Limits of Historical Criticism* by William J. Abraham. Copyright 1982 by Oxford University Press. Used by permission of Oxford University Press. *A Handbook of Christian Theologians*, enlarged edition by Dean G. Peerman and Martin E. Marty (eds): Copyright 1984. Abingdon Press. Used by permission.

FOREWORD

—·ᴡᴡᴘᴘᴏᴬᴬᴬᴬᴡᴡ·—

Books in Christian theology today are often either driven by the
ideological market (for example, theologies *of* . . . feminism, liberation,
ecology etc.) or co-opted by a helping discipline (for example, theology *and* . . . literary theory, social theory philosophy etc.). The aim of
the present series, however, is to do theology *as such*. While neither
disparaging engagement with current issues nor abstaining from inter-
disciplinary reflection, each volume in this series begins with confidence
in the continuing relevance of Scripture and Christian tradition for
today.

The volumes in this series provide more than methodological
studies or descriptions of religious belief, more than reminders of the
problems facing theology or of the inevitability of negative theology.
They aim to demonstrate the possibility of a genuinely constructive
theology in what has increasingly become a deconstructive situation.
To be constructive, theology must be *done*. Throughout, the goal has
been to look in the first place to the transformative resources inherent
in the Christian tradition itself. The underlying conviction of the series
is that the central tenets of the Christian faith, far from being exhausted,
are as relevant as ever.

Doctrinal provincialism has often been the bane of theology, and
the current theological landscape remains polarised. The volumes in
this series display a scholarly concern with the basic truth-claims of
the Christian faith, though not in a doctrinaire or narrowly dogmatic

fashion. Rather than staking out yet another position to be defended against its competitors, each study searches out, in the first instance, as much common ground as possible between various positions on the basis of a charitable reading of the classical works of the theological tradition – Orthodox, Roman Catholic and Protestant. These studies are primarily *creedalist* rather than confessionalist.

Each volume is constructive, and this in several senses. (1) Each study *surveys* the past history and the present condition of a particular doctrine, in particular the critical problems and possibilities to which modernity and postmodernity have given rise. (2) Each study is guided by and *builds on* the past, mining the tradition for its liberating potential. (3) Each study *reconstructs* Christian doctrine in a creative appropriation of the biblical text and church tradition in the light of the contemporary situation. Authors do not simply describe but further develop the tradition. Special attention is given to the contemporary context and to challenges which provide the backdrop for each book in the series. This reconstructive task also includes questions of theological method; an author's implicit metaphysical and epistemological positions are not assumed, but explained. (4) Each study seeks to *fit together or configure* the relevant parts of the Christian Scriptures (for example, symbols, metaphors, narrative, teaching) into a meaningful whole. Authors are sensitive to the ways in which the Bible's diverse literary forms and contexts contribute to and shape its theological content. (5) Each study shows how its specific doctrine *reinforces the overall structure* of Christian theology and displays the systematic nature of Christian doctrine. What would be lost without a particular doctrine? This emphasis on systematicity reveals whether a given doctrine is only ornamental or whether it is essential to the structural integrity of the whole. 'Constructive' here means presenting a doctrine in its coherence with other central Christian beliefs. (6) Each study tries to be *relevant*, suggesting connections with current concerns and consequences for present faith and life. One of theology's functions is to educate; another is to solve real problems. The volumes in this series advance understanding not only for the sake of satisfying intellectual curiosity, but also in order to provide concrete directions for thought and action. The authors indicate what ethical and socio-political commitments follow from their doctrinal reconstructions.

Philip D. Clayton and Kevin J. Vanhoozer

ACKNOWLEDGEMENTS

This book has been long aborning. It was originally planned as the third volume of my multi-volume systematics, *The Christian Story*. The invitation by co-editors Clayton and Vanhoozer to write on the subject for the important *Constructive Theology* series, however, took clear precedence. It meant that the years of research already invested in the inquiry could now be directed instead towards this volume. Long subsequent work on it and the valuable feedback of the co-editors have deepened and reshaped my initial purposes.

Class settings at Andover Newton and in the Boston College-Andover Newton joint doctoral programme have been important testing grounds for many drafts of the chapters on Barth, Tillich, Rahner and Henry. I am very grateful to students in the 1986–95 seminars on revelation for their probing comments. These materials were also developed and refined in the Kaye lectures at Vancouver School of Theology, the Scott lectures at Brite Divinity School, Texas Christian University, the Day-Higgenbottom lectures at Southwestern Baptist Seminary, the Osterhaven lectures at Western Theological Seminary, the Staley lectures at Catawba College, a presentation at the conference on 'Christian Theology in a Post-Christian World' at Wheaton College, Illinois and a paper at the first 'Christian Theology and the Bible Consultation' of the North American Society of Biblical Literature.

The sections on the grand figures of the twentieth century were also scrutinised by those familiar with their thought. James Luther

ACKNOWLEDGEMENTS

Adams, Tillich translator and specialist and my University of Chicago teacher, read key portions of that chapter, as did colleague Max Stackhouse and friend George Tavard. Carl Henry reviewed in an earlier form the material here on Carl Henry, as did biblical scholar Willis Elliott. In Boston, no-one knows the theology of Karl Barth better than Pastor Joseph Bassett, who conducts yearly seminars on Barth. He reviewed with a critical eye my chapter on Barth.

Ideas for this book have gone through the fires of 'Theological Tabletalk', a group of Boston-area pastors, teachers and graduate students that has met weekly for twenty-five years, reading major works of many of the figures cited here. A co-founder of that group, my former pastor Herbert Davis, has been a constant and valued interlocutor. Theological colleagues in the the American Theological Society, the Boston Theological Society and Andover Newton Theological School have had their impact on my understanding of revelation, especially so Avery Dulles, Mark Heim, George Peck and Robert Daly. Ecclesial testing grounds for these theses have been the 'centrist' theological renewal movements and ecumenical ventures in which I have been involved over the past decade, especially colleagues Frederick Trost, Llewellyn Smith, Richard Floyd, Kathryn Greene-McCreight, Joseph Burgess and Diane Kessler.

Labouring long and hard with a barely legible text, Sheila Lloyd, our Andover Newton faculty secretary, brought order to its form and efficiency to its production.

Closest to home and, humanly speaking, most formative of my thinking is the theological companionship of my spouse, Dorothy. The books we have written together, the daily colleagueship and conversation on both ultimate and penultimate matters and the disciplines of daily prayer make this work and all my writing and teaching a joint ministry.

Gabriel Fackre
Easter 1996

Introduction

MODELS OF REVELATION: A NARRATIVE INTERPRETATION

—∿∿∿ℝℝℚ∿∿∿—

The christological controversies of the early centuries, the split between the Churches of East and West, the struggles of the Reformation, today's divisions among orthodox, modern and postmodern, experiential and evangelical, retrievalist and revisionist, are inescapably linked to the question of *revelation*. Avery Dulles goes even further:

> The great theological disputes turn out, upon reflection, to *rest* on different understandings of revelation, often simply taken for granted.[1]

This work is a search for those underlying 'understandings of revelation'. And more. A proposal is made on how to evaluate and interrelate them.

'Authority . . . inward light, reason, self-evidencing Scripture, or the combination of the four, or some of them, or in what proportion . . . ?' So asks Mark Pattison in his review of disputes on the doctrine of revelation from 1688 to 1750.[2] D. E. Nineham observes that the same partisans appear in the period from 1700 to 1960, as surveyed by H. D. McDonald.[3] *The Doctrine of Revelation: A Narrative Interpretation* turns up similar points of view, and ventures an answer to Pattison's 'which? . . . what?' questions. Along with the reply is a framework for understanding why these four perspectives recur, and why they must

1

be accompanied by a resolute reach beyond to matters of 'combination' and 'proportion'.

The imperial claims of one or another part of the Corinthian church (1 Cor. 12) have their counterparts in the history of Christian theology. The christological controversies of the early centuries are a showcase of the reductionist temptation, with Ebionism, Docetism and their increasingly sophisticated heirs censoring or muting either the human or the divine natures of the Person of Christ. So emerges 'heresy' as a partial truth with inordinate claims. Struggles over the doctrine of revelation have had equivalent tendencies, with one or another 'only this, or mostly this, and no more'. Could it be that, as in the christological debates, each major advocacy is right in what it affirms but wrong in what it denies?

The alternative to partial truth is more than a matter of addition: authority plus inner light plus reason plus Scripture equals . . . revelation. Complex issues of priority and interrelationship are entailed. Indeed, the quadrilateral cited by Pattison itself needs scrutiny. Another way of sorting out the claimants, their limitations and contributions, is here pursued. This other route is the way of *narrative*.

NARRATIVE THEOLOGY

'Narrative' is a recurring subject in the theological conversation of the late twentieth century, with varying understandings of 'narrative theology'.[4] Narrative as a literary form is 'the presence of a story and a storyteller'.[5] That could include history and reportage – a 'news story' – but, as the word functions in most narrative theology, the account defers to the narrator's vision rather than to presumed fact. The narrative pattern, as a recital of happenings with a beginning and an ending, becomes a plot in which characters and events move over time and space through conflict towards resolution. While not precluding 'history', story takes its coherence, meaning and directionality from the storyteller.[6]

Why narrative now? Theories abound. Narrative is more faithful to the engaged, affect-drenched push and pull of human existence than the abstractions and manipulations of the failed culture of technocracy. Narrative reflects the drama of the times, the century of magnified horror and hope. Narrative is an attempt to find coherence in apparent incoherences, personal and social, staying close to the temporal givens rather than choosing flight to the atemporal or irrational.

All of these are considerations in the use of narrative in this work,

2

but not decisively so. Given the 'covenant with Noah' to be discussed, cultural analyses of this sort do have a catalytic role in the formulations of Christian theology, but not a controlling one. The use of narrative is determined, finally, by the shape of faith itself. For one, Scripture is full of narratives, definitively those of Jesus, living, dying, risen. But more than that, the Bible is a book that tells an 'overarching story'.[7] While imaginatively portrayed, it is no fictive account, having to do with turning points that have 'taken place' and will take place, a *news* story traced by canonical hand.[8] Its '*good* news' is about events in meaningful sequence, unrepeatable occasions with a cumulative significance internal to their narration (in contrast to 'myth' that dissolves uniqueness, expressing what is always and everywhere the case).[9] Following this narrative in both form and content, the ecumenical creeds (Apostles and Nicene) growing out of the early baptismal rules of faith bespeak a three-act drama, the 'missions' of the triune God. Historic and contemporary confessional lore, catechesis and liturgy also follow the course of this story/drama. Classical Christian doctrine, while cast in discursive language and set forth in the standard *loci* of systematic theology, may be understood as 'chapters' in the biblical and ecclesial macro-narrative: creation, fall, covenant, Jesus Christ, church, salvation, consummation, with the triune God as prologue and epilogue.[10]

Modernity 'eclipsed' the biblical narrative (Hans Frei),[11] and postmodern premises collide with its assertion of overarching coherences. This work joins a growing company of ecumenical, evangelical, catholic and postliberal voices that are speaking again of the Story, seeing a corona at the very moment of modern and postmodern eclipse.[12] Thus narrative, testimony to the biblical tale of an inextinguishable Light, and in touch with twentieth-century sensibilities, provides here the interpretive framework.[13]

Through the formative work of Hans Frei and George Lindbeck, 'postliberal' understandings have come front and centre in the late twentieth-century theological discussion of narrative. However, the more recent turn to narrative began with a 'story theology' that focused experientially on narrative as either the shape of our 'storied' world, or the articulation of personal and social identity, or in biblical forms the evocation of reader healing and hope.[14] It continues as a voice in the narrative conversation.[15] For all that, theological reference to the topic turns regularly instead to the postliberal proposal.[16] While some of its leading exponents distance themselves from the self-description of 'narrative theology',[17] a cluster of theologians in this recent Yale tradition represent the most vigorous expression of the rubric adopted in this work.[18] Clarification of the interrelationships is, therefore, in order.[19]

In *The Eclipse of the Biblical Narrative*,[20] Frei shows how Enlightenment strategies to make Scripture persuasive to moderns eliminated the narrative world of the Bible and with it the singular understandings of the biblical God and the person of Christ. For Frei, the integrity of Scripture is assured and the faithfulness of the theological task is maintained when the internal biblical world 'redescribes' what is beyond it. The modern eclipse entails a reversal of the relationship. Scripture is best read as a 'history-like' narrative along the lines of nineteenth-century realistic novels in which the identity of characters emerges in their interaction with the common ventures of life. Thus the storied world of the canon, read typologically, with special reference to the micro-narratives within it, is the given for Christian theology, not to be dissolved by efforts to confirm or disconfirm its authority by arguing its correspondence with exterior referents, either historical or metaphysical. In subsequent work, Frei carried forwards his proposal by indicating how the identity of Christ, the one whom Christians know as their orienting Presence, is 'rendered' in the stories of Jesus, especially the passion and resurrection narratives. Frei argues for a 'literal reading' of Scripture as against its subversion by external warrants and frameworks.[21] All this does not preclude an 'ad hoc apologetics' that appropriates selectively cultural disciplines and insights to enable biblical faith to state its case better (as with Erich Auerbach's literary skills and the model of English and French nineteenth-century novels).

George Lindbeck's *The Nature of Doctrine* marked an important turn in theological conversation when ground-breaking agreements in ecumenical dialogue that reversed long-standing polarisation prompted his 'cultural-linguistic' alternative to 'experiential-expressive' and 'cognitivist' understandings of Christian doctrine.[22] When Christian discourse is conceived as a language world in its own right embodied in its biblical charter, worship patterns, traditions and behaviour – with doctrine as its grammatical rules – Lindbeck's call to maintain Christian identity converged with Frei's quest for biblical integrity. In like manner, Lindbeck spoke for an 'intratextual' reading of Scripture that absorbed the world, rather than the other way around. An 'overarching story' came to higher profile in Lindbeck, with more development of the place of Israel and the church as the community of 'honorary Jews', but a story always read, as with Frei, through a christological lens, one shaped by the discernment of his 'unsubstitutable personal

4

identity' in the Jesus stories. The church and its traditions as the context for reading Scripture also comes further forwards, for the plain meaning of Scripture is what the Christian community takes it to be at a given point in time, under the guidance of a doctrinally - ruled reading.[23]

Many of the postliberal refrains are to be heard in this narrative interpretation of the doctrine of revelation. Stated in the latter's terms, these are:

1. the entry, with Barth, into the 'strange new world of the Bible' to learn who God is and what God did, does and will do;
2. the understanding of the biblical world as an overarching narrative that renders the identity of the Christian God;
3. the centrality of its chapter on Jesus Christ as the interpretive key to the whole narrative;
4. the place of Israel in the purposes of God;
5. the resource role of the Christian community and its ecumenical doctrine in the interpretation of Scripture;
6. the rejection of the premises of culture as the framework for understanding the biblical source, christological centre and ecclesial resources of authority, and the doctrinal substance related thereto;
7. an eclectic use of extrabiblical experience and categories comparable to postliberal 'ad hoc apologetics'.

Along with the convergences, there are differences from, and questions put, to the postliberal perspective.

A Difference

'Narrative' here is related, first and foremost, to theological content, not literary form. While borrowing an interpretive literary concept from culture – 'narrative' – as does the postliberal perspective, its conversion and baptism in Christian context here have to do with identifying the pattern of God's decisive actions among us, not primarily the genre in which multiple descriptions of these actions are cast. As in the distinction between 'history' as events in their own right and 'history' as the account of these events, so too here 'story' refers to the unfolding drama of divine deeds, not the many and varied instantiations of the literary form in which they are described.

Storytelling, as noted earlier, is different from history-writing in the degree to which the narrator's vision shapes the account. Both postliberal narratology and the one here set forth deploy the term 'narrative' in this way. The focus of the former, however, tends to be on the *stories* within Scripture that render a character, definitively those about Jesus. The latter focuses on the encompassing biblical *Story* that runs from Genesis to Revelation, with its centrepoint in Jesus Christ. This overarching story appears *in nuce* only fugitively in New Testament summary, as for example in the prologue of John. The understanding of Scripture in these terms comes from its canonical shape and thus from the early process of the Christian community's self-definition vis-à-vis its surroundings. Concurrently, it developed its 'rule of faith' and subsequent creedal refinements including its doctrine of the Trinity, economic and immanent, all formulations of the biblical Storyline from creation to consummation. Thus the 'Great Tradition' as embodied in this early defining ecumenical consensus enables us to see the *Great Narrative* within Scripture. The Story told by the authoritative canon is hearable by us through the Storytelling community. Why the canon is source and the community is resource are questions that take us to Chapters 6 to 9, on inspiration and illumination.

Some Questions

First, a developing theme in postliberal narrative is the interpretation of the 'plain sense' of Scripture as

> what a participant in the community automatically or naturally takes a text to be saying on its face insofar as he or she has been socialized in a community's conventions for reading the text of Scripture.[24]

If the authoritative plain sense of Scripture is tied so closely to the community and its socialisation processes, how can Scripture exercise its magisterial role vis-à-vis the community? We shall return to this question in Chapter 7 on church, one that Barth puts to those who locate final authority in the church. The primacy of Scripture and its critical role vis-à-vis the Christian community has to do with the relation of biblical inspiration to ecclesial illumination.

Second, postliberal narratology, making use as it does of realistic novel and cultural-linguistic analogies, is regularly suspected of denying basic points of historical reference in the Jesus story or even metaphysical Reference – the reality of the narrative's chief character, God.[25] Both Lindbeck and Frei have denied these charges,[26] and Bruce

Marshall has made a compelling case for Lindbeck's propositional assumptions, the correspondence truth-claims of Christian language being established by the coherence of its assertions with the 'web of belief', not by norms extraneous to it.[27] However, persisting unclarity invites the question of reference/Reference to the 'real order' in postliberal perspectives.

Third, what is the revelatory warrant for the authority granted to Scripture? What are the theological grounds for the judgment that the biblical world must absorb and redescribe the world beyond it? Chapter 6, on inspiration, is an attempt to answer that question.

Fourth, what is the revelatory warrant for the authority granted to the church in postliberal perspective? Chapter 7, on ecclesial illumination, is an attempt to answer that question.

Finally, where is the biblical chapter on Noah in postliberal narrative? The influence of Barth is evident in the sharp juxtaposition of the biblical world with that of the world beyond it, with suspicions of any claim to epistemic graces in the latter. The invasion of the church by 'the world beyond' in Barth's time and our own makes the case for *againstness* compelling. However, 'the biblical world' includes Noah and the Noachic covenant as is argued here. Indeed, 'ad hoc apologetics' assumes some such theological rationale for selective borrowing from that world. The later Barth sought its equivalent in the concept of 'free communications' and 'parables of the kingdom', ideas to be discussed and critiqued later.

THE GREAT NARRATIVE OF REVELATION

Inextricable from the drama of *reconciliation* set forth in Scripture, classical tradition and standard dogmatics, is the 'Great Narrative' of *revelation*. Every chapter in the story of God's *deeds* includes *disclosures*. The doctrine of revelation developed in this work will, therefore, retell the Story with an eye to the revelatory disclosures amid the reconciling deeds.

The 'Great Narrative' structure can also serve as a framework for locating and engaging the partisans in the traditional debates about revelation. Historic disputants appear at each turn in the tale. Put positively, the varied points of view to be encountered each bear special witness to some phase of the narrative of revelation. Put negatively, those that define revelation in terms of this or that chapter to the exclusion or reduction of others censor the full story. In Paul's

Corinthian imagery, each perspective is an organ in the body of truth. The eye cannot say to the hand, '"I have no need of you" . . . If all were a single member, where would the body be?' (1 Cor. 12:21,19).

William Abraham, commenting on historic controversies, speaks of the quest for catholicity in fitting narrative terms:

> Divine revelation must not be approached in independence from delineating the divine activity through which God reveals Himself. To pick out any one act or activity as the essence of revelation is to miss the total picture, yet this is what has happened in the history of the doctrine of revelation. One generation focuses on divine creation as the bearer of revelation; another in reaction focuses on divine speaking to prophets and apostles; another focuses on Jesus Christ as the bearer of revelation; another highlights the supreme significance of the inner illumination of the Holy Spirit; yet another argues that revelation comes only at the end of history . . . What unites each element to the other is a narrative of God's action that stretches from creation to the end.[28]

Colin Gunton, in his more recent *A Brief Theology of Revelation*, develops a theological epistemology that centres on an encompassing view of a 'narratively identified God'. Critiquing narrative theologies that confine the rendering of that identity to New Testament stories or to the Exodus-Easter range of 'history of salvation' views, his own soteriological and trinitarian perspective reflects Abraham's inclusive narratology and with it 'necessary reference to the economy of creation, salvation and final redemption of all things'.[29] Accordingly, Gunton proceeds along a revelatory line from 'creation to the end', with its christological centrepoint, and its biblical, creedal, confessional, propositional and personal aspects, all of which reflect the historic advocacies to which Abraham alludes.

Abraham points out specifically the tendency to fix upon one or another revelatory 'act or activity' of God: 'creation'; 'speaking to prophets and apostles';'Jesus Christ as bearer of revelation';'illumination of the Holy Spirit'; and 'revelation that comes only at the end of history'. These are recurring themes in the historic discussion because they are all integral parts of the Great Narrative of disclosure, luminous moments, *phases* in the unfolding story of revelation. In the typology to be developed, these four and their subsets come into focus as: *preservation* (described by Abraham as 'creation', but with the fall taken into account); *action* ('Jesus Christ' in Abraham's sequence, but also to include 'Israel'); *inspiration* ('prophets and apostles'); and *illumination* (personal and ecclesial 'illumination by the Holy Spirit', and its eschatological fulfilment, 'revelation that comes at the end of history'). The retelling of the Christian Story in *revelatory* terms – highlighting these luminous moments – will, accordingly, appear this way: prologue, creation, fall, covenant with Noah, covenant with Israel, Jesus Christ, scripture, church, salvation, consummation, epilogue.

Abraham is correct that theologies of revelation do tend to focus on, or reduce to, one or another theme. To construe the doctrine narratively enables us to expose this tendency and press beyond it to a more encompassing view. Further, it clarifies the relationships among partial perspectives and enables us to see priorities within them. The identification of turning points within this *epistemological* narrative also provides a way of appropriating the contributions of historic positions while recognising the need for correction and complementarity.

'Epistemology' is a hoary topic in Western philosophy and theology. Narrative, as here conceived, has significant implications for the use of this term. Since Kant, much modern theology has assumed that religious knowledge is a subset of a general theory of knowledge with the conclusion drawn that its Object is cognitively inaccessible, allowing for 'faith' but not 'knowledge'. A *narrative* of divine disclosure as here understood rejects the Kantian veto. The latter, a creature of a period of Western culture – itself part of the fallen world into which a disclosive Word must be spoken – is not the arbiter of ultimate truth-claims. Narrative epistemology is not a species of the genus, philosophical epistemology. The being and doing of God are knowable – under the conditions of finitude and sin to which Kantian modesties do point – in particular turns in the revelatory Story. Assertions about who God is and what God does are true to the extent that they conform to those narrative norms, not to criteria external to them. This does not preclude, however – on the basis of the common grace of the covenant with Noah to be discussed – the possibility of making a plausible though not 'knock-down' post-Kantian case for knowledge-claims, including Christian ones.[30]

INTERLOCUTORS

The twentieth-century controversies on revelation are a laboratory for learnings about both the search for wholeness in the doctrine and the temptation to reduce the narrative to one or another chapter. On the eve of a new century, the recollection of the strengths and weaknesses of our immediate inheritance is in order. Thus the positions of various twentieth-century theologians will be engaged with representative citations from their writings. Quotations from, rather than summaries of, important works are to the fore in this work in order to give first-hand acquaintance with relevant influential writings of the era. Special attention will be given to the work of four major figures: Karl Barth, Karl Rahner, Paul Tillich and Carl Henry. The depth and degree of the investigations into the doctrine of revelation by these four theologians are one measure of their stature. No traveller into the next century of Christian theology should be without lessons learned from their struggle with, and enrichment of, Christian doctrine, especially its epistemological undergirding. To encourage in-depth but accessible encounter with these figures, one key volume of each author's work will be the focus of detailed inquiry and evaluation. Each theologian represents the concentration on one of the four phases of the narrative of revelation. Although occasional reference is made to antecedents, choosing here the intensive encounter with key twentieth-century theologians precludes surveys of the development of the doctrine of revelation found in the histories of the doctrine and also in current systematic treatments. The best of the latter reviews is in Volume 1 of Pannenberg's *Systematic Theology*.[31]

Of course, the four twentieth-century theologians in question are creatures of their locations: white, male, middle-class, Eurocentric. They share in the conditioning factors of their day and age, exposed as such by current hermeneuticians of suspicion. The recognition of the limitations of each perspective is integral to the analysis that follows. However, each figure bears testimony to an aspect of the doctrine of revelation that cannot be ignored. After examining a position in detail, *contributions* to the overarching narrative of revelation will be discussed and *problems* attendant to it will be examined.

Some might wonder: do we focus on these giants of another day because so few contemporaries can help us in this journey? Ronald Thiemann, in his recent work *Revelation and Theology*, comments:

> Despite the prominence of the doctrine of revelation in nearly every modern theology written prior to 1960, very little clarity has emerged regarding the possibility and nature of human knowledge of God . . . A sense of revelation-weariness has settled over the discipline and most theologians have happily moved on to other topics of inquiry.[32]

Ironically, Thiemann's own important work on this subject has been part of a new spurt in the investigation of the doctrine of revelation.

The momentum began a few years earlier in theologians across the spectrum, from Roman Catholic Avery Dulles' durable *Models of Revelation*[33] to evangelical Carl Henry's six-volume *God, Revelation and Authority.*[34] Spanning this period, although beginning earlier, are the important writings on revelation of Wolfhart Pannenberg and Thomas Torrance.[35] Other significant new contributions include the works of William Abraham, Richard Swinburne, George Mavrodes, Keith Ward and Colin Gunton.[36] And beyond particular studies in this doctrine, every one of the full-scale projects in the current revival of systematic theology – over sixty in the past fifteen years – includes a locus on the doctrine of revelation.[37] The same interest in the subject can be seen in the rash of new catechetical literature in churches seeking to rein-terrogate their traditions, most notably the section on revelation in the *Catechism of the Catholic Church.*[38] While not developing the doctrine systematically, the outpouring of works on religious pluralism deals in one way or another with the issues of revelation.[39]

While the increased attention to the doctrine of revelation lays athwart Thiemann's judgment about the disinterest of theologians in the topic, no work on revelation by figures as formative of twentieth-century theology as our interlocutors has appeared.[40] Understanding both their contributions and their shortcomings can be an important resource to the now-intensified epistemological inquiry.

The ferment in the doctrine of revelation is related to current challenges to Christian faith, modern and postmodern. What can we hold to be true in a world secular and relativist, a 'culture of disbelief', yet one marked, paradoxically, by the rise of religious passions and the retrieval of ancient religious traditions? Integral to this question of *what* we can believe are the prolegomenal issues of *where, how* and *why.* 'Where do we go to find out what is so?' is the question of *authority,* with three major types of answer emerging in the history of Christian thought: 'Bible', 'Church', 'World' – Scripture, tradition and human experience in its various forms.[41] 'How do we interpret those privileged places?' is the question of *hermeneutics,* with historic answers constituting multiple subsets of each of the major types of authority. 'Why do we go where we go and interpret it the way we do?' is the question of *revelation.* Many works on that subject also attempt to deal with the contiguous issues of authority and interpretation. However, while revelation, authority and interpretation are inseparable, they are also distinguishable, requiring a depth of analysis not possible in the compass of this work. The writer's *The Christian Story,* vol. 2, *Authority: Scripture in the Church for the World* is a companion piece that deals with the issues of 'where' and 'how'.[42] Their presuppositions in *revelation* are the burden of this book.

DISTINCTIONS AND DEFINITIONS

Avery Dulles observes in *Models of Revelation* that

> biblical authors and theologians prior to the sixteenth century rarely used the term 'revelation' in the modern sense as a technical concept to designate whatever is needed to make something a matter of divine and Christian faith.[43]

While the technical term is more recent, the subject has been a theological constant, having to do with the *warrants* for the basic beliefs of the Christian church. Something accounts for matters 'of divine and Christian faith' being *knowledge of God*. Revelation is the presupposed divine activity that assured the church of the reliability of its affirmations, and thus their *truth*.

The subject took initial shape in the history of Christian thought in connection with the questions of *authority and interpretation,* 'the media by which the original revelation was preserved and handed down in the Church . . . [and] the principles by which these media were interpreted'.[44] So J. N. D. Kelly observes as he begins his inquiry into early Christian doctrines with an exploration of the earliest norms of doctrine – 'Tradition and Scripture' – and their revelatory presuppositions. The three interrelated themes – 'media', 'principles by which these media were interpreted' and 'original revelation' – constitute prolegomena in works of systematic theology, identified here as the *where*, the *how* and the *why* of the matter. Sometimes they are spoken of as 'theological method' in contrast to 'theological content', the latter being the *what* of the specific doctrines of God, Christ, church, etc. The distinction, however, is far from absolute, for each methodological assertion presupposes some doctrinal content, as will be noted. The focus of this work is the Why? question that underlies 'Tradition and Scripture' and to whatever else appeal is made as touchstone of belief: give us the theological warrant *why* Scripture is the mediate source of authority (God, of course, is, in P. T. Forsyth's words, the *fontal* source of authority), and tradition is the resource for interpreting it. Those who hold that the Bible and its classical exposition in Christian tradition are authoritative do so because of their answer to the Why?: the triune God by the light and power of the Holy Spirit has revealed defining truth through them. Others who look to different sources of authority do so because another revelatory process is identified or presupposed. In each case, therefore, a *doctrine of revelation* is the underpinning of a concept of authority and its interpretive principles.

Yet things are not 'one on top of another', as it might appear. For example, to assert that 'God reveals truth in the Bible' assumes something about God, something about where we receive this Word, and something about how we understand what is so received. Thus the revelatory Why is inextricable from the authoritative Where of Scripture (and/or tradition), a hermeneutical How of interpreting Scripture (and/or tradition), and a doctrinal Who and What about God. Those who advocate other sources of authority, whether they be other sacred books or figures, or some aspect of human experience – rational, moral, affective – are faced with the same circularity: authority presupposes revelation which in turn relies on assumed sources of authority that require interpretation and are founded on belief in a Reality who/which discloses truth through sources of authority which, in turn . . . and so on. Every claim to know something about ultimate states of affairs entails a leap of faith into an epistemological circle of this sort. As such, the circle is not vicious, but universally functional and logically necessary.[45]

The doctrine of revelation is a photograph that stops the travel within that circle at a critical point, answering the question of the disclosive Why: Why has the triune God (the Who and What) chosen a given Where and How? That photograph will be taken here with a wide-angle lens that captures the panorama of background authority and interpretation. Such a panoramic view will take into account the sources of authority. (In this work, Scripture is the 'source', the Church with its classical tradition is the 'resource' and the world of human experience beyond their bounds is the 'setting').[46] In the exposition to follow, therefore, Scripture will play a magisterial role, the church's tradition and conversation a ministerial one, with general human experience as catalytic and contextual. The Scripture that is cited presupposes a canonical-cum-christological hermeneutic. That is, the text is read in the light of the overall narrative pattern of teaching that unifies the two Testaments, with its defining centre, Jesus Christ.[47] 'Tradition' and 'conversation' include the ecumenical consensus points of Christian doctrine and the running theological commentary on them, with the accent on conversation with the four major figures.

These interrelationships can be portrayed in two diagrams, as developed in companion works to which cross-references will be made from time to time.[48]

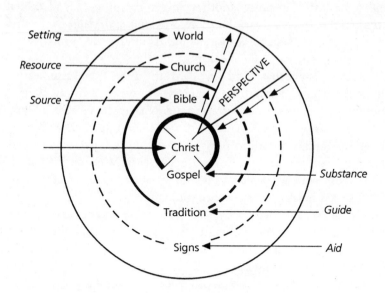

Authority and Interpretation

The primacy of Scripture, as resourced by tradition, will appear in the treatment of each chapter of the Story. That means following step by step the overall narrative flow of biblical stories and their revelatory images: the tree of the knowledge of good and evil, the rainbow sign, the pillar of fire, the promised dawn, the incarnate Light, the pentecostal flames, the eschatological Day, etc. In these stories, light imagery is pervasive, associated as it is with knowledge in both Scripture and tradition, centrally so with regard to Jesus Christ. As Jaroslav Pelikan points out,

> the image of light and the radiance was assuredly one of the most important . . . One of the earliest known Christian hymns was the *Phos hilaron*, which hailed Christ as
> Serene light of the Holy Glory
> of the Father Everlasting
> Jesus Christ.[49]

Each chapter will take up the thread of the biblical narrative of revelation with accompanying theological exposition. The extensive use of Scripture's own accounts and imagery is an attempt to stay within the 'strange . . . world of the Bible' (Barth), so old in itself but so 'new' to the regnant modern/postmodern culture.

14

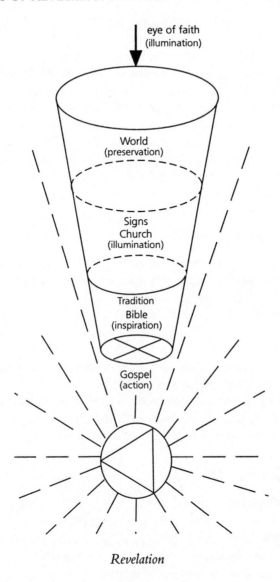

Revelation

Revelation, therefore, is narrative-specific, the story of the triune God's self-disclosure, the gift of the knowledge of God given in the history of God with human beings to human beings. The doctrine of revelation explores why we turn where we do to know who God is and what God does among us from creation to consummation. As such, the narrative of revelation is about, and coordinate with, the narrative of reconciliation.

MODELS OF REVELATION

To make initial contact with the twentieth-century discussion, and to provide data for the interpretation of the 'phases' of revelation, we draw on Avery Dulles' review of an array of points of view on the present theological scene in *Models of Revelation*.[50] 'Models' are intellectual constructs that express major tendencies in a field of inquiry. As in his study, *Models of the Church*, so here also, Dulles' identification of five models with figures that illustrate them – and his own evaluations – represents an ecumenical approach to current understandings of revelation.

Revelation as 'Doctrine'

In this view, God's disclosive work is the provision of information about deity and the divine purposes, as that is cast in clear-cut and abiding 'propositions'. Such propositions are 'timeless truths' to be found either in Scripture or in the dogmatic formulas of the historic church. Dulles alludes to various evangelicals, notably Carl Henry, as representative of a 'conservative evangelical' version of this model. The Roman Catholic Hermann Diekmann illustrates a neo-scholastic Roman Catholic expression of revelation as doctrine. The former looks to verbally-inspired and inerrant autographs of the Bible as the locus of revealed propositions, and the latter finds revealed information in the official deposit of dogma of the Roman Catholic Church.

Revelation as 'History'

Often developed in opposition to the first model, this *Heilsgeschichte* view finds God's disclosive work not in infallible words or statements but in decisive divine deeds, primarily those in the history of Israel and in the life, death and resurrection of Jesus Christ. Not what God says but what God does constitutes revelation, although note is regularly taken of the need to explain the meaning of the events and thus the importance of the biblical interpreters proximate to the determinative events. The mid-century 'biblical theology movement' exemplifies this perspective, although Dulles also links Wolfhart Pannenberg's 'universal history' view with the 'acts of God' theologians G. Ernest Wright, C. H. Dodd and Oscar Cullmann.

Revelation as 'Inner Experience'

God's disclosure comes through an experience variously characterised as the numinous, the holy, absolute dependence, ultimate concern, etc., a 'religious a priori' at the core of all particular religions. The historic faiths are species of the genus religious experience, rich and varied expressions of a universal awareness of the divine. Friedrich Schleier-macher is cited as representative with his focus on 'God-consciousness', a pious feeling available to all, albeit shaped communally. Other theologians holding this view are George Tyrrell, August Sabatier, William Ernest Hocking, Wilhelm Hermann and their heirs.

Revelation as 'Dialectical Presence'

Again, emerging as counterpoint to then-current notions (Inner Experience or Doctrine) are the 'neo-orthodox' theologies, among whom Dulles includes a spectrum from Karl Barth to Rudolf Bult-mann. Revelation in this model is understood to be the Word of God that confronts us in Scripture and overturns our agendas and expecta-tions. For Barth, the great No to our plans and pieties and Yes to God's purposes is said in the Word enfleshed, Jesus Christ. For Bultmann, the emphasis is on the decision of faith to be made in response to the Word addressed to us in a demythologised Scripture.

Revelation as 'New Awareness'

Here, God is conceived as immanent in nature and history, moving the world forwards to its intended goal. Revelation is the sensitising of human beings to the divine activity and an invitation to participate in its purposive work. Disclosure is affective rather than cerebral, working through performative symbols rather than propositional statements, although 'giving rise' to the latter. Dulles includes in this camp such thinkers as Pierre Teilhard de Chardin, Gregory Baum, Gabriel Moran, Leslie Dewart and John Hick.

Dulles discovers things to affirm in all these views. Yet, as total solu-tions, each has serious limitations. Drawing insights from each, Dulles proposes the integrating theme of 'symbolic mediation'.[51] The Roman Catholic tradition, rich in symbol and thus with affective power, is able to accommodate the insights of New Awareness. But symbolic mediation entails also faithfulness to the determinative deeds of God of the historical model, the truth-claims of the propositional model, the 'overagainstness' of the Word of Scripture in the dialectical model, and the mystical and personal dimensions of Inner Experience, while avoiding the reductionist temptations of each.[52]

The ecumenical intention of Dulles is kindred to the present work in two respects: learning by listening to a variety of points of view in the Christian community, past and present; and seeking to avoid reductionism in doctrine by honouring the insight of a model without collapsing the doctrine into it. Here, however, the 'models' are transposed into the narrative terms earlier indicated: *phases* of revelation in the story of reconciliation. Dulles' phenomenological survey – models discerned empirically in a given time and place – appear as disclosive *moments* within a comprehensive narrative.

The transposition and reconfiguration appear this way:

1. *Preservation* refers to revelation vis-à-vis universal human experience – moral, affective, rational. Inner Experience and New Awareness are Dulles' models that relate to this phase.
2. *Action* refers to revelation in definitive historical deeds of God, the election of Israel and incarnation in Christ. Dulles' models of History and Dialectical Presence are expressions of it.
3. *Inspiration* has reference to privileged accounts and interpretations of the deeds of God in Scripture. The evangelical version of Dulles' model of revelation as Doctrine points to this act of disclosure.
4. *Illumination* is a rubric for the light given on all the foregoing in sequel acts of disclosure. Dulles' scholastic model of Doctrine is witness to the ecclesial phase of this age of the Spirit. The personal appropriation aspect of Dialectical Presence corresponds to the chapter on salvation, and the eschatological dimension of Pannenberg's thought points to the revelatory consummation.

As the use of 'Great Narrative' with its four turning points is an unconventional way of interpreting the doctrine of revelation, a more traditional division of this book will be employed to demonstrate its connection with the standard treatment of the subject matter. Thus the chapters in the Story will be subsumed under Parts I, II and III, with their respective rubrics 'General Revelation', 'Special Revelation' and 'Revelation as Reception'.

Employing a narrative framework, the contributions, limitations and interrelationships of historic perspectives can be identified and the search for fullness in the doctrine of revelation pursued.[53] As in Dulles' effort to incorporate the richness of the varied perspectives and to avoid their reductionist tendencies by venturing an encompassing view, so also here the goal is an ecumenical doctrine of revelation. Each partial perspective will be encountered at a juncture in the fuller narrative of revelation. And as no ecumenical approach is without roots in a particular ecclesial tradition (Dulles writes self-consciously from within his Roman Catholic matrix), so this work draws upon the author's Reformed heritage, with attention to both its strengths and its limitations.

In sum, the aim of this work is to contribute to the church's search for the meaning of revelation by: the location of the question and the historic answers in a narrative framework; the identification of those answers in a typology that relates them to phases in the unfolding noetic drama; the use of a twentieth-century conversation with formidable thinkers who represent the four basic phases of the revelation narrative; and the quest for a fuller reading of the narrative by drawing on the strengths of each conversation partner and perspective and recognising their weaknesses, with the prayer of Taize ever at hand:

> Spirit of wisdom and understanding, Spirit of counsel and strength, Spirit of knowledge and devotion, Spirit of obedience to the Lord . . . Sanctify us, O Comforter!

NOTES

1. Avery Dulles, *Models of Revelation*, 2nd edn (Maryknoll, NY: Orbis, 1992), p. xix. Author's italics.
2. Cited by D. E. Nineham in H. D. McDonald (ed.), *Theories of Revelation: An Historical Study 1700–1960* (Grand Rapids: Baker Book House, 1979), Foreword.
3. D. E. Nineham, ibid., Foreword. In briefer form, John Baillie surveys similar developments in his 'Historical Reminder', *The Idea of Revelation in Recent Thought* (New York: Columbia University Press, 1956), pp. 3–18.
4. For a discussion of narrative, see the writer's 'Narrative Theology: An Overview', *Interpretation* 36:4 (October 1983), 340–52. The varieties of narrative theology are sometimes identified as 'biblical narrative' and 'story theology', or 'pure narrative' and 'impure narrative' – characterisations of the views of Hans Frei and Paul Ricoeur, as in Gary Comstock, 'Two Types of Narrative Theology', *Journal of the American Academy of Religion* 55:4 (Winter 1987), 687–717; and Mark Ellingsen, *The Integrity of Biblical Narrative: Story in Theology and Proclamation* (Minneapolis:

Fortress, 1990), pp. 53–61. The writer's typology is threefold: 'biblical stories', 'life story' and 'community story'.

5. Robert Scholes and Robert Kellog, *The Nature of Narrative* (London: Oxford University Press, 1966), p. 4. While some distinguish 'story' from 'narrative', they are treated here synonymously following most usage in narratological discussion. On the proposed distinction, see Mark Ellingsen, op. cit., p. 57ff. and passim.

6. Is the writing of history itself, finally, 'story' so understood? Postmodern historians think so, and thus a great debate is current within the discipline. On these distinctions, see James Barr, 'Story and History in Biblical Theology', in idem (ed.), *The Scope and Authority of the Bible* (Philadelphia: Westminster Press, 1980), pp. 1–17.

7. In Christian discourse, as in George A. Lindbeck, *The Nature of Doctrine: Religion and Theology in a Postliberal Age* (Philadelphia: Westminster Press, 1984), p. 120 and passim.

8. No juxtaposition of 'story' with 'history' does justice to the biblical metanarrative. The former's recognition of the imaginative role of the narrator in telling the tale does not preclude the historical core of the account. No history, then no biblical *God of history*, with its gnostic entailments and ethical consequences.

9. On this distinction, see Karl Barth, *The Doctrine of the Word of God, Prolegomena to Church Dogmatics*, I, 1, trans. G. T. Thomson (New York: Charles Scribner's Sons, 1936), pp. 375–8.

10. As in the framework of the writer's developing systematics, *The Christian Story*, vols 1, 2 (Grand Rapids: Eerdmans, 1978, 1984, 1987, 1996).

11. Hans W. Frei, *The Eclipse of Biblical Narrative: A Study in Eighteenth and Nineteenth Century Hermeneutics* (Philadelphia: Fortress Press, 1975).

12. For evidence of growing convergences of these constituencies, see Timothy R. Phillips and Dennis L. Okholm (eds), *The Nature of Confession: Evangelicals and Postliberals in Conversation* (Downers Grove, IL: InterVarsity Press, 1996); and Carl Braaten, 'Renewal in Theology for the Church', *Pro Ecclesia* 3:2 (Spring 1994), 136–40.

13. Narrative/story as a self-conscious interpretive framework was given impetus by the Reformation and post-Reformation covenant theologies, and reappeared in the *Heilsgeschichte* schools of the nineteenth and twentieth centuries. The mid-twentieth-century 'biblical theology' movement made use of the 'acts' and 'drama' metaphors, as in G. Ernest Wright and Reginald H. Fuller, *The Book of the Acts of God: Contemporary Scholarship Interprets the Bible* (Garden City, NY: Doubleday & Co., Anchor Books, 1960); and Bernhard Anderson's still durable study book, *The Unfolding Drama of the Bible*, 3rd edn (Philadelphia: Fortress Press, 1988). Anderson divides the biblical drama into three acts each with two scenes, set within a prologue and epilogue (p. 15 and passim). J. Richard Middelton and Brian J. Walsh in *Truth is Stranger Than It Used*

to Be: Biblical Faith in a Postmodern Age (Downers Grove, IL: InterVarsity Press, 1995), pp. 182–3 and 240, following N. T. Wright, and in conversation with postmodern trends, speak of 'an unfinished dramatic script . . . in six acts with a multiplicity of scenes' (creation, fall, Israel, Jesus Christ, church as 'faithful improvisation' and 'climactic finale'). Their Wright source is 'How Can the Bible be Authoritative?', *Vox Evangelica* 21 (1991), 7–32. See also N. T. Wright, *The Climax of the Covenant* (Minneapolis: Fortress Press, 1991), pp. 263–7 and passim.

Postmodern thinkers – Jacques Derrida, Michel Foucault, Jean-François Lyotard – are scornful of 'metanarratives', holding them to be illegitimate claims of access to reality and universality, smokescreens for agendas of power and violence. Better 'small stories' with pragmatic or playful purpose. The call for epistemic modesty, the warnings of covert self-interest, and the attention to micro-narratives, especially those of the marginalised, all cohere with chapters in the Great Narrative to be explored with its eschatological proviso, understanding of the fall, and ecclesial catholicity. However, the attack on metanarrative is full of irony, for

> the postmodern answers . . . make sense only in terms of a postmodern metanarrative, though this narrative is surreptitiously introduced and remains implicit. The very term *postmodern* implies a discernment of a particular stage in world history, that we live after or at the end of modernity. (Middelton and Walsh, op. cit., p. 76.)

Comparably, Richard Rorty, tracing his postmodern convictions to a University of Chicago exposure by philosopher Charles Morris to the writings of Charles Peirce, William James, John Dewey and George Herbert Mead, announces that 'There's No Big Picture' ('There's No Big Picture', *The University of Chicago Magazine* 86:4 (April 1994), 18–23). The writer, attending the same classes of Professor Morris, learned that an incipient postmodernism was itself a very Big Picture, a totalising schema of how the world works. Further, as Cornel West has pointed out, Rorty's postmodern pragmatism provides no norms from judgment of the cruel and unjust, and invites either moral paralysis or the raw play of power.

14. See, for example, James Wiggins (ed.), *Religion as Story* (New York: Harper and Row, 1975); Sallie McFague, *Metaphorical Theology* (Philadelphia: Fortress Press, 1982); the works of John S. Dunne, *Time and Myth* (Garden City, NY: Doubleday & Co., 1973) and *A Search for God in Time and Memory* (Notre Dame: University of Notre Dame Press, 1977); J. B. Metz, *Faith and Society*, trans. David Smith (New York: Seabury Press, 1980); Robert McAfee Brown, 'My Story and the Story', *Theology Today* 22 (July 1975), 166–73; Thomas Groome, *Christian Religious Education: Sharing Our Story and Visions* (New York: Harper & Row, 1980); John Navone and Thomas Cooper, *Tellers of the Word* (New

York: Le Jaq Publishing House, 1981); Richard Jensen, *Telling the Story* (Minneapolis: Augsburg Press, 1980); James McClendon Jr, *Theology as Biography* (Nashville: Abingdon Press, 1974); and David Tracy, *The Analogical Imagination* (New York: Crossroad Publishing Co., 1981). Formative figures in literary and philosophical disciplines and their representative works that have influenced the discussion of narrative theology include Robert Alter, *The Art of Biblical Narrative* (London: George Allen & Unwin, 1981); Erich Auerbach, *Mimesis*, trans. Willard Trask (Princeton: Princeton University Press, 1953); Northrop Frye, *The Great Code: The Bible and Literature* (New York: Harcourt Brace Jovanovich, 1983); and Paul Ricoeur, *Essays on Biblical Interpretation*, ed. Lewis B. Mudge (Philadelphia: Fortress Press, 1980). Amos Wilder, pioneer in parable study, in *Jesus' Parables and the War of Myths* (Philadelphia: Fortress Press, 1982), represents the accent on the disclosive and transformative power of story.

15. The most articulate in formulation and in engagement with the Frei–Lindbeck and other perspectives is Stephen Crites. See his essays, 'The Narrative Quality of Experience' and 'A Respectful Reply to the Assertorical Theologian', in Stanley Hauerwas and L. Gregory Jones (eds), *Why Narrative? Readings in Narrative Theology* (Grand Rapids: Eerdmans, 1989), pp. 65–88, 293–302.

16. As in Colin E. Gunton, *A Brief Theology of Revelation* (Edinburgh: T. & T. Clark, 1995), pp. 5–6, 49–52.

17. As in Hans W. Frei, '"Narrative" in Christian and Modern Reading', in Bruce D. Marshall (ed.), *Theology and Dialogue: Essays in Conversation with George Lindbeck* (Notre Dame: University of Notre Dame Press, 1990), pp. 160–1; and Stanley Hauerwas, 'The Church as God's New Language', in Garrett Green (ed.), *Scriptural Authority and Narrative Interpretation* (Philadelphia: Fortress Press, 1987), pp. 188–9.

18. The leading figures in what is sometimes called 'the New Yale theology' have been students of Frei and Lindbeck, edit the deceased Frei's work, and write in concert or in collections in tribute to their mentors, as in Green, op. cit.; Marshall, op. cit.; George Hunsinger and William C. Placher (eds), *Types of Christian Theology: Hans W. Frei* (New York: Yale University Press, 1992); George Hunsinger and William C. Placher (eds), *Theology and Narrative: Selected Essays, Hans W. Frei* (New York: Oxford University Press, 1993).

19. A discussion by the writer of the convergences and some differences among 'ecumenical', 'evangelical' and 'postliberal' narrative theologies constitutes the chapter 'Narrative: Evangelical, Postliberal, Ecumenical' in Timothy R. Phillips and Dennis L. Okholm (eds), *The Nature of Confession*, op. cit.

20. Frei, *The Eclipse of the Biblical Narrative*, op. cit.

21. Hans W. Frei, *The Identity of Jesus Christ: The Hermeneutical Basis of Dogmatic Theology* (Philadelphia: Fortress Press, 1975); and 'The "Literal

Reading" of Biblical Narrative in the Christian Tradition: Does it Stretch or Will it Break?' in Frank McConnell (ed.), *The Bible and the Narrative Tradition* (New York: Oxford University Press, 1986), pp. 36–77.

22. Lindbeck, *The Nature of Doctrine*, op. cit., pp. 30–45.

23. On the latter points, see 'The Story-Shaped Church: Critical Exegesis and Theological Interpretation', in Green (ed.), *Scriptural Authority and Narrative Interpretation*, op. cit., pp. 161–78.

24. Kathryn E. Tanner, 'Theology and the Plain Sense', in Green (ed.), *Scriptural Authority and Narrative Interpretation*, op. cit., p. 63.

25. As in Wallace, 'The New Yale Theology', op. cit.; Julian Hartt, 'Theological Investments in Story: Some Comments on Recent Developments and Some Proposals', op. cit.; in Hauerwas and Jones (eds), *Why Narrative?*; Carl Henry, 'Narrative Theology: An Evangelical Appraisal', in *Gods of This Age or . . . God of the Ages?* (Nashville: Broadman and Holman, 1994), pp. 257–76; and Avery Dulles, 'Observations on George Lindbeck's *Nature of Doctrine*' (paper given at the Divinity School, Yale University, 14 September 1984).

26. As in Frei's reply to the criticisms of Carl Henry in 'Response to "Narrative Theology: An Evangelical Appraisal"', in *Theology and Narrative*, op. cit., pp. 207–12. So too Lindbeck's agreement with Marshall's defence of the propositional aspect of Lindbeck's view in 'Response to Bruce Marshall', *Thomist* 53:1 (July 1989), 403–6.

27. Bruce Marshall, 'Aquinas as a Postliberal Theologian', *Thomist* 53:1 (July 1989), 353–402.

28. William J. Abraham, *Divine Revelation and the Limits of Historical Criticism* (Oxford: Oxford University Press, 1982), p. 13.

29. Colin E. Gunton, *A Brief Theology of Revelation* (Edinburgh: T. & T. Clark, 1995), p. 112.

30. For an example of such, see Avery Dulles, *Models of Revelation*, 2nd edn (Maryknoll, NY: Orbis, 1992), pp. 50, 132, 247, 258, 271–2, 288, 289 and passim. Dulles draws heavily on Michael Polanyi, *Personal Knowledge* (New York: Harper Torchbooks, 1964). See also Richard Swinburne, *Revelation: From Metaphor to Analogy* (Oxford: Oxford University Press, 1992); and George I. Mavrodes, *Revelation and Religious Belief* (Philadelphia: Temple University Press, 1988).

31. Wolfhart Pannenberg, *Systematic Theology*, vol. 1, trans. Geoffrey W. Bromiley (Grand Rapids: Eerdmans, 1988), pp. 63–258.

32. Ronald F. Thiemann, *Revelation and Theology: The Gospel as Narrated Promise* (Notre Dame: University of Notre Dame Press, 1985), p. 1.

33. Avery Dulles, *Models of Revelation* (Garden City, NY: Doubleday, 1983), 2nd edn (Maryknoll, ny: Orbis, 1992).

34. Carl F. H. Henry, *God, Revelation and Authority*, vols 1–6 (Waco, TX: Word Books, 1978–83).

35. From Wolfhart Pannenberg (ed.) in association with Rolf Rendtorff,

Trutz Rendtorff and Ulrich Wilkens, *Revelation as History*, trans. David Granskou (New York: Macmillan Co., 1968) to Wolfhart Pannenberg, *Systematic Theology*, vol. 1, trans. Geoffrey W. Bromiley (Grand Rapids: Eerdmans, 1988), pp. 1–257. And from T. F. Torrance, *Theological Science* (New York: Oxford University Press, 1969) to idem, *The Trinitarian Faith: The Evangelical Theology of the Ancient Catholic Church* (Edinburgh: T. & T. Clark, 1988), pp. 13–46, 52–84, 133–8, 202–15, 245–7, 285–91, 310–11.

36.   Abraham, *Divine Revelation and the Limits of Historical Criticism*, op. cit.; Swinburne, *Revelation: From Metaphor to Analogy*, op. cit.; George I. Mavrodes, *Revelation and Religious Belief*, op. cit.; Keith Ward, *Religion and Revelation* (Oxford: Clarendon Press, 1994); Colin E. Gunton, *A Brief Theology of Revelation*, op. cit.; and a forthcoming work by David S. Cunningham.

37.   For a running account of this phenomenon, see the writer's essays, 'The Surge in Systematics: A Commentary on Current Works', *Journal of Religion*, 73:2 (April 1993), 223–37; 'In Quest of the Comprehensive: The Systematics Revival', *Religious Studies Review* 20:1 (January 1994), 7–12; 'The Revival of Systematic Theology', *Interpretation* 49:3 (July 1995), 229–41.

38.   Articles 1–3, *Catechism of the Catholic Church* (Liguori, MO: Liguori Publications, 1994), pp. 19–38.

39.   An exception would be Ninian Smart and Steven Konstantine, *Christian Systematic Theology in a World Context* (Minneapolis: Fortress, 1991), declaring itself to be 'perhaps the first comprehensive attempt to place the Christian faith in its real new context: that is, in the milieu of the plural and postcolonial world, and intellectually in the light of the modern studies of religions' (p. 17). While new in these respects, it stands in the Tillichian tradition to be discussed.

40.   Wolfhart Pannenberg might be an exception to this generalisation, although he has not yet had the widespread influence of our four figures.

41.   See the writer's detailed typology in *The Christian Story*, vol. 2, *Authority: Scripture in the Church for the World* (Grand Rapids: Eerdmans, 1987), pp. 60–156.

42.   Ibid.

43.   Dulles, *Models of Revelation*, op. cit., p. 18.

44.   J. N. D. Kelly, *Early Christian Doctrines* (New York: Harper & Brothers, 1958), p. 29.

45.   On this matter, three of our four major interlocutors agree. See Karl Barth, *Church Dogmatics*, III/1, trans. and ed. G. W. Bromiley and T. F. Torrance (Edinburgh: T. & T. Clark, 1958), pp. 359–61; Paul Tillich, *Systematic Theology*, vol. 1 (Chicago: University of Chicago Press, 1951), p. 9; and Karl Rahner, *Foundations of Christian Faith: An Introduction to the*

Idea of Christianity, trans. William V. Dych (New York: Seabury Press, 1978), p. 372.

46. For background on these distinctions, see Fackre, *The Christian Story*, vol. 2, op. cit., pp. 341–50.

47. Ibid., pp. 176–210.

48. The first diagram can be refined to include other hermeneutical aspects, as in Gabriel Fackre, *Ecumenical Faith in Evangelical Perspective* (Grand Rapids: Eerdmans, 1993), pp. 69–70.

49. Jaroslav Pelikan, *The Light of the World: A Basic Image in Early Christian Thought* (New York: Harper & Brothers, 1962), pp. 30–1.

50. My in-depth exposure to the doctrine of revelation began as the Protestant reader of the manuscript of *Models of Revelation* that developed in 1981–2 while Dulles was in residence at nearby Boston College. For more commentary on revelation, see the Dulles essay in Francis Schüssler Fiorenza and John P. Galvin (eds), *Systematic Theology: Roman Catholic Perspectives*, vol. 1 (Minneapolis: Fortress Press, 1991), pp. 89–128; and *Assurance of Things Hoped For: A Theology of Christian Faith* (New York: Oxford University Press, 1994), passim..

51. In the updated edition of this work, Dulles faults commentators on the first edition for describing his views as a separate model: Dulles, *Models of Revelation*, 2nd edn, op. cit., p. viii.

52. See Dulles, *Models of Revelation*, 2nd edn, op. cit., pp. 131–54.

53. A case can be made that 'phases' of a full narrative constitute an attempt at 'typology', in the sense that all conceivable theological options are included rather than only the historical occasion of phenomenological 'models'. In *The Christian Story*, vol. 2, *Authority: Scripture in the Church for the World* (Grand Rapids: Eerdmans, 1987), the writer delineates a comparable overarching typology on the question of authority, based on the categories of 'Bible', 'Church' and 'World'. Cf. Karl Barth, *Church Dogmatics*, IV/3, first half trans. G. W. Bromiley and T. F. Torrance (Edinburgh: T. & T. Clark, 1961), pp. 96–101, 114–20.

Prologue

GOD: THE TRINITARIAN
SOURCE OF DISCLOSURE

⎯⎯ᴧᴧᴧᴿᴿᴀ◎ᴀᴿᴿᴧᴧᴧ⎯⎯

> Go therefore and make disciples of all nations, baptising them in
> the name of the Father and of the Son and of the Holy Spirit.
> (Matt. 28:19)

Who is the God named 'Father, Son and Holy Spirit'? In narrative
terms, the answer is in the trinitarian prologue telling us of the One
who does the deeds that constitute the Story. The 'economy' of the
divine doing is rooted in the 'ontology' of the divine Being.

Yet what we say about who God is presupposes the course of the
Christian story itself. Our knowledge of God's being grows out of the
disclosures that accompany the divine deeds. The chief Character
becomes clear as the drama unfolds. But to tell the story aright we
must begin at the beginning, as 'the order of being' is different from
the 'order of knowing'. The prologue is about who God *is* as the font
of what God *does*. In the narrative of *revelation*, we give primary attention to the revelatory aspects of the inner essence, the 'being' of God
– the *immanent* Trinity that account for the revelatory phases of God's
outreach to and history with us, the 'doing' of God – the *economic*
Trinity. But we do so only by anticipating chapters to come, and centrally so the one in which the defining Word, Jesus Christ, is spoken
that illumines God's self-revelatory Being.

26

THE TRINITY AS GOD'S IMMANENT SELF-REVELATION

Almighty and everlasting God, who has given to us your servants grace by the confession of a true faith to acknowledge the glory of the eternal Trinity, and in the power of the divine majesty to worship the Unity . . . (*Book of Common Prayer*)

How to honour the Three and worship the One? In the late twentieth century, the struggle with the triunity of God has come to the theological foreground. In theologies as disparate as Eastern Orthodox, Roman Catholic, liberation, feminist, political, evangelical and ecumenical, the divine Triad has been re-examined and its ecclesial and cultural implications pursued.[1] Heated debates have also taken place about language for the Trinity, both that of the universal baptismal formula and other references to Deity considered to be exclusive and patriarchal.[2] One common thread in the recovery of the doctrine of the Trinity, with origins deep in the history of Christian thought, has important implications for the narrative of revelation: the incomparable mutuality of the Persons.

In contrast to the Western Christian preoccupation with the divine unity, much trinitarian theology today has given new attention to the patristic and Eastern focus on the three Persons. Thus a retrieved 'social analogy' is adduced as support for communitarian understandings of both church and society. Political and liberation theologies find grounding for egalitarian commitments in the co-equality of the Persons, and ecumenical theologies relate the *koinonia* willed for the Churches to the divine *Koinonia*.

The difficulty that attends too-quick passage between human social and ecclesial experience and the doctrine of God is the same that has plagued the 'psychological analogy'. In the Christian story, with its chapters on creation (finitude) and the fall (the universality of sin), no direct crossover is possible from human experience – social or psychological – to the being of God. The meaning of 'social' or 'psychological' in God must be taken from the disclosure of what God does in the narrative to define these terms.[3]

With due acknowledgement of the chasm unbridgeable from our side, Jürgen Moltmann and others have drawn on the patristic refrain of *perichoresis* and *circumincessio* to explore, though not explain, the trinitarian mystery. The Persons are 'coinherent', 'compenetrating' one another. Father, Son and Spirit 'inexist'. Attempts to construe them as a sequential Trinity were early exposed and rejected as Sabellianism. Binitarian tendencies that depersonalise the Holy Spirit, or restatements that identify the Persons as 'modes of being' of the one personal God, have been put into question.[4] In contrast, 'coinherence' is a neologism created in recognition that *no* human experience of total reciprocity can be found in which one 'inexists' another with each maintaining its identity and integrity, but there is such *in God*. There is that 'in God' because, in the Great Story, God is Three Persons in one Being, a *Thou* not a *They*.

Coinherence, as the integrity of each and mutuality of all, does have import for the being of the church and the life of the world: a gift and mandate of co-equal, co-present 'life together', as contemporary eccle-siologies and socio-political theologies have rightly asserted. These are not replications of, but derivations from, the co-equal, compenetrating Being of God, mandates for a fallen and finite creation. They can have this derivative status, challenging the imperialisms and hierarchies of this world, because the 'image of God' in human beings, while damaged by the fall beyond our repair, is not destroyed. In narrative terms, it is preserved through the 'covenant with Noah' and restored in Jesus Christ. In these chapters of the revelatory narrative, God enables us to use finite and fallen language, albeit converted and baptised.

The triune coinherence has implications for epistemology. The mutual love of the Persons is inextricable from the mutual *knowledge* of the Persons. Reciprocal love means reciprocal transparency. Inner-trinitarian *perichoresis* entails the total intercommunication of the Persons. Because we know in Jesus Christ that 'God is *love*' (1 John 4:8), we also know by the revelation of God in Jesus Christ that God is *also* '*light* and in him there is no darkness at all' (1 John 1:5). Love and light are inseparable (1 John 2:7–11). What God does in deeds of reconciling love among us is grounded in the inter-Personal Love that God is. In *like* manner, the disclosures of God in the story of revelation have their origin in the mutual transparency of the Persons. The acts of revelation among us rise from the divine self-knowledge, under-stood in its tri-Personal sense. What we are given to know is a promise anchored in the divine Being. As Thomas Torrance expresses it,

> The economic forms of God's self-communication to us in history derive from and repose upon a communion of the Persons immanent in the Godhead. It is as our knowing of God passes from what is called the 'economic Trinity' to the 'ontolog-ical Trinity' that we have *theologia* in the supreme and proper

sense, knowledge of God on the free ground of his own Being, knowledge of him which is controlled and shaped by relations eternally immanent in God. Without this advance from knowledge of God in his relations toward us (*quoad nos*) to at least some knowledge of God in himself (*quoad se*), knowledge of God is not ontologically grounded in God, but is at the mercy of our knowledge of ourselves. If God is not inherently and eternally in himself what he is toward us in Jesus Christ, as Father, Son and Holy Spirit, then we do not really or finally know God at all as he is in his abiding Reality.[5]

Duns Scotus long ago traced all the acts of disclosure among us to the inner-trinitarian Life and Light Together, *theologia in se*. And again, as Torrance points out, the early church fathers deployed the doctrine of the Trinity to challenge mystical and philosophical tendencies of their time that placed Deity beyond the reach of reliable knowing. Our access to God is rooted in the inner-revelatory relations of the Persons. *Theologia nostra*, clouded as it is by the conditions of finitude and sin, is grounded in the divine *theologia in se*.[6]

While the doing of God is traceable to the triune being of God, as stated, we know that being only through the deeds done, and in particular the defining deed, Jesus Christ. The use of the term *logos* in the gospel of John to interpret the centrepoint of the Story is New Testament witness to God's self-communicative nature. In the prologue of John, the lineage of the Word enfleshed (John 1:14) is traced back into the Godhead, where 'In the beginning was the Word, and the Word was with God, and the Word was God' (John 1:1). The 'Word' spoken to us in Christ is the outworking of the God whose nature it is to be self-disclosing. Indeed, the prologue of John is the narrative of revelation in microcosm. From the inner Life and Light that God is comes 'the life ... the light of all people ... the true light which enlightens everyone ...' (John 1:3, 9), the witness to the true light, John the Baptist (John 1:6-9), and finally light and life enfleshed, the 'glory as of a father's only son, full of grace and truth' (John 1:14). Theophilus of Antioch so followed the journey that went from the indwelling Word, the *Logos endiathetos*, to the outgoing Word, *Logos prophorikos*, to the *Logos spermatikos*, the inseminating Word that enlightens all humanity, to the *Logos ensarkos*, the enfleshed Word in Jesus Christ. We shall develop the same narrative, enlarging it in accord with the testimony of the full canon. But the epistemological point of the prologue here germane is that what we can say about the inner-trinitarian life and light comes from centre of the Story. Jesus Christ, as the 'effulgence of God's splendour, and the stamp of God's very being' (Heb. 1:3 NEB), discloses to the eye of faith the God in whom there is no shadow, 'God of God, Light of Light, very God of very God . . .'.

Throughout the gospel of John, the knowledge of God – both *theologia nostra* and *theologia in se* – is a refrain. In the early verses of a long soliloquy in the 'Book of Signs', Christ declares the mutual indwelling of the Father and the Son:

> If you know me, you will know my Father also . . . (14:7); Whoever has seen me has seen the Father (14:9); Do you not believe that I am in the Father and the Father is in me? The words that I say to you I do not speak on my own; but the Father who dwells in me does his works (14:10); Believe me that I am in the Father and the Father is in me (14:11); All that the Father has is mine . . . (16:15)

Wherever the truth is spoken, therefore, the Son of the Father, the Word of the Father, Jesus Christ speaks it. Truth is the gift of the *Logos* at work in the narrative of revelation . . . by the power of the Holy Spirit.

THE SPIRIT AND THE WORD

The third Person, co-present, co-equal, coinherent in the mutual Life of the immanent Trinity is the empowering agent in the economies of both revelation and reconciliation. In the narrative of revelation, the third Person is the 'Spirit of truth':

> And I will ask the Father, and he will give you another Advocate, to be with you forever. This is the Spirit of truth . . . (14:16–17); But the Advocate, the Holy Spirit, whom the Father will send in my name, will teach you everything . . . (14:26); When the Advocate comes, whom I will send to you from the Father, the Spirit of truth who comes from the Father, he will testify on my behalf (15:26); When the Spirit of truth comes, he will guide you into all the truth . . . (16:13)

Coming from the Father, sent by the Son, the Person of the Spirit is the Power at work in the disclosure. The trustworthiness of the revelation so given to us is established by the Spirit's eternal bonding within the Family that God is.[7]

Every phase of disclosure in the grand narrative of revelation is the work of the Spirit of the Son of the Father.[8] It is in intention at creation, after the fall in preservation, in the election of Israel and the incarnation of the Word in Jesus Christ, in the inspiration of Scripture and in the illumination of the church militant and triumphant. As the Persons have their special missions in the divine economy, the Holy Spirit 'comes front and centre' in the third act of the unfolding drama. In our reading of the Story, the revelatory gifts of *inspiration* and *illumination* are there given. Yet no work of creation and reconciliation – the missions of the Father and the Son – is without the Spirit; for, as in the ancient 'law of the Trinity', all the works of the Trinity are one. Thus every empowerment of the revelatory Word of the Father is the work of the Spirit – the preservation of a rainbow light after the fall, the pillar of fire among an elect people and the enfleshed Word in Jesus Christ.

GRACE AND KNOWLEDGE

As the Giver is the Spirit of the triune God, the gifts are those of divine love. As undeserved, they are *gracious*. We learn the meaning of such unmerited and vulnerable Agape at the heart of the Christian story on Calvary, and hear its echoes in Paul's hymn to a love that is 'patient . . . kind . . . does not insist on its own way . . . bears all things, believes all things, hopes all things, endures all things' (1 Cor. 13:4, 5, 7). The vulnerable love that God is expresses itself in gifts offered, but gifts that can be refused. The grace of revelation, as well as the grace of salvation, invites our 'yes' or our 'no'. Noetic gifts are offered throughout the narrative, but the offer becomes true knowledge *for us* only when received in faith. Thus the reciprocity integral to sexual union – a mutuality of 'knowing' – becomes an apt biblical metaphor for the reciprocity intrinsic to fulfilled acts of revelation.

The understanding of revelation as a gracious offer inviting the response of faith has important implications for each turn of the revelatory tale. As receiving faith is *itself* a gift of grace and not a human work, theological reflection on the Spirit's epistemic gifts must acknowledge the same ultimate mystery about this presence as that confessed about the soteric gifts of the Spirit:

> But by the grace of God I am what I am, and his grace towards me has not been in vain. On the contrary, I worked harder than any of them – though it was not I, but the grace of God that is with me. (1 Cor. 15:10)

Donald Baillie, in his searching comments on the 'paradox of grace', sheds light as well on the epistemological antinomies, for 'ascribing all to God . . . does not abrogate human personality nor disclaim human responsibility'.[9] The faith that *knows*, as with the faith that *saves*, is at one and the same time divine initiative and human act. We face here a final mystery before which predestinarian, Arminian, synergist and semi-Pelagian rationalisms must maintain a respectful silence in matters of both soteriology and epistemology.

THE ANGELS AND THE WORD

The trinitarian work of communication is not without the activity of the 'messengers of God'.[10] The Scripture bears witness to the instrumental work of the angels in the economy of revelation as well as reconciliation:

> Where God is – the God who acts and reveals Himself in the world created by Him – heaven and the angels are also present . . . At bottom a piety or theology in which there is no mystery, which lacks the mirror of self-representing deity, in which there are therefore no angels, will surely prove to be a godless theology.[11]

Wherever messages are given by the triune God, the messengers are there, agents of the Word empowered by the Spirit. In their prophetic office,[12] they bring good news:

> Do not be afraid. I know that you are looking for Jesus who was crucified. He is not here; for he has been raised . . . (Matt. 28:5–6)

and bad:

> The third angel poured his bowl into the rivers and the springs of water, and they became blood . . . (Rev. 16:4)

Throughout the metanarrative of revelation, wherever the Spirit of the Son brings things to light, only a 'godless theology' would deny an angelic work. Yet the angels are on the margins of the Story, in the stained-glass windows of the sanctuary and not on its altar. We shall presuppose their presence throughout wherever the truth is told, but give central attention to the work of their Source. To the work of the Spirit of the Son of the Father in the narrative of disclosure that rises from the inner-trinitarian Light we now turn.

NOTES

1. The range of important recent writings on the doctrine of the Trinity includes Torrance, *The Trinitarian Faith*, op. cit., and idem, *The Christian Doctrine of God: One Being in Three Persons* (Edinburgh: T. & T. Clark, 1995); Jürgen Moltmann, *The Trinity and the Kingdom: The Doctrine of God*, trans. Margaret Kohl (San Francisco: Harper & Row, 1981); Pannenberg, *Systematic Theology*, vol. 1, op. cit., pp. 259–448; John D. Zizioulas, *Being as Communion* (Crestwood, NY: St Vladimir's Seminary Press, 1985); Eberhard Jüngel, *The Doctrine of the Trinity: God's Being Is in Becoming*, trans. Scottish Academic Press (Grand Rapids: Eerdmans, 1976); Catherine Mowry LaCugna, *God for Us: The Trinity and Christian Life* (New York: HarperSanFrancisco, 1991); Colin E. Gunton, *The One, the Three and the Many: God, Creation and the Culture of Modernity* (Cambridge: Cambridge University Press, 1993); Elisabeth Johnson, *She Who Is: The Mystery of God in Feminist Theological Discourse* (New York: Crossroad, 1992); Leonardo Boff, *Trinity and Society*, trans. Paul Burns (Maryknoll, NY: Orbis, 1988); John J. O'Donnell, *The Mystery of the Triune God* (New York: Paulist Press, 1989); Christoph Schwoebel (ed.), *Trinitarian Theology Today* (Edinburgh: T. & T. Clark, 1995); Millard J. Erickson, *God in Three Persons: A Contemporary Interpretation of the Trinity* (Grand Rapids: Baker Book House, 1995).

2. Two major works representing polar opposites are Alvin J. Kimmel (ed.), *Speaking the Christian God* (Grand Rapids: Eerdmans, 1992) defending the classical formula, and Ruth C. Duck, *Gender and the Name of God* (New York: The Pilgrim Press, 1991) arguing for its alteration. See also, on the trinitarian language question, Donald G. Bloesch, *The Battle for the Trinity: The Debate over Inclusive God-Language* (Ann Arbor, MI: Servant Books, 1985). For a survey of the various positions on inclusive language, see the writer's 'Inclusivity: The Language Debate', *Prism* 9:1 (Spring 1994), 52–65.

3. This is an appropriation here in narrative form of Karl Barth's important distinction between the 'analogy of being' and 'the analogy of faith'. This has implications also for the language debate, for the trinitarian name of God – Father, Son and Holy Spirit – does not derive from our experiences of fathers, sons or spirits, but from meanings brought to them from God's narrative deeds that challenge and alter our human experiences of the same.

4. See Jürgen Moltmann on Karl Barth, in *The Trinity and the Kingdom: The Doctrine of God*, op. cit., pp. 140–4.

5. Thomas Torrance, *Reality and Evangelical Theology* (Philadelphia: Westminster Press, 1982), p. 24. This has a long tradition. See Thomas Aquinas, *Summa Theologica* (London: Blackfriars in conjunction with Eyre & Spottiswoode, 1964), Ia, 14, 1–5, pp. 4–17. The Protestant discussion focused on the distinction between *theologia archetypa* – 'the

knowledge God has of Himself and in Himself' and *theologia ectypa* – our human knowledge of God. See Heinrich Heppe, *Reformed Dogmatics*, revised and edited by Ernst Bizer, trans. G. T. Thomson, foreword by Karl Barth (Grand Rapids: Baker Book House, 1978), pp. 5, 106–8.

6. Torrance, *Reality and Evangelical Theology*, op. cit., pp. 21–51.

7. See the development of the Johannine family imagery for the Trinity in Royce Gordon Gruenler, *The Trinity in the Gospel of John: A Thematic Commentary on the Fourth Gospel* (Grand Rapids: Baker Book House, 1986).

8. This is a formulation proposed by Jürgen Moltmann that takes into account the Eastern Orthodox critique of the double procession. See Jürgen Moltmann, *The Spirit of Life: A Universal Affirmation*, trans. Margaret Kohl (London: SCM Press, 1991), pp. 306–9.

9. Donald Baillie, *God Was in Christ: An Essay on Incarnation and Atonement* (New York: Charles Scribner's Sons, 1948), p. 114.

10. On the three-fold office of angels that draws on Karl Barth's searching discussion of 'the Whence', see the writer's 'Angels Heard and Demons Seen', *Theology Today* 51:3 (October 1994), 345–66.

11. Karl Barth, *Church Dogmatics*, III/3, trans. and ed. G. W. Bromiley and T. F. Torrance (Edinburgh: T. & T. Clark, 1960), p. 477.

12. For a discussion of the 'three-fold office' of angels, and in this case the prophetic office, see Fackre, 'Angels Heard and Demons Seen', *Theology Today*, op. cit., pp. 348–54.

PART I

General Revelation

1

CREATION: THE INVITATION
TO KNOW GOD

———〰〰ᎡᏢ⊙ᎡᎡ〰〰———

Day-to-day questions about goodness and truth beyond the borders of Christian faith and the Christian church are forcefully posed by the reality of contemporary religious pluralism.[1] A narrative response to these issues lies in the opening chapters of the biblical story – creation, fall and the covenant with Noah – and the corollary phase of revelation here discussed as the common grace of *preservation*. The economy of trinitarian revelation begins in the chapter on creation, but includes the chapter on the fall in which the original vision experiences its ocular damage[2] and the promise to Noah of enough of the original light for the world's pilgrimage to go forwards. Thus major questions in classical and contemporary theology identified variously as 'reason and revelation', 'natural theology', 'the natural knowledge of God', 'general revelation', 'common grace', 'God's free communications', the 'supernatural existential', 'human experience and revelation', 'Christ and other religions', 'the state of the *imago Dei*' etc. will be examined in a preliminary conversation with a spectrum of views in Chapter 2, on the fall, and in a sustained conversation with Paul Tillich in Chapter 3, on the covenant with Noah. The present chapter on creation – with no interlocutors – will set the stage for things by reference to the Genesis accounts.

'Creation' in the narrative of revelation has to do with the original disclosive *intention* of God. As the doctrine of revelation is related to the *human* realm within creation – *our* knowledge of God, not the epistemology of angels or atoms – the focus here will be on the human dimension of the created order. If creation is tridimensional – 'nature', 'human nature', 'supernature' – nature and supernature will enter the picture only where germane to the revelatory encounter between God and the creature with the human face.[3]

BIBLICAL BEGINNINGS

'In the beginning...'(Genesis 1:1, John 1:1). Who God is comes to expression in what God wills. The one who is Life Together brings to be a world willed, in turn, to be together. The *koinonia* for which we are destined by the divine *Koinonia* is suggested by the wave of part-nerships brought to be in creation. 'Waters' above and below, and the companion Earth and Seas, are called to be together (Genesis 1:6–10). So, too, light was separated from darkness, and two 'great lights' were made for joint rulership of the partners Night and Day. To render hospitable the earth, on which a special drama is to be played out, 'vegetation' was created with its own duality in the unity of 'plants yielding seed, and fruit trees of every kind on earth that bear fruit ...' (Genesis 1:12). Associated with this terrain are 'swarms of living creatures': 'the fish of the sea', 'the birds of every kind', 'cattle and creeping things and wild animals of the earth of every kind' (Genesis 1:20–5). Each is called to live in its respective habitat and in harmony with one another. The world so declared to be 'good ... very good' (Genesis 1:12, 25, 31) is in accord on the plane of nature with what God is, the loving coinherence of the Persons.

The life together intended for nature that derives from the harmonies of the divine *perichoresis* comes to special focus in *human* nature:

> Then God said, 'let us make humankind in our image, according to our likeness ... So God created humankind in his image; in the image of God he created them ... (Genesis 1:26, 27)

The 'image of God' in which humans are made, according to this rendering of the first chapter of the Story, is in the likeness of God's own social Being. Whether or not the priestly writer intended (by the 'us') that God be understood in divine colloquy, a canonical-cum-trinitarian reading of Genesis 1:26 coheres with the collegial character of the *imago Dei*. (We follow here Karl Barth's exegetical lead.[4]) Human existence shares in the *koinonia* pattern of all creation, but in a special way.

In our sociality, we are called to be representative and steward of creation, and thus given a *capacity* to choose to accept this role. God in sovereign freedom is *Free* to be Together. God gives to those made in the divine image a derivative freedom for partnership, and invites us to exercise it towards the end of life together with God and one another. Nature, created 'good', as God is, is not denied a hint of that capacity, for even the good 'creeping things' include the serpent capable of the use and abuse of respondability.[5] Yet in human beings there is a unique freedom. As representative and custodian of creation, the human race is called to mirror God's own watch-care of the world and capacitated to serve the divine purposes.

Partnership is stamped on all creation, nature with nature and even nature with humanity. Living creatures come to be as 'helpers', for 'it is not good that the man should be alone' (Genesis 2:18). Yet in the animal world 'there was not found a helper to be his *partner*' (Gen. 2:20). Only a *co*-humanity which mirrors the divine coinherence is so fit. Paradigmatic of a partnership in which humans are free-to-be-together is the union of 'Man' with 'Woman' (Gen. 2:23):

> So God created human beings in his own image, in the image of God he created them; male and female he created them (Gen. 1:27) . . . When God created humankind, he made them in the likeness of God. Male and female he created them and he blessed them and named them 'Humankind' when they were created (Gen. 5:1.2). . . . Therefore a man leaves his father and his mother and clings to his wife, and they become one flesh. (Gen. 2:24)

'One flesh' – a life together in which 'the two shall become one . . . no longer two, but one flesh' (Matt. 19:5, 6) – is a knowing together as well as a being and doing together.

> Now the man knew his wife Eve . . . (Gen. 4:1)

'Knowing' is the biblical description of the quintessential union and communion of male and female. The cognitive co-knowing of distinguishable persons in 'one flesh' communion is the image and likeness of the co-knowing God under the conditions of finitude, a mirror of the transparency of the Persons to one another.

The mirror is a *dim* mirror, for there is no *coinherence* of the persons in the human one-flesh communion. The 'moral union' of the conjugal state is different in kind from the 'ontological union' of the triune Being, ours by grace, and God's by nature. The finitude of conjugal knowing is underscored in the dominical declaration that this union is penultimate, but not ultimate, for 'the dead neither marry nor are given in marriage' (Luke 20:35). Yet the language of 'image' (and 'likeness') in Scripture and tradition allows the light given in the most intimate of human knowing to point beyond itself to the inner-trinitarian Light.

As a concordance quickly reveals, biblical knowing moves beyond its one-flesh meaning in both horizontal and vertical directions: human knowledge of the world and human knowledge of God. In this mobility, the analogy becomes further qualified. To know the world – persons, events, objects, ideas etc. – is to 'understand' along a spectrum that runs from distant acquaintance to intimate friendship, as in Martin Buber's distinction between the 'I–It' relation and the 'I–Thou' encounter. And none in this continuum entail the unity of 'one flesh' knowing. To speak of *knowing* God requires the same contextual reserve. While eschatologically 'I will know fully, even as I have been known' (1 Cor. 13:12), this ultimate knowledge of God is still that of a finite knower, different in kind from the self-knowledge of Infinite Being. And in the knowledge of God short of that End, Paul returns us to the mirror imagery, albeit a clouded one (1 Cor. 13:12).

In a narrative interpretation of the doctrine of revelation, the biblical description of the knowledge of God in creation – its pre-fall condition – is a logical place to look for the divine intention. Traditional theologies have sought to find it there with 'original wisdom' keeping company with 'original righteousness'.[6] What God wills for the world is perfect knowledge as well as holiness. Yet neither the Genesis accounts nor random proof-texting from the canon will bear the weight of detailed descriptions of a state of virtue and knowledge attributed in Christian tradition to Adam and Eve in Paradise.[7] The specifics of the Garden tale fix upon the obedience expected of its human inhabitants with the accent on what should not be done, then the disclosure of our non-compliance, the consequent rebuke and the punishment exacted (Genesis 3:3, 9–19). 'Knowing' is entailed in these imperatives and their human rejection. But it has to do with a divine command *not* to know:

> And the Lord commanded the man, 'You may freely eat of every tree of the garden; but of the tree of the knowledge of good and evil you shall not eat' . . . (Gen. 2:16–17)

Indeed, it is not God but the serpent who is the epistemological agent! (Genesis 3:1–5).

But is the story of the tree temptation about 'the knowledge *of* God'? No, it is about knowledge *as* God:

> when you eat of it your eyes will be opened, and you will be like God, knowing good and evil. (Gen. 3:5)

In narrative terms, to eat of the tree is to have the knowledge reserved only for the prologue of the Story, to know as God only knows in the inner-trinitarian Life and Light. To eat of this tree is to want to know, to claim to know, as God alone knows, and thus to commit the primal sin of playing God, idolatry in its epistemological dress (or undress). Here we anticipate the fall, as the chapters of the Story flow into one another, paralleling the interrelationship of all Christian doctrines.

'Original wisdom' is included in the classical concept of *iustitia originalis*, original righteousness before the fall, dissociating the act of cognitive idolatry from the primal 'knowledge of God' given to humans in a good creation. The Genesis stories themselves presuppose that knowledge, the awareness of the divine presence by Adam and Eve and a hearing of the commands of God as to what is 'good' and what is 'evil' – eat of every tree but not this tree – including a hearing of a word from God that eventuates in an obedient naming of the animals (Genesis 2:20). Thus, within the confines of the Genesis accounts themselves, the distinctions made in our narrative reading of revelation emerge: the privileged divine self-knowledge – *theologia in se* – and the knowledge of God purposed for us – *theologia nostra*.

Do the Genesis descriptions of the knowing of God by Adam and Eve, when read as saga not science, still require a *state* of being in human history that has not yet suffered the consequences of the fall? As creation is intrinsically good (*esse est bonum qua esse* – Augustine), creation and fall cannot be coterminous. God's intention must, therefore, correspond to *some* temporal state before the human race's first act of idolatry. In revelatory terms at the very least, there is a *posse cognoscere*, an ability to know the truth, corresponding to a pre-fall 'innocence' as the capacity to do the truth. That there is such a possibility before the fall (with the fall bringing *non posse cognoscere*) is the premise of classical Christian teaching. But what its nature is is not required of that teaching, and is not integral to a theological-cum-critical exegesis of the Genesis tale.[8]

The Genesis chronicles only hint at who God is. The Story must unfold for the chief Character to become clear. Similarly, as noted, the creation stories are modest in their descriptions of our intended knowledge of God. We await the eschatological chapter, for the end of all things is *telos* as well as *finis*. The consummation, when God 'will wipe every tear from their eyes' (Revelation 21:4), will reveal the *visio*

Dei for which we are intended, knowledge in which we 'will know fully, even as [we] have been known' (1 Cor. 13:12).

But now the plot thickens.

NOTES

1. For a comprehensive survey of the issues of salvation as well as revelation prompted by Christian claims to the 'scandal of particularity', and historical and contemporary responses to them from within the Christian community, see John Sanders, *No Other Name: An Investigation into the Destiny of the Unevangelized* (Grand Rapids: Eerdmans, 1993). For a current evangelical-ecumenical exchange of views, see Gabriel Fackre, Ronald Nash and John Sanders, *What About Those Who Have Never Heard?* (Downers Grove, IL: InterVarsity Press, 1995). Mark Heim's important new work, *Salvations* (Maryknoll, NY: Orbis Books, 1995), reviews and critiques a range of pluralist theologies (notably John Hick, W. C. Smith and Paul Knitter) and develops an alternate view that seeks to maintain the primacy of Christian soteric and noetic claims while acknowledging the validity of multiple though secondary salvations and revelations.
2. The plea of Matthew Fox for a 'paradigm shift' from 'original sin' to 'original blessing' eliminates the second chapter of the Christian story. See Matthew Fox, *Original Blessing* (Sante Fe, NM: Bear & Co., 1983).
3. On these distinctions, see Gabriel Fackre, *The Christian Story*, vol. 1, *A Narrative Interpretation of Christian Doctrine*, 3rd edn (Grand Rapids: Eerdmans, 1996), pp. 66–75.
4. Karl Barth, *Church Dogmatics*, III/1, trans. and ed. G. W. Bromiley and T. F. Torrance (Edinburgh: T. & T. Clark, 1958), p. 191f., and *Church Dogmatics*, III/2, trans. H. Knight, G. W. Bromiley, J. K. S. Reid and R. H. Fuller (Edinburgh: T. & T. Clark, 1960), pp. 323–4.
5. Fackre, *The Christian Story*, vol. 1, op. cit., pp. 66–7.
6. See Heinrich Heppe, *Reformed Dogmatics*, op. cit., pp. 238–50.
7. For such, see Augustus Hopkins Strong, *Systematic Theology: A Compendium* (New York: Fleming Revell Co., 1907), pp. 514–32. Strong adduces original righteousness from such texts as 'Eccl. 7:39 – 'God made man upright': ibid., p. 517.
8. Arguments that employ the assumptions of modernity as an alternative to treating the Genesis stories as 'literal' accounts of human beginnings – for example, postulating a stage of purity or innocence in evolution – are unpersuasive. The proposal that the pre-fall state is the *possibility* before the fall of knowing and doing aright, is less so. But finally we are left with the importance of the *that* and the impenetrability of the *what*. On 'critical' and 'theological' exegesis, see the author's exploration of four-fold exegesis of Scripture in *The Christian Story*, vol. 2, op.cit., pp. 157–254.

2

THE FALL: THE NOETIC CONSEQUENCES OF SIN

In the narrative of *reconciliation*, 'the fall' is the No said by the world to the divine invitation to life together. God brought the world to be for a mutuality that mirrors the divine Mutuality, a partnership with God and one another that manifests in finite terms the Infinite Community that God is. In this chapter, the world 'shakes its fist' in the face of God (the metaphor of the African-American poet, James Weldon Johnson, in his poem *God's Trombones*), turning on its heel from the divine beck-oning.[1] Not life together but life alone – the *incurved* life (Luther), the *shutup* way (Kierkegaard): 'There is no-one who is righteous, not even one' (Rom. 3:10). 'Sin' in the narrative is self-*idolatry*, the self – not God – at the centre, the inreach that forswears outreach, the universal *incurvatus in se* that refuses the invitation to community. And its most subtle form is the denial of culpability: 'The man said, "The woman you gave to be with me, she gave me the fruit of the tree" . . . the woman said, "The serpent tricked me"' (Gen. 3:12, 13).

The consequence of the universal No is the estrangement of humanity from Deity and all the intended partners to God's purposes (fellow-humanity, and the realms of nature and supernature). Alienation is death: 'the wages of sin is death' (Rom. 6:23). Death as separation takes many forms. The Genesis tale graphically depicts them:

- the estrangement of humans from God: 'Therefore the Lord God sent him forth from the Garden of Eden . . . He drove out the man . . .' (Gen. 3:23, 24).
- the estrangement of humans from one another: in the place of the unity of 'one flesh . . . and not ashamed' (Gen. 2:24, 25) comes separation and shame (Gen. 3:7), and the rulership over, not the partnership of, one another (Gen. 3:16).
- the estrangement of humans from nature: 'I will greatly increase your pangs in childbearing . . . in toil shall you eat of it all the days of your life; thorns and thistles it shall bring forth for you' (Gen. 3:16, 17, 18).
- the estrangement of nature itself: 'cursed is the ground because of you . . .' (Gen. 3:17).
- the estrangement of humanity from supernature and the hope of eternity: 'and at the east of Eden he placed the cherubim, and a sword flaming and turning to guard the way to the tree of life' (Gen. 3:24).

The *alienation* that marks this second chapter is why Christian faith has to do with a narrative of *reconciliation*.

The inextricability of the narrative of *revelation* from that of reconciliation is strikingly displayed in the Genesis description of the fall. At the centre of this tale is the issue of knowledge. Our *hubris* has to do with the will to know as God alone knows. As indicated in Chapter 1, on creation, the divine intention is not to deny to humanity the knowledge *of* God, but rather knowledge *as* God. The primal sin of playing God is wanting to have our 'eyes opened, and . . . be like God' (Gen. 3:5). The forbidden fruit of 'the tree of the knowledge of good and evil' (Gen. 2:17) is the divine prerogative. God alone dwells in the inner-trinitarian Light. In this sense, too, 'God is known by God alone'.[2]

The invitation to sin in the Genesis story is the 'crafty' serpent, historically portrayed as the devil. As noted, this character plays the role of formulating the nature of human sin – idolatry, ontic and noetic – wanting to be God in wanting to know as God. The role of the devil also signals the weight placed on epistemological deceit, for the serpent's forecast – 'you will not die' (Gen. 3:4) – does not come true. Thus Satan, in Christian theology, is conceived not as a true angelic messenger of God exercising a prophetic office, but as 'the father of lies' (John 8:44).

Sin is estrangement from the divine intention of 'original wisdom' as well as 'original righteousness'. Adam and Eve run from their destiny of knowing and being known by God: 'And the man and his wife hid themselves from the presence of the Lord' (Gen. 38). The One they finally meet is the One they fear, the God of wrath: 'I heard the sound of you in the garden, and I was afraid' (Gen. 3:10). Their will to know as God knows results in knowing the Night of judgment but not the Light of mercy, not knowing the divine Love on the further side of the divine Wrath.

In the Christian story, the non-knowing of God as the God of inner-trinitarian Life and Light is more than 'ignorance'. Finitude, as the limitation of even the sharpest eye of faith by locations biological, social, historical, is the lot of creaturely knowledge of God all along the narrative line of revelation that follows, thus the element of ignorance in every disclosure. Ignorance is our sight of revelation 'in a mirror dimly' (1 Cor. 13:12) short of the final Clarity. On the other hand, the non-knowing coordinate with sin is not ignorance but *error*, a mis-knowledge not the lack of knowledge. 'Original error', therefore, keeps company with 'original sin' – missing the *sight* coordinate with missing the *mark*. The gravity of error is compounded when it is declared to be true knowledge, which assertion becomes *lie* – thus the evasive declarations of Adam and Eve before the questioning of God, the lies that follow in train from their Tempter, the 'father of lies'.

HOW FAR THE FALL?

The question of the consequences of universal sin is taken up in the history of theology as the present state of the 'image of God'. What is its condition 'after the fall'? Destroyed? Damaged, but not destroyed? If damaged, to what extent? Or perhaps it survives the fall intact? The answer depends on what is meant by the *imago Dei*.

In our narrative reading, the *imago* of the chapter on creation was related to the prologue of the Story: the image of God as one flesh union, the paradigmatic 'life together' intended for a world called into being by the ultimate Life Together. As the *intention* of God for the world is embodied in the structure of this co-humanity, the *imago Dei* is inviolate. In this respect, human sin does not impair it. As the *capacity* to fulfil the intention, the image of God has been seriously affected. Called to be *free* to be together, our will is in slavery. Human bondage affects our knowing as well as our being. To what degree?

A CONVERSATION

Our method of inquiry in this work is to enter into conversation with twentieth-century theologians who have given attention to one or another chapter of the revelation Story. The first entry into this forum is an exchange on the question of 'How far the fall?' We choose here as dialogue partners representatives of the Reformed tradition known for its sobriety about the human state, convinced that 'the image of God has been seriously affected'. However, even with this common premise, a range of opinion appears, one that reflects that of the wider Christian conversation. Although the twentieth-century Reformed discussion is our showcase of traditional options, that debate has its antecedents in major figures in the history of the doctrine to which reference will also be made.

While the doctrine of the fall (as part of theological anthropology) is the customary place to explore the question of the present state of the *imago Dei* as capacity, the discussion in the Reformed family takes up also a grace of God that counters the effects of the fall, a 'common grace' with its issue in 'general revelation'. In a narrative understanding of revelation, these have to do with the *next* chapter in the Story, the 'covenant with Noah'. Thus the present conversation anticipates things to come, especially so in the assessment of respective positions. What is often described abstractly as the 'effects of original sin' – the more or less impairment of the capacities of the *imago Dei* – is, in the narrative, not understood without attention to the 'grace of preservation'. As noted earlier, the interrelationship of the chapters in the Story runs parallel to the interrelationship of the doctrines of the church.

FORMATIVE FIGURES

Augustine

Augustine (354–430) significantly shaped Western Christian understandings of the Trinity, grace, the church, baptism, history, human nature and destiny. Interlaced with these classical topics (doctrinal loci, or, narratively described, chapters in the narrative of *reconciliation*) are Augustine's views on the doctrine of revelation. We attend here to those aspects that bear on this chapter of the narrative of revelation, the effects of the fall on the *imago Dei*.

Augustine was an exuberant expositor of the teaching of *iustitia originalis*, the condition of 'original righteousness' before the fall. The perfections of Adam were both spiritual and physical, a will in allegiance to its Maker, desires ordered to their proper end, a state of *posse non peccare*, an ability not to sin, and thus a making of us in the divine likeness, enabled by both creative and preserving graces. The seat of these perfections is the *imago Dei*:

> that image of the Creator, that has been implanted immortally in its own immortality, must be found in the soul of man, that is in the reasonable or intellectual soul . . . that it is able to use its reason and intelligence to understand and behold God.[3]

For all that, humankind mysteriously fell from the original state, indeed 'fell from grace'. The fault belonged to Adam and Eve alone. And what was it?

> nothing else than pride. For 'pride is the beginning of all sin' (Eccl. 10:15). And what is pride but an appetite for inordinate exaltation? Now, exaltation is inordinate when the soul cuts itself off from the very Source to which it should keep close and somehow makes itself and becomes an end in itself.[4]

And none of us is guiltless. We were all co-present in that first fatal choice, ours also the originating sin.

The effects of the fall are a disordered desire, a concupiscence that fixes on the mutable and evanescent, with its final issue, death and damnation. But our concern here is with the noetic consequences. The *imago Dei* as the original capacity for the knowledge of God coordinate with the original righteousness before God is seriously defaced. Ignorance of God is its lot, only to be remedied by the act of God in Jesus Christ, and testimony thereto in Scripture as construed by a magisterial Church. Yet

> so even though reason or intelligence is now dormant . . . yet the human soul is never anything but reasonable and intellectual; and therefore if it were made according to the image of God . . . whether this image be so effaced as almost to amount to nothing, or whether obscured or disfigured, or whether it be clear and beautiful – it always is.[5]

The Augustinian *imago*, deformed but not destroyed, accounts for the sense of incompletion we have, the 'groaning with inexpressible groaning' which he himself experienced in his spiritual journey towards faith and his memorable testimony that 'our hearts are restless 'til they find their rest in thee'. It also enabled him to speak of 'the vestiges of the Trinity' discernible in the created order, including our own introspective depths, and to honour truth wherever found among the philosophers, and for him 'particularly the Platonists'. Be it noted, extrabiblical truth is entrammelled in a fallen state

> improperly and unlawfully prostituted to the worship of demons. The Christian, therefore, can separate these truths from their unfortunate associations, take them away, and put them to their proper use for the proclamation of the gospel.[6]

Commentators such as Reinhold Niebuhr and Colin Gunton have argued that Augustine's stated intention to let 'the proclamation of the gospel' control and relativise his philosophical borrowings regularly faltered and failed.[7] Be that as it may, we are dealing here with the structure of his thought on the *imago* and its destiny after the fall. As J. N. D. Kelly describes it, for Augustine 'human nature has been terribly scarred and vitiated. Augustine does not inculcate a doctrine of "total depravity" . . . Nevertheless the corruption has gone far enough'.[8] As such, his thought anticipates the 'minimalist' themes to be explored.

Thomas Aquinas

While Thomas Aquinas (1225–74), like Augustine, left his mark on a range of Christian teaching in the West, theological epistemology, especially the relation of faith to reason, remains a critical legacy. In a narrative interpretation of revelation, he appears in the discussion of the *imago Dei* and the effects of the fall on it.

The influence of Aristotle is evident in his understanding of the *imago* 'primarily' in terms of its 'intelligent nature'.[9] Yet, with regard to Adam before the fall,

> there are so many authorities of the holy Fathers attesting that man had grace in the state of innocence . . . this rightness was a matter of reason being submissive to God, the lower powers to the reason, body to soul . . . Now it is plain that submission of body to soul and lower powers to reason was not by nature; otherwise it would have persisted afer sin . . . From this it is plain that the primary submissiveness in which reason put itself under God was not something merely natural either, but was a gift of supernatural grace.[10]

The rightness of original reason was dependent on a supernatural endowment.

48

The fall was marked by the entrance of concupiscence, a self-love that turns from God to things mutable, begun in Adam and continuing in us:

> Properly speaking, the cause of sin is assigned by reason of man's turning to perishable good, and from this point of view every sin presupposes an inordinate desire for some temporal good. Man's inordinate desire for a temporal good comes from an inordinate love of himself . . . inordinate self-love is the cause of all sin.[11]

And the noetic effects? The Adamic rectitude made possible by a supernatural endowment was lost as a result of the fall, and with it went the saving knowledge of God. Its effects can only be altered by an act of special revelation and reconciliation, that accomplished in Christ and communicated in Scripture as rightly interpreted by the teaching office of the Church. Yet, the loss of the *donum superadditum* does not destroy the natural capacities of reason (and virtue). In their present state, even after the fall, a 'natural theology' is within the competence of human beings, as reflected in the 'five ways' of plausible argument for the existence of God, and an understanding of 'natural law' as the ways of virtue discernible through reason unaided by revelation.[12] The influence of this anthropology can be seen not only in the teachings and traditions of the Roman Catholic Church but also in the 'maximalist' view to follow of those who sought to reform those teachings and traditions.[13]

THE REFORMED CONVERSATION

A Rejectionist View

Reformed thought includes the assertion of a radical fall, the destruction of the image as *capacity*. Karl Barth represents a version of this view. Later in this volume, we shall engage in detail his alternative christocentric epistemology, including a feature of his later thought that appears to qualify his earlier outright rejection of revelation 'in reason, in conscience, in the emotions, in history, in nature, and its culture and its achievements and developments'.[14] In this rejectionist mode, Barth sternly warns of the enticements of 'natural theology':

> The logic of the matter demands that, even if we only lend a little finger to natural theology, there necessarily follows a denial of the revelation of God in Jesus Christ . . .[15]

Karl Barth's passionate No! to claims of universally discernible creational light requires a different reading of the biblical passages often cited as supportive of it. He acknowledges their existence, especially so the Romans passages, but these are sidelined by 'a deciding line, the chief line of the biblical message'.[16] The Romans 1 and 2 references to 'heathen' knowledge of God are not to be understood as revelation given prior to Christ, but

> the truth ascribed to, reckoned to and imputed to the heathen over and above himself . . . read-into man in the cosmos by the sovereignty of the prophetic-apostolic authority.[17]

That is, only after the incarnate Word do 'the heathen know God', even though they do not realise it.[18] A similar argument is made about the Psalms that have been read as warranting a belief in a knowledge of God from nature. Barth holds that without the revelation of God in Israel's history, the psalmist would not know that the heavens reflect God's glory:

> In itself, and as such, the text of the cosmos is dumb, as is clearly stated in Psalm 19:3. 'There is no speech nor language; their voice is not heard'.[19]

We shall return both in description and evaluation to Barth's alternative understanding of revelation in Chapter 5, on Jesus Christ, noting here his espousal, especially in his earlier writing, of the right end of the Reformed spectrum of thought on the extent of the fall.

A Minimalist View

The Dutch Calvinist, G. C. Berkouwer, is a critic of Barth, turning to this subject in one of the volumes in his series on Christian doctrines, *General Revelation*.[20] Reviewing the passages in question, particularly those in Romans, Berkouwer declares that Barth's exegesis

> is more the result of an a priori view of revelation than an unprejudiced reading of the text itself . . . (and) is isolated from the stream of the history of exposition.[21]

Berkouwer wants to defend the validity of 'general revelation', the activity of God in nature, history and the human conscience, that discloses to the ready eye the being, attributes and expectations of God. Following the teaching of the Johannine prologue and other texts, he views this will-to-disclose as from Christ himself, the pre-existent

Logos. However, 'knowledge and revelation are not identical'.[22] A fundamental distinction must be made between the ontic and the noetic, what is real in the intention and action of God in creation, and what is known of it by universal humanity. Because of the fall, the human organ for perceiving the work of the triune God in the *creation, preservation* and *governance* of the universe'[23] has been incapacitated. The eye designed to receive the revelatory sights has been blinded. Interpreting article 2 of the Belgic Confession accordingly, Berkouwer holds that the

> activity of God in created reality is not *observed* and *acknowledged* ... due ... to the radical darkening of the human heart which did, and does still, withdraw itself from full communion with him, who is very close to the world in all his actions.[24]

Because the objective revelation is not received by the necessary subjective response, there is 'no true knowledge' of God available to humans through the revelation offered universally to them.

For all that, general revelation does have its meaning and even fruitful consequences for a humankind that cannot recognise it for what it is: 'Man can never remove himself so far that the light of revelation no longer shines on his life'.[25] The results of the divine persistence to disclose even in the state of the fall are five-fold.

First, there is an accountability to God for the sin to which humanity succumbs. If there were no objective reality to revelation, then humanity would not be responsible for its rebellion against the will and way of God. But with the ontology of revelation, its givenness in the world's creation, preservation and governance, humanity is now 'without excuse'.[26] This is a major aspect of the disagreement with Barth, Berkouwer holding that Barth wrongly relieves humanity of its culpability.

Second, the shining of the light also leaves a burning in the heart. One effect of a persisting objective revelation is an uneasiness with our state, a longing and groping. We are restless with our condition, 'knowing' we are made for more, in a quest for 'transcendence', and engaged in speculation about human homelessness in the philosophies of our own time.

A third effect is the sense of guilt that rises in the human heart. Thus Berkouwer cites the concealments sought by Adam and Eve after the Fall: 'We do still hear the voice of God after the Fall ... The presence of God, his being not *far*, but *near*, becomes a *problem* for the first time in the trouble[d] conscience'.[27] Our conscience includes a longing for release from the guilt of which we are dimly aware, a quest for a home beyond our homelessness.

Fourth, more than the negative awareness of incompletion are the positive traces left in human consciousness:

> It is indeed remarkable that human life, in manifesting an innate aversion to God and his holy will . . . still stands for right and justice, for punishing that which is evil and rewarding that which is good (cf. Romans 13:3, 4). There is still an appreciation of . . . human community. There is still a searching for truth and knowledge. In short, there is still a *working* of the law written in human hearts which neither know God nor serve him.[28]

The functioning of revelatory disclosure of the law makes possible 'civic virtue', the resistance of 'individualistic self-annihilation', the preservation of the rudimentary conditions of human community. So human beings are aware of the social orderings of God that make governance possible and create the conditions for a livable culture. Such modest attainment of civility and humanity presupposes not only some knowledge of the will of God for human life, albeit not the 'true knowledge' of God and the intended commonwealth of God, but also some capacity to do what is disclosed. Thus the 'common grace' of God in creation makes possible fragmentary knowing and doing, sufficient for a continuing life and life together that avoids 'bestiality' in a fallen world.

Finally, both the judgments of God experienced in the guilty conscience and the restless soul, and the sustenance of God manifest in the elementary civilities of life of which even a rebel world is capable, are evidences of the disclosive patience of Deity. And the biblical account of God speaking to Adam and Eve in their attempted concealment, revealing to them the scope of their offence, and disclosing to us the same in our flight, puts humanity on 'the pathway' towards the long-suffering God's revelatory deeds to come:

> In this revelation lies the beginning of the particular dealings with God, which in the midst of the universal doings of God among all peoples, paves the way for the particularism of salvation in Israel . . . and this history of special revelation leads to, and ends in, the fullness of times: God revealed in the flesh (1 Timothy 3:16).[29]

But we can never forget that we are still in general revelation, far from the endpoint of this journey. Thus the modest effects of the objective divine disclosure among us are themselves subject to the perversity that marks a fallen humanity. The very compass within us that is to aim towards transcendence is deflected to other ends, indeed other gods. Hence the history of idolatries, both those that appear in the world's religions and those that show up in our personal and social demonries, a 'many-sided heathendom and a multi-formed idolatry'.[30]

The import of the Noachic covenant to be discussed in the next chapter is anticipated in the foregoing analysis of Berkouwer. Thus he argues for the reality of divine disclosure in the 'doings of God' to and in creation. Further, he stresses its limits in both intention and exercise: general revelation as the basis for the accountability of humans to God, its negative function being to remind us of our sin, and its positive function giving us enough light and power to know and fulfil in a broken way the norms of human life together. And with that comes the *sensus divinitatis*, but one that occasions the idolatry into which sinners transmute this God-given gift.

With the insights come oddities and inadequacies. Berkouwer's separation of the ontic from the noetic, and his denial of any 'true knowledge' in the human subjectivity receiving the objective acts of revelation, do not comport with the effects of general revelation that he finds in humans, both negative and positive. Transcendent longing and guilt, on the one hand, and the 'actual working of the law' written in our hearts, on the other, are not inconsequential acts of knowing (and being). While they do not constitute knowledge of God or the good of the sort that comes from 'special revelation', they are a knowledge – a reception of revelation – that belies a too-sharp juxtaposition of the ontic and the noetic.

Further, the work of Providence in common grace is not sufficiently credited as the source of the implied knowledge of God. That is, if the ontic and noetic are not functionally as separate as he formally asserts, and if a positive as well as negative role is played by a noetically-effective objective revelation in human affairs (the knowledge of justice and the power to pursue it haltingly), then there is no reason to deny to humans some broken 'vertical' awareness of God, comparable to the broken 'horizontal' awareness of the good:

> Ever since the creation of the world his eternal power and divine nature, invisible though they are, have been understood and seen through the things he has made (Romans 1:20) . . . For what can be known about God is plain to them, because God has shown it to them (Romans 1:19).

What humanity does with this ontic-cum-noetic disclosure is something else: 'For though they knew God they did not honour him as God or give thanks to him' (Romans 1:21). The consequences of that are found in both human knowing and being, namely a misdirection of the worship of God to idolatry:

> Their senseless minds were darkened . . . they became fools; and they exchanged the glory of the immortal God for images resembling a mortal human being or birds or four-footed animals or reptiles (Romans 1:23).

Aspects of the good creation of Genesis are here transformed into gods: humanity, the occupants of the Heavens, the Earth, the Seas. And concurrently, a rupture takes place of the co-humanity for which they were made, both in the male–female paradigm (Romans 1:26–7) and the larger sociality, life together being subverted by the way of 'covetousness . . . envy, murder, strife, deceit . . .' (Romans 1:29).

Pauline characterisations of the estrangement of human beings from one another, and the distortion of the male–female relationship, are reversals of the *imago Dei* in which we are made. With the bondage of the will, the capacity for life together is lost. However, the *form* of the image is untouched, even as the *matter* is seriously damaged. And that form asserts itself in the self-destruction that accompanies refusal to pursue the purpose of human sociality. Humanity knows enough of the purposes for which it is made to have the modicum of life together that enables a continuation of the Story. But no knowledge of the triune Being mirrored in human togetherness is available after the fall. It must await subsequent decisive deeds and disclosures. Berkouwer's restraint as to the knowledge available for us in general revelation is a proper reminder of light and power yet to be. But, for a greater acknowledgement of the awarenesses given to humans in a Noachic covenant, we go to a third partner in the Reformed conversation.

A Maximalist View

With Aquinas as exemplar, we turn to Bruce Demarest, a North American evangelical whose work *General Revelation* examines alternative positions in both classic and contemporary Christian thought and then sets forth a view of God's universal disclosure that goes beyond the minimalist view of Berkouwer.[31] Indeed, Demarest, while critical of Aquinas for failing 'to account sufficiently for the debilitating affects of the Fall on man's cognitive faculty',[32] can yet say: 'Thomas Aquinas must be commended for stressing the rationality of the Christian faith'.[33] Demarest's affirmation includes an approval of 'natural theology', albeit one of more modest scope than that proposed by Aquinas. He departs in this respect from other conservative evangelicals who trace the roots of 'secular humanism' to the thought of Thomas Aquinas himself.[34] Thus Demarest argues:

> although Francis Schaeffer's paradigm of 'nature eating up grace' is certainly true of Enlightenment humanism and later liberal theology, it is unjustly applied to the Angelic Doctor himself . . . Thomas painstakingly delineated the upper limits of reason's competency.[35]

Demarest finds in the biblical passages in question two kinds of universal revelation: a *sensus divinitatis* in each human soul, and manifestations of God's reality and truth in creation (both nature and history), each accessible to humankind even in its fallen state. In the former case, 'man created in the image of God and universally illumined by the Logos, effably intuits the reality of God as a first truth'.[36] This is a 'timeless truth', a knowledge of God given and received in immediacy 'from the first moment of mental and moral self-consciousness'.[37] Such an intuition also 'involves consciousness of God's moral law, written in the heart'.[38] In the latter case, 'Man by common grace not only intuits the reality of a Supreme Being . . . but also infers the existence and character of God by rational reflection on the date of the created universe'.[39] The data from which humans can draw these inferences are the world of nature, on the one hand, and the dynamics of history, on the other. From these '*indicia*' which reinforce the intuitive a priori, the existence of God can be argued and some of the divine attributes discovered. Sifting through such passages as Psalms 19:1, 8:3–4, 29:4, 104:24, 93:2; Acts 17:24–7, 14:15–16; Romans 1:18–20, 32, 2:15–16, Demarest contends not only that humans can discover that God exists, but also that Deity is uncreated Creator, Sustainer and universal Lord, One who is self-sufficient, transcendent, immanent, eternal, great, majestic, powerful, wise, good and righteous, has standards of right and wrong, should be worshipped, should perform the good, and will judge evil:

> In sum: God's glory (Psalm 19:1), divine nature (Romans 1:20), and moral demands (Romans 2:14–15), are to some extent known through general revelation.[40]

And

although the arguments for God's existence have fallen on hard times at the hands of modern liberal and neo-orthodox theologians, they undoubtedly are useful apologetic tools by which a rationally significant case for biblical theism can be advanced . . . Scripture thus upholds a natural theology. . . .[41]

In these assessments of fallen humanity's access to the knowledge of God, we are a long way from the rejectionist view. Not all the way to the Thomistic version of natural theology, according to Demarest, because the latter seeks to prove its case by airtight argument. Also it denies the intuitive aspect of religious epistemology, basing its arguments only on evidence of the senses. As such, it is a speculative rationalism that 'lacks immediacy and warmth', bifurcating nature and grace. These tendencies are related to the Thomistic lack of biblical realism about human sin, grounding assertions of the natural knowledge of God in a theory about the fall which holds that only the added gift, *donum superadditum*, was lost. With a nature/grace distinction before and after the fall, traditional Roman Catholic theology leaves in doubt the divine initiative, one that must be presupposed as general revelation coming from a common grace that gives light to human reason.

General revelation in Demarest's perspective means disclosure at both ontic and noetic poles. What God wills in the face of human resistance is what God does. Thus the light that shines in creation, contrary to Berkouwer, *is* perceived through a human epistemological sight dimmed but not destroyed. The merit of the maximalist interpretation is a recognition that noetic grace, as all grace, is *power* as well as *favour*, as befits its agent, the Holy Spirit. The power of God at this stage of the Story is the sustenance of creation in preparation for deeds and disclosures to come.

Demarest indicates three places where the Spirit's nurturing work is stated or implied: the inner life of the self and the outer worlds of nature and history. Revelation given to all has to do with both horizontal and vertical reality: knowledge of the things in human relationships that make life livable, and enough awareness of a Presence to which it is accountable to sustain the human journey forwards. God keeps the promise to provide for creation the necessities of life. Demarest thus makes a good case for the inseparability of the ontic and noetic. However, it is accompanied by an inflated estimate of fallen humanity's cognitive capabilities. While criticising Thomas for an inordinate confidence in human reason and diminishment of the effects of the fall, 'natural theology' makes a bold entrance. In the covenant with Noah to be explored, 'general revelation' and 'common grace' are bashful not bold, far short of the warrants needed for a 'natural theology' that can establish by reason the existence and attributes of God, or a 'natural law' that can discern in detail norms of human behaviour.

In a narrative interpretation of both reconciliation and revelation, the state of the image of God cannot be abstracted from the Story. What we are and what we know have to do with the forbearance of God in the unfolding of the divine purposes. That patience with the human race is reported in Scripture as a 'rainbow sign', the promise of God to keep the Story moving ahead, and to provide the conditions for the pursuit of that journey. Thus the capacities of the *imago Dei* to know and to do will be set in the midst of the sustaining promise to be taken up in the next chapter.

Before proceeding to that chapter, a comment on a literary feature of the emerging narrative of revelation is in order.

METAPHOR AND MEANING

The citation and interpretation of Genesis in these early chapters have fixed on its rich theological metaphors. Such figures, and the extended metaphors we call stories, pervade Scripture. In Chapter 6, on the authority of the Bible, their role in 'inspiration' will be explored. Here we note how Donald Baillie, in *God Was in Christ*, brings together in a metaphor-rich parable the early chapters in the narratives of both reconciliation and revelation.[42] It summarises, in biblical light–imagery and the language of his day, the course of the 'sacred story' we have traversed to this point,

> a tale of God calling his human children to form a great circle for the playing of His game. In that circle we ought all to be standing, linked together with lovingly joined hands, facing toward the Light in the centre, which is God . . . seeing our fellow creatures all round the circle in the light of that central Love, which shines on them and beautifies their faces; and joining with them in the dance of God's great game, the rhythm of love universal. But instead of that, we have, each one, turned our backs upon God and the circle of our fellows, and faced the other way, so that we can neither see the Light at the centre nor the faces on the circumference. And indeed in that position it is difficult even to join hands with our fellows! Therefore instead of playing God's game

we play, each one, our own selfish little game . . . Each one of us wished to be the centre, and there is blind confusion, and not even any true *knowledge* of God or our neighbors. That is what is wrong with mankind. Of course a man is not really happy in that attitude and situation, since he was created for community with God and man. Moreover the light of God is still shining from the true centre upon his back, though not on his face. It throws his own shadow on the ground in front of him, and the shadow is contorted into grotesque shapes with every movement that he makes until his whole world looks queer and unfriendly (it is indeed a fallen world, a ruined world). He knows, dimly or clearly, that not all is well . . . But God has not given mankind up.[43]

In this imaginative rendition of the Story, Baillie takes us from the loving Light of the Prologue through creation's intention of life and light together with God and one another, to our narcissistic about-face – *incurvatus in se* – and its night of estrangement. But there is also the lingering awareness of our destiny, for God 'has not given . . . up' on us. About that steadfast love and light, the next chapter speaks.

NOTES

1. So portrayed visually in Dorothy and Gabriel Fackre, *Christian Basics* (Grand Rapids: Eerdmans, 1994), p. xv.
2. An adaptation to the inner-trinitarian Life of Karl Barth's christocentric epistemological refrain.
3. St Augustine, *The Trinity*, trans. Stephen McKenna (Washington: Catholic University of America Press, 1963), Book XIV, Chapter 4, (6), p. 417.
4. St Augustine, *The City of God*, trans. Gerald G. Walsh and Grace Manahan (Washington: Catholic University of America Press, 1952), Book XIV, Chapter 13, p. 380.
5. *The Trinity*, op. cit., p. 418.
6. Ibid. Alister McGrath quotes this passage as representative of Augustine's intentionally selective use of philosophical sources: 'Augustine on Philosophy and Theology', in Alister McGrath (ed.), *The Christian Theology Reader* (Oxford: Blackwell, 1995), p. 6.
7. See Reinhold Niebuhr, *The Nature and Destiny of Man: A Christian Interpretation*, vol. 1 (New York: Charles Scribner's Sons, 1945), pp. 153–9; and Gunton, *A Brief Theology of Revelation*, op. cit., pp. 43–6.
8. Kelly, *Early Christian Doctrines*, op. cit., p. 364.
9. St Thomas Aquinas, *Summa Theologiae*, vol. 13, trans. Michael Cardinal Browne and Fr Aniceto Fernández (London: Blackfriars in conjunction with Eyre & Spottiswoode, 1963), First Part, Question 93, Article 3, p. 57.

10. Ibid., Question 95, Article 1, p. 109.

11. St Thomas Aquinas, *Summa Theologiae*, vol. 25, trans. John Fearon OP (London: Blackfriars in conjunction with Eyre & Spottiswoode, 1968), First Part, Question 77, Article 4, p. 173.

12. For an extract on 'the five ways', see McGrath, *The Christian Theology Reader*, op. cit., pp. 10–12.

13. There are many historical anticipations of views that move beyond Augustine and Aquinas and the points of view to be discussed in 'the Reformed conversation'. Thus a forerunner of the variety of views represented in the next chapter, that restate revelation in the categories of reason or some other form of human experience, is the deism of Matthew Tindal, for whom revelation is the 'republication' of the purities of reason. He contended

> that the religion of nature is absolutely perfect Religion; and external Revelation can neither add to, nor take from its Perfection; that True Religion, whether internally or externally reveal'd must be the same.

Matthew Tindal, *Christianity as Old as the Creation: A Republication of the Religion of Nature* (London: n.p., 1730), p. 58.

14. Karl Barth, *Church Dogmatics* II/1, trans. T. H. L. Parker, W. B. Johnson, H. Knight and J. L. M. Haire (Edinburgh: T. & T. Clark, 1957), p. 173. Bruce Demarest, critic of Barth, notes the 'new emphasis' that appears in the volume we shall examine, IV/3/1, commenting however that in a subsequent work, *Evangelical Theology*, the new tack is not taken up. Bruce A. Demarest, *General Revelation* (Grand Rapids: Zondervan Publishing House, 1978), p. 128.

15. Karl Barth, *Church Dogmatics* II/1, op. cit., p. 173.

16. Ibid., p. 112.

17. Ibid., p. 134.

18. See also ibid., p. 335, and *Church Dogmatics*, II/2, trans. G. W. Bromiley, J. C. Campbell, I. Wilson, J. Strathearn McNab, H. Knight and R. A. Stewart (Edinburgh: T. & T. Clark, 1957), pp. 345–54; and *Church Dogmatics*, I/2, trans. G. W. Bromiley and T. F. Torrance (New York: Charles Scribner's Sons, 1956), pp. 304–7.

19. Barth, II/1, p. 123.

20. G. C. Berkouwer, *General Revelation*, trans. from the Dutch edn (Grand Rapids: Eerdmans, 1983).

21. Ibid., p. 154.

22. Ibid., p. 314.

23. Ibid., p. 291.

24. Ibid., p. 291.

25. Ibid., p. 130.

26. Ibid., p. 228.

27. Ibid., p. 309.

28. Ibid., p. 202.
29. Ibid., p. 310.
30. Ibid., p. 151.
31. Demarest, *General Revelation*, op. cit.
32. Ibid., p. 42.
33. Ibid., p. 41.
34. As, for example, Tim LaHaye in *The Battle For the Mind* (Old Tappan, NJ: Fleming Revell, 1980), pp. 27–30, and behind his views those of Francis Schaeffer.
35. Demarest, *General Revelation*, op. cit., p. 42.
36. Ibid., p. 228.
37. Ibid., p. 228.
38. Ibid., p. 231.
39. Ibid., p. 233.
40. Ibid., p. 243.
41. Ibid., p. 240.
42. Baillie's story has had wide influence in catechesis and in evangelism in North American mainline churches, viz. the United Church of Christ, *Evangelism for a New Day* (New York: United Church Board for Homeland Ministries, 1973), passim.
43. D. M. Baillie, *God Was in Christ: An Essay on Incarnation and Atonement* (New York: Scribner's, 1948), pp. 205–6.

3

THE COVENANT WITH NOAH: THE GRACE OF PRESERVATION

———〜〜ЯЯ⊙ЯЯ〜〜———

How does the world fare after the fall? A sorry picture develops. In the Genesis drama, God warns that 'sin is lurking at the door' (Gen. 4:7) and Cain proves it by slaying his brother Abel (Gen. 4:8), reaping the divine punishment (Gen. 4:9–16). Generations come and go without narrator comment on the fallen condition of the world except for the reminder of 'the ground that the Lord has cursed' (Gen. 5:29), until the divine lament:

> The Lord saw that the wickedness of humankind was great in the earth, and that every inclination of the thoughts of their hearts was only evil continually. And the Lord was sorry that he had made humankind on the earth, and it grieved him to his heart. So the Lord said, 'I will blot out from the earth the human beings I have created – people together with animals and creeping things and birds of the air, for I am sorry that I have made them'. (Gen. 6:5–8)

And again

> Now the earth was corrupt in God's sight, and the earth was filled with violence. And God saw that the earth was corrupt; for all flesh had corrupted its ways upon the earth. (Gen. 6:11–12)

Yet a turn comes in this sorry tale: 'Noah was a righteous man, blameless in his generation; Noah walked with God' (Gen. 6:9). While punishment is wreaked upon the corrupt world, God relents. Noah is saved, creation is sustained – and a *covenant* comes to be:

> I will establish my covenant with you; and you shall come into the ark, you, your sons, your wife, and your sons' wives with you. And of every living thing, of all flesh, you shall bring two of every kind into the ark, to keep them alive with you; they shall be male and female. (Gen. 6:18–19)

'Covenant', *berith*, as initiated by God, is a solemn promise to carry out a divine purpose. It bonds God to a people: 'I will take you as my people, and I will be your God' (Exodus 6:7). This divine will-to-life-together is the issue of God's own Life Together. In this sense, God *is* Covenant, willing for and doing with the world what is commensurate with the divine Being. Thus the history of God with the world can be, and has been, construed as a series of covenants, beginning with creation itself, or with Adam as a 'covenant of works', continuing through Noah, Abraham, Moses, Aaron, Phineas, David, Jesus Christ, the church etc.[1] And each of these covenants with the world can be grounded in a pre-temporal covenant between the Father and the Son.

Following explicit biblical usage and the overarching narrative of revelation, we locate the chapter on covenant where it first appears in Scripture – in the promise made to Noah. The 'people' whom Noah represents are the generations to come, the whole world after the fall. In the initial reference to the bonding of God with Noah, we hear echoes of God's original intent, the willing of 'male and female', life together at every level, with its capstone in co-humanity. Recruitment for a new faithfulness to the unconditional love of God in the two-by-two companionship of male and female of all species continues the hope of God recorded in Genesis accounts of Eden. Noah and spouse, sons and daughters, are the germ of a reoriented race with a potential for the life together ordained by God. With them, the disordered creation is called to a similar bonding, the various species of non-human life paralleling those of the original creation entering the ark:

> Of the birds according to their kinds, and of the animals according to their kinds, of every creeping thing of the ground according to their kinds, of every creeping thing of the ground according to its kind, even the serpents, two of every kind shall come in to you to keep them alive. (Gen. 6:20)

The writer then tells of the work of devastation done by the flood, God's judgment on the sin of the world, blotting out

> every living thing that was on the face of the ground, human beings and animals, creeping things and birds of the air . . . Only Noah was left, and those that were with him in the ark. (Gen. 7:23)

Thus, after the deluge, the rescue and promise.

The covenant with Noah carries with it a characteristic of all God's covenant-making: irrevocability. God does not go back on the divine intention. The No of the world cannot turn aside the Yes of the Word. Covenants are for keeps. This unconditionality of the divine love in the economy *ad extra* is again rooted in the unreserved self-giving of the Persons, one to Another in the immanence of divine Love, *ad intra*. And now, after the fall, the depths of that bonding love are demonstrated as mercy toward sinful stewards, divine love absorbing divine wrath, giving the world yet another chance.

We note in passing that in these remarkable chronicles of Israel, the ancient writers have laid the epistemological foundations of the Great Story. As we shall contend in a subsequent discussion of the inspiration of Scripture, the Holy Spirit is active in the formation of a creaturely-conditioned tradition, disclosing to the eye of faith who the source of our world is, what Deity intends for this world, created good in nature and supernature, with a human nature made in the divine image, a world resisting the divine purposes but not abandoned to self-destruction. Employing the cosmology of its time with its Seas, Heavens and Earth, its levels of inanimate and animate existence, its Edenic garden with walking deity and talking serpent, and its archetypal figures such as Adam, Eve, Abel, Cain and Noah, it gives a glimpse to the eye of faith of the divine purposes on their way.

The lasting universal covenant with Noah is the promise of *preservation*. Preservation is the work of the triune Providence sustaining the world in its journey towards its purposed End. The gift given by the Spirit of the Father of the Son is a *common grace* that both enables and enlightens. The latter is our focus in the narrative of revelation which we are tracing here.

THE NOACHIC COVENANT OF REVELATION

What revelatory light is shed on our way by the rainbow sign? As noted in Chapter 2, this question is answered in the Christian tradition by a doctrine variously called 'general revelation', 'natural revelation', 'the natural knowledge of God', 'natural theology', 'natural law' etc., with different degrees of confidence in the accessibility of that light. We began our investigation of the question with a conversation on the present state of the *imago* and now reframe these themes in terms of the Noachic narrative:

> Then God said to Noah and to his sons with him, 'As for me, I am establishing my covenant with you and your descendants after you, and with every living creature that is with you . . . This is the sign of the covenant that I make between me and you and every living creature that is with you, for all future generations: I have set my bow in the clouds, and it shall be a sign of the covenant between me and the earth'. (Gen. 9:8–10, 12–13)

The long-suffering God will not give up on a rebellious creation.

The promise of the world's continued being includes the promise of the world's continued knowing. The rainbow is a 'sign' – for God (Gen. 9:16), but also for us (Gen. 9:14). We are not left 'without a witness' (Acts 14:17) to those things necessary to know for the Great Narrative to go forwards. What are 'those things'?

Inextricable from the covenantal promise are covenantal imperatives. Genesis 9:1–7 enjoins Noah's heirs to raise new generations, care for the earth and respect human worth, 'for in his own image God made humankind' (Gen. 9:6). The hate and hurt of humans by humans is a violation of the image of dignity and divine sociality in which this race of beings is made. As God is lovingly free to be together, so we are designed in that image in creation now reaffirmed in the Noachic covenant. And when we violate that purpose, we pay the consequences.

For the narrative to continue, therefore, enough moral and rational light must be cast on the path ahead, and enough of a glimpse of the goal given for humans to make their way. Allusion to this light is made throughout Scripture. Thus the injunctions in Proverbs, Job and Ecclesiastes to find wisdom, seek justice, care for those in need, strive for peace, speak the truth, share one's substance, love honesty, be slow to anger and forgive readily. These are the elementary laws of life together, without which both self and society are destroyed. G. C. Berkouwer delineates them in his modest view of general revelation. Indeed, when the universal light so given is scorned, judgment falls upon 'the transgressions of Damascus, Gaza . . . Edom . . . the Ammonites . . . Moab . . .' (Amos 1–2). The knowledge of the laws of life together in a rabbinic tradition functioning as early as the second century Chanina ben Gamaliel is identified as 'the Noachian precepts'. As such, humanity beyond the singular history of God with Israel is not excluded from knowledge of the 'Noahide laws' that make and keep life human.[2]

The noetic aspect of the covenant with Noah is reflected in the New Testament allusions to revelatory light available to human beings outside the particularity of Israel and Christ to which references has been made, especially John 1:9, Romans 1:19–20, 2:14–15, 12:17, 13:1–6, Acts 14:17, 17:22–8, 1 Cor. 11:14–16, 15:31, 1 Peter 2:12, Mark 10:1–9, Matt. 5:16, 7:11, 16, 19:1–9, Luke 12:5, 14:8–10.[3] They are modest indicators, given by Providence, to the standards of a sustainable life in the face of the threat to that life by the imperial self-will at work in a fallen world.

The biblical reference to the sensibilities – moral, affective, rational – that sustain human life speak of, or presuppose, an awareness of their Source. Thus in the Noah story, the promises and mandates are given in the context of a word from God: 'God blessed Noah and his sons, and said to them . . .' (Gen. 9:1). In like manner, Paul's references to Gentile knowledge 'since the creation of the world' allude to aware-nesses of God – 'they know God . . .', however qualified by 'minds . . . darkened' and 'futile . . . thinking' (Romans 1:19–22). Thus, as devel-oped in the 'yes and no' conversation with Berkouwer and Demarest, a common grace is at work in fallen creation discomfiting secular certainties, opening hearts and minds to the possibility of Another with whom we have to do. In their stumble and fall, humans are too prostrate to see the Source of the light they have, the rational aspects of their *imago* too damaged to construct persuasive arguments for the existence or attributes of God. But there is enough light from 'the rainbow' to point them beyond, bestirring them to 'search for God and perhaps grope for him and find him' (Acts 17:27).

The rainbow is a apt light-symbol for expressing the modest dis-closive grace given in this phase of the revelatory Story. It speaks of a light given against the background of the storm and darkness of the fall. Not 'twilight knowledge' (Emil Brunner) left over at the end of the day, but a new gift given, pointing forwards with the promise of things to come.

Faithfulness to this chapter of the Christian story has implications for many current and future theological questions. Is there a basis for common conversation across diverse cultures, traditions and religions?

Are there warrants within Christian faith for collegialities and mutualities across those same boundaries? If there is reason for such concourse, what is the criterion we bring to it?

In this reading of the Christian story, as in a parallel reading of the 'Jewish story',[4] the 'Noahides' are partners in the biblical journey. To them is given a universal covenant, the promise of enough noetic light and soteric power to keep the drama moving towards its End. As gifts of the triune God, truth, goodness and beauty, wherever they are found are to be honoured. Because they are gifts of the Spirit of the Son, the *criterion* by which such offerings are discerned and judged is Jesus Christ. And because this chapter is part of the Christian story, conversation across culture and tradition is warranted, and collegiality and mutual enrichment is possible. Indeed, God can raise up an 'Assyria' as the 'rod' of divine anger (Isaiah 10:5) to call Christians to account before their own standards, as secular movements of justice and peace in the twentieth century have done. Often, graced human experience beyond the boundaries of Scripture and church functions as catalyst for the recovery of forgotten Christian commitments. Yet the biblical witness to Jesus Christ is the standard before which all such claims to 'liberation' and 'reconciliation' must pass, one which accordingly transforms and conforms whatever is given in the 'general revelation' of a fallen world to the disclosures of 'special revelation' in Jesus Christ.

The covenant with Noah has similar implications for Christian witness and relationships in a religiously plural world. God has not left the world without a witness to the divine Presence. Conversation across the boundaries between Christian faith and the world religions is legitimate, for the triune God is the universal giver of transcendent as well as immanent light and power. As in the case of justice and truth, so also with 'the holy', the standard by which other religious claims are assessed in interfaith dialogue is Jesus Christ as witnessed to in Scripture and illumined by the church and its traditions. Common cause as well as common conversation is legitimate and necessary, for convergences on critical issues of justice and peace, as normed by the Gospel, invite Christians into partnership in a shared struggle for a livable planet. And mutual enrichment is possible as well, for interreligious dialogue and collegiality can help Christians recover neglected aspects of their own tradition, and in turn enable others to do the same.

Because the covenant with Noah is only an early phase in the narrative of both reconciliation and revelation, the noetic and soteric gifts given are far short of the Light and Power yet to come. While the common grace of preservation is a 'scandal of *universality*', and thus a judgment on all imperialisms that deny truth beyond Christian boundaries, and all social solipisms that deny the possibility of cross-cultural communication, the longer Story will tell of a 'scandal of *particularity*' in Jesus Christ. With it comes an enlightening and saving grace to which Christians joyfully witness in all conversations, colleagueships and mutualities made viable by the grace of preservation.[5]

In the narrative we are following, the thought of Paul Tillich appears in this chapter on the covenant with Noah. Tillich did not, in general, think narratively and would resist location at this point in the Story. Yet his probe into the role of philosophical, moral and affective sensibilities and his exploration of 'ultimate concern' witness in their own way to the universal noetic gift. At the same time, his rereading of the Story in these categories seriously foreshortens the narrative of revelation. As with our other three major interlocutors, we shall investigate his position in detail, drawing on a key volume of his work on the subject of revelation.

PAUL TILLICH

In *A Directory of Systematic Theologians in North America*, Paul Tillich is cited as mentor more often than any other theologian.[6] Well beyond that, his influence lives on in a variety of existential, secular and pluralist theologies. Tillich's impact is directly related to his thought on this doctrine. For a succinct statement of it, we turn to Volume 1 of his *Systematic Theology*.[7] As the concept of authority is inseparable from the doctrine of revelation, we begin with Tillich's treatment of the 'sources' of authority.

THE WORLD OF EXPERIENCE

The three dimensions of human experience – rational, moral and affective – appear in the Tillichian terms of metaphysical, ethical and mystical and their equivalents.[8] And he deals with the substance of each under yet other rubrics: the role of 'the situation', the contextual 'question' which a 'theology of culture' (an 'answering theology') seeks to identify in an epoch like ours that gives prominence to moral/ethical issues; the place of rational/metaphysical investigation, as in the role of philosophy vis-à-vis theology; and the place of 'experience' (the affective/mystical) in the work of theology.

CONTEXTUALITY: THE SITUATION

The responsible theologian works in the framework of 'the situation' – 'the totality of man's creative self-interpretation in a special period'.[9] Tillich contends that political, psychological, sociological and artistic commentary on the dynamisms of a particular time and place can identify the historical context to which faith must speak. Thus Picasso's Guernica, Sartre's No Exit, Karen Horney's theory of anxiety, Marx's concept of estrangement and other cultural indicators are 'temperature tests' (James Luther Adams) of the time.[10] To ignore this reading of the current situation is to turn theology into barren self-preoccupation: 'Fundamentalism and orthodoxy reject this task, and in doing so they miss the meaning of theology'.[11]

The 'kerygmatic theology' of Karl Barth is similarly indicted. While Tillich believes that Barth intuitively draws on discernments of the cultural situation, he holds that Barth rejects their relevance and falls into 'orthodox fixation'.[12] Sound theology attends to the cultural issues and is therefore 'apologetic' theology. It must retain the intent of 'kerygmatic' theology, however, by being faithful to the 'Christian message'. With these two reference points, theology employs the 'method of correlation', seeking to ascertain the question put forward by the situation, then bringing to bear on it the 'Christian message . . . the eternal truth of its foundation'.[13]

Tillich, writing in the mid-twentieth century, finds the cultural question to be 'self-estrangement':

> It is not an exaggeration to say that today man experiences his present situation in terms of disruption, conflict, self-destruction, meaninglessness, and despair in all realms of life. This experience is expressed in the arts and in literature, conceptualized in 'existential' philosophy, actualized in political cleavages of all kinds, and analyzed in the psychology of the unconscious. It has given theology a new understanding of the demonic-tragic structures of individual and social life.[14]

Other eras of the church's life were confronted with different issues, and had to make commensurate response. But we cannot repeat their answers.

> The question arising out of this experience is not, as in the Reformation, the question of a merciful God and the forgiveness of

> sin . . . It is a question of a reality in which the self-estrangement of our existence is overcome, a reality of reconciliation and reunion, of creativity, meaning and hope. We shall call such a reality the 'New Being'.[15]

To the pervasive cultural question of *non-being* must come the answering theology of *New Being*.

The theological work of appropriating cultural commentary entails a 'theology of culture',

> the attempt to analyze the theology behind all cultural expressions, to discover the ultimate concern in the ground of a philosophy, a political system, an artistic style, a set of ethical or social principles . . . It has become an important part of many critical analyses of the present world situation, of the cultural decline of the West, of developments in special realms . . . The style of a period expresses itself in cultural forms, in its choice of objects, in the attitudes of its creative personalities, in its institutions and its customs.[16]

In many of his writings, Tillich seeks to 'read the style' of his own time in its art forms, political movements and social and psychological disciplines.[17]

Tillich's incorporation of 'the situation' into theology (and preaching and teaching in the church) presupposes a view of revelation. Before examining it, however, a closer look at the concept of *experience* is in order. 'Experience' makes its appearance in Tillich's critique of the mid-century 'empirical theologies' of Alfred North Whitehead, Henry Nelson Wieman and William Ernest Hocking. He holds that an 'ontological shock' lies behind their architectonic theories,

> another kind of experience, an immediate participation in religious reality . . . their religious experience in a mystical sense . . . their personal religious life.[18]

The 'mystical sense' alluded to here is kindred to Friedrich Schleiermacher's 'sense of absolute dependence' or Rudolf Otto's experience of the holy. Tillich has his own special language for this 'awareness of something unconditional':[19] *ultimate concern*.

Affective terms abound in his description of ultimate concern – anxiety, longing, ecstasy. While illustrating his thesis from the mystical, spiritual, 'enthusiastic', pietist and existentialist traditions, he insists that the clothing of this experience cannot be mistaken for its body. Unconditional concern is a quality of all human experience, as humans are 'grasped' ultimately through varied penultimate claimants.

In his *Systematic Theology*, Tillich clarifies an ambiguity in his description of the experience noted by critics of his earlier work. The term 'unconditional' is rendered adjectivally, and its use as a noun ('the Unconditioned') is abandoned. This move is made to avoid the misunderstanding of the awareness as an encounter with a transcendent Entity. Unconditional concern is an experience of 'the holy', rather than 'the Holy One' the existence of which we could doubt or argue about.[20] The latter would, according to Tillich, be making God 'an object among other objects'. Ultimate concern is an experience of 'depth', one that takes place at a level below the subject–object distinction.

Another unclarity persists, however: the relation of the experience of ultimacy to the varying historical contexts. Does the experience change with each new 'situation'? Many of Tillich's characterisations of ultimate concern are couched in the language of 'being' vis-à-vis 'non-being'. Thus the human encounter with *finitude* is regularly associated with the experience of the unconditional. What ultimately counts is what gives us 'the courage to be' in the face of non-being, a common refrain in the existential philosophy of his period. We shall return to this interrelationship of experience and interpretation in the next section on the role of philosophy in Tillich's theology.

Tillich's *Systematic Theology* is marked by another development in his thought on the place of experience in matters of authority. In Volume 1, he applies the term 'medium' to experience in order to distinguish it from the 'sources' of theological construction. At the same time, however, he 'denies the assertion that experience is in *no* sense a source'.[21] Tillich's ambivalence has to do with the formative role which he wants to assign to experience, even though he judges that 'experiential theologies' have been so open to new experiences – from world religions, for example – that they 'might even pass beyond the confines of Christian experience',[22] and seek to exercise hegemony over it. Thus he asserts that the integrity of the Christian message must be protected, and accountability to the christological norm maintained. Christian theology is based on the unique event,

> Jesus the Christ. In spite of the infinite meaning of this event it remains *this* event and, as such, the criterion of every religious experience. This event is given to experience and not derived from it.[23]

For all that, experience does affect our understanding of the event, Jesus the Christ. Indeed, it 'transforms' the message: 'The medium colours the presentation and determines the interpretation of what it receives'.[24] This transformation is necessary, according to Tillich, in order to avoid a lifeless repetition of the message. But we must be wary of going too far by making the result 'a new production instead of a transformation'.[25] Experience is always a 'dependent medium', relying on the 'objective sources' as they are interpreted by the christological norm.

While the theologian's *personal* experience is the focus of Tillich's developed section on this subject, 'collective experience' – the characteristic modes of life and thought of a given culture – is drawn into the discussion of 'medium'. 'Collective as well as individual experiences are the mediums through which the message is received, coloured and interpreted'.[26] Used in this way, 'experience' and 'situation' overlap. What receives, colours and transforms the presentation of the message, therefore, are situational factors, ones which include the interpretive frameworks that identify the regnant cultural question. Important implications for the doctrine of revelation follow from this contention.

Philosophy is one of the resources for identifying the cultural problematic. We turn next to its place in Tillich's view of authority.

PHILOSOPHY

Philosophy, for Tillich, is rooted in the larger concept of 'ontological reason'. In contrast to 'technical reason' – reasoning about means, attentive to evidence and the laws of logic – ontological reason is 'the reason that knows being'. As such, it is the human engagement with the *logos* of being, a 'subjective reason' that has access to, and seeks unity with, the 'objective reason' that constitutes the vertebrae of reality. Ontological reason expresses itself in 'cognitive', 'legal', 'aesthetic' and 'communal' functions. Each has its own ends: the cognitive seeking 'truth-itself', the legal seeking 'justice-itself', the aesthetic seeking 'beauty-itself' and the communal 'love-itself'.

Philosophy is the deepest form of cognitive encounter with reality. It analyses and gives us knowledge of the 'structure of being', formulating it in categories, laws and concepts, universal in nature. While 'metaphysics' is the classical name for this pursuit, the word today wrongly suggests 'a duplication of this world by a transcendent realm of beings'.[27] Tillich replaces the word with the term 'ontology'.

Ontology requires 'detached objectivity' and seeks universal truth. Tillich distinguishes philosophy from theology in that the latter begins in ultimate concern with the particularities of cult and myth. But there is an overlap, for the philosopher is moved by ultimate concern and is also influenced by historical circumstance.

The theologian must respect the terrain and contribution of the philosopher, drawing upon those insights when making assertions about the nature of being.

> He can do this only in an attitude of detachment from his exis-
> tential situation and in obedience to the universal logos . . . The
> philosophical basis is the ontological analysis of the structure of
> being. If the theologian needs this analysis, either he must take it
> from a philosopher or he must himself become a philosopher . . .
> He is obliged to argue for a philosophical decision in the name
> of the universal logos and from the place where there is no place:
> pure reason.[28]

How philosophical analysis works can be seen in the way in which Tillich defines key terms in his system, especially as they are related to the cultural questions of his own historical situation. His understanding of 'ultimate concern' is a case in point.

> *Our ultimate concern is that which determines our being or not-being.*
> *Only those statements are theological which deal with their object in so far*
> *as it can become a matter of being or not-being for us* . . . The term
> 'being' means the whole of human reality, the structure, the
> meaning, the aim of existence. All this is threatened; it can be lost
> or saved. 'To be or not to be' in *this* sense is a matter of ultimate,
> unconditional, total and infinite concern.[29]

Philosophy's age-old question – Why is there something and not nothing? – is given here an 'existential' turn with the self peering ahead on its journey towards nothingness, a being-towards-death (Heidegger). Elsewhere, Tillich describes the question as 'ontological shock', 'the shock of possible non-being'.[30] Thus the 'mystical a priori' at the root of all philosophy and historical religions is 'the ultimate question, although fundamentally it is a state of existence rather than a formulated question'.[31]

In these various sorties into the topic, *finitude* emerges regularly as *the* human problem, and despair is its failed answer. In our time, we are overwhelmed by this universal human condition and thus find 'mean-inglessness and despair in all realms of life'.[32] Existential philosophy, especially in its Heideggerian form, has given powerful articulation to 'this question implied in our present situation and in every human situation'.[33] In Tillichian terms:

> Finitude is the possibility of losing one's ontological structure, and with it, one's self. But this is a possibility, not a necessity. The anxiety of finitude is not the despair of self-destruction.[34]

Being-towards-death is the future we face. Despair and self-estrangement are its consequences, making their presence felt in the mentalities and movements of the day.

While philosophy helps us to formulate 'the question', we must look elsewhere for the answer. 'New Being' is the word of courage to be spoken in the face of the threat of non-being. New Being is the theological 'norm' within the sources of Christian theology.

THE SOURCES AND NORM OF THEOLOGY

The Bible and the Church appear alongside the 'World' or experience and philosophy in Tillich's scheme of authority. Scripture has a privileged place, as 'the Bible . . . is the basic source of systematic theology'.[35] Its primacy derives from being 'the original document about the events on which Christianity is based'.[36] The definitive happenings to which Christianity points are reported and interpreted by first-hand witnesses, constituting thereby the 'original revelation' to which all subsequent 'dependent revelation' must orient. As a human document, the Bible needs to be studied critically, with the 'detached' tools of scholarship. However, a 'devotional-interpretive' approach, one moved by ultimate concern in the context of situational questions, is also needed.

Contrary to the *sola scriptura* of 'neo-orthodox biblicism', and 'evangelical biblicism', theology needs 'church history' as a second source. Any attempt to overleap the centuries with claims to direct access to the truths of Scripture (the temptation of Protestantism) fails to understand how much the intervening history shapes our perception of biblical contents. Others (Roman Catholics), who rightly assign the church a role, err in giving undue authority to 'the decisions of councils and popes'. While the theologian's own tradition should find a place in the work of interpreting the message, the whole history of Christian thought, critically appropriated and existentially read, must be taken into account.

A third source is 'broader' than the previous two, ranging far beyond

Bible and Church. It is constituted by 'the material presented by the history of religion and culture'.[37] The religious tradition into which we are born, and the religious influences that work on us in the society in which we live, shape our ways of thinking and being. So also do all the cultural forces that impact on us. But these broader streams constitute a normative as well as a descriptive source, functioning intentionally as well as circumstantially. The theologian must actively appropriate those religious and cultural expressions that can contribute to the responsible communication of the Christian message.

Included in the appropriation process are theological histories of religion and culture that investigate both the demonic and the creative aspects of these phenomena. Especially important is the effort to develop a 'theology of culture' that seeks to identify the ultimate concern and existential questions in a given culture.

We note in passing that the contextual, experiential and philosophical aspects of the 'world' discussed earlier make a reappearance here in the category of 'source'. Implied, however, is their tertiary place in the structure of authority.

> Bible, church history, history of religion and culture . . . There are degrees of importance in this immense source material, corresponding with its more direct or more indirect relationship to the central event on which the Christian faith is based, the appearance of the New Being in Jesus as the Christ.[38]

With this reference to 'the New Being in Jesus as the Christ', we arrive at 'the norm' and 'criterion' of Tillich's systematic theology.

THE NORM

The norm is the standard by which the sources are appropriated and interpreted, determining the way in which the Christian answer is given to the questions posed by each historical situation. Tillich observes that 'very early in the history of the church . . . it received a material and a formal answer'.[39] The first was a 'doctrinal norm' found in baptismal confessions and set forth in an early creed 'with Jesus the Christ as the centre'.[40] The second was 'a hierarchy of authorities – bishops, councils, pope – who were supposed to safeguard the norm against heretical distortions'.[41] However, over time, the first dissolved into the second, with the Council of Trent establishing the Roman Catholic church papal decisions as finally normative.

However, Tillich believes that the material norm has had a life of its

74

own, the fruit of 'the Spiritual life of the church',[42] mutating according to the issues of time and place: the message of immortal life and truth being the church's response to the Greek preoccupation with mortality and error, the sacramental sacrifice of the God–Man in the medieval church responding to the experience of guilt, the Reformation themes of justification, divine mercy and forgiveness speaking to the issue of personal sin, the synoptic Jesus answering the nineteenth-century questions of personal and social existence, the prophetic message of the kingdom of God responding to social injustice in recent Protestantism.

Our own time also has its developing norm, 'adequate to the present situation and to the biblical source'.[43] If the present question is one of disruption, self-destruction, conflict, meaninglessness and despair, then the answer must be about a reality of reconciliation and reunion, of creativity, meaning and hope. Before the threat of non-being: New Being. So Christians see it, for they find in their biblical source just that reality, Jesus the Christ.

The Pauline 'doctrine of the New Creation in Christ' is the biblical symbol for the New Being, 'which included the "prophetic-eschatological message" of the "new aeon"'.[44] Thus the 'apologetic situation' in which we find ourselves points to *this* perspective on Christ (rather than justification, incarnation, sacramental sacrifice, kingdom of God etc.), preserving as it does the substance of earlier responses. We shall paint in more detail the New Testament 'picture of Christ' that constitutes this norm in the subsequent section on revelation.

There is a certain puzzle here to which we shall return in our assessment of Tillich's thought on revelation. How can the norm, 'Jesus as the Christ', function as criterion for the use of the sources and the medium, if the cultural source and the experiential medium enter significantly into the formulation of the norm? How can the 'eternal message' be correlated with the cultural question if the centre of that message is already defined in terms provided by an analysis of the cultural question?

REVELATION

All the foregoing discussion of the *where* and *how* of authority – sources, medium, norm – presupposes answers to the *why* of revelation. The implicit is rendered explicit in the stipulated section on revelation in the first volume of *Systematic Theology*. It begins with an analysis of the relation of reason to revelation. Tillich focuses on 'ontological reason', that capacity of the mind in which the human logos reaches towards the universal Logos – a 'subjective' reason that is our human access to the 'objective' Reason in the nature of things. Always standing in the wings is the temptation to allow 'technical reason' to come centre stage, replacing ontological reason's quest for the ends of life with its own preoccupation with means.

Ontological reason gives us knowledge of the structure of reality, being united in its very depths with this reality. But entry to it is impeded by the splits that plague reason-in-existence. The existential conflicts of 'actual reason' include the polarisations of autonomy and heteronomy, relativism and absolutism, formalism and emotionalism. These false alternatives prompt a question for 'revelation', as the ambiguities of reason put it on course for a quest for revelation with its answering themes of theonomy, concrete absolute and reunion.

The revelation which an estranged reason needs and seeks does not displace the role of reason with revealed 'information' about how the world works. Ontological reason retains its privileged access to the structures of being. Revelation has no 'epistemology' of its own, giving it knowledge of the meaning of being or the processes of nature and history. It verifies its own assertions about truth, goodness and beauty by attention to empirical data and the laws of logic – an 'experimental' means, or 'controlling knowledge', and the more elusive yet profound test of 'efficacy in the life-process of mankind' – an 'experiential' means, or 'receptive knowledge'.[45]

If revelation does not give us information about God, what does it unveil? It opens up the *mystery* of the ground and abyss of being. This is 'knowledge' in the sense that

> its reality has become a matter of experience [and] . . . our relation to it has become a matter of experience. Both of these are cognitive elements. But revelation does not dissolve the mystery into knowledge. Nor does it add anything directly to the totality of our ordinary knowledge . . .[46]

For Tillich, we cannot know about a divine being with certain attributes through the process of revelation. For example, the classical teaching about the omniscience of God

> is not about the faculty of a highest being who is supposed to know all objects, past, present and future . . . The absurdity of such an image is due to the impossibility of subsuming God under the subject–object scheme, although this structure is grounded in the divine life. If one speaks, therefore, of divine knowledge and

the unconditional character of the divine knowledge, one speaks symbolically... Nothing falls outside the logos structure of being. The dynamic element cannot break the unity of the form; the abysmal quality cannot swallow up the rational quality of the divine life.[47]

In the same way, any theological doctrine of human nature cannot tell us something about the structure of human beings or the human condition that we could not otherwise know from ontological reason: 'One should not confront Socrates with Paul in order to show how much more realistic Paul was'.[48]

How does revelation happen? It takes place in an objective-subjective simultaneity. The objective pole of revelation Tillich calls 'miracle', and the subjective 'ecstasy'. Ecstasy includes the 'ontological shock', the threat of non-being. But it also

unites the experience of the abyss, to which reason in all its functions is driven with the experience of the ground in which reason is grasped by the mystery of its own depth and the depth of being generally.[49]

Tillich believed that Rudolf Otto was right in his linkage of 'annihilating power' (the *mysterium tremendum*) with 'elevating power' (*mysterium fascinosum*).

Two misunderstandings must be avoided, Tillich asserts. One is to confuse ecstasy with emotion. While affectivity is entailed, as the word itself suggests, ecstasy cannot be psychologised. Another misunderstanding is to claim special deliverances of truth about another realm of being, as is done in conventional notions of 'inspiration'. The latter is 'demonic' for it replaces the legitimate function of reason with false claims to information about a transcendent realm. 'Miracle' is the objective pole of the event of revelation. Rather than being the violation of natural law,

a genuine miracle is... an event which is astonishing, unusual, shaking, without contradicting the rational structure of reality... It is an event which points to the mystery of being, expressing its relation to us in a definite way... it is an occurrence which is received as a sign event in an ecstatic experience.[50]

A miracle presupposes the 'negative side of being' as does ecstasy. 'There is a stigma that appears on everything, the stigma of finitude, or implicit and inescapable non-being'.[51] As the occasion for the disclosure of the ground of being, the abyss opens up in the event as well as in the response to it.

Where do miracle and ecstasy take place? The answer is that 'there is no reality, thing, or event which cannot become a bearer of the mystery of being and enter into a revelatory correlation'.[52] 'Nature', from stones and stars to human bodies can become vehicles for the disclosure of mystery. Personal and national history can become 'transparent to the ground of being', and the word in both vocal and written form can be an occasion for ultimate disclosures.

Another aspect of the 'where' of revelation is the important distinction between 'original' and 'dependent' revelation.

> An original revelation is a revelation which occurs in a constellation that did not exist before. This miracle and this ecstasy are joined for the first time.[53]

Tillich illustrates this by comparing the original revelation in the miracle of Jesus with its ecstatic reception by the apostolic community, and the history of dependent revelation that came after in the history of the church in every moment when 'the divine Spirit grasps, shakes, and moves the human spirit'.[54] Prayer is an example of that continuing dependent revelation:

> If it is brought down to the level of a conversation between two beings, it is blasphemous and ridiculous. If, however, it is understood as the 'elevation of the heart', namely, the center of the personality, to God, it is a revelatory event.[55]

Tillich concludes his analysis on the meaning of revelation by underscoring yet again the temptation to confuse it with 'revealed knowledge'.

> Knowledge of revelation is knowledge about the revelation of the mystery of being to us, not information about the nature of beings and their relation to one another . . . Propositions about a past revelation give theoretical information; they have no revelatory power. Only though an autonomous use of the intellect or through heteronomous subjection of the will could they be accepted as truth.[56]

Further, true knowledge always employs *symbols* which carry their own 'cognitive' weight in the sense that they bring us into relation with ultimate reality in ways that no 'non-symbolic' language ever could.

ACTUAL REVELATION

In the section on authority, we examined the christological criterion, and now we return to it, this time as the definitive 'sign-event', the 'decisive, fulfilling, unsurpassable revelation'.[57] Why so?

> A revelation is final if it has the power of negating itself without losing itself.[58]

The bearer must be willing to sacrifice all claims to special wisdom, virtue and piety, life itself. The revealer is such by becoming entirely 'transparent' to the ground and abyss of being. Such self-surrender is possible only if the person is already joined to being-itself. Uninterrupted unity with the ground of ultimacy makes possible the ultimate sacrifice.

> In the picture of Jesus as the Christ we have the picture of a man who possesses these qualities, a man, who, therefore, can be called the medium of final revelation.[59]

Throughout his whole life as it is given to us in the New Testament portrait, Jesus exemplifies this self-surrender, and does so supremely on the cross. He releases us from any idolatry of his theology or ethics, as if these had an absolute status, 'can claim finality or even claim superiority' over other world-views.[60]

> Jesus of Nazareth is the medium of the final revelation because he sacrifices himself completely to Jesus as the Christ.[61]

The particularity of this final revelation cannot be sundered from a 'history of revelation'. Without this more wide-ranging disclosure, the claims to a unique revelatory event would constitute

> a strange body which has no relation whatsoever to human existence and history . . . Without the symbols created by universal revelation, the final revelation would not be understandable . . . The question of the final revelation would not be have been asked . . .[62]

That universality can happen in the same kind of variety noted earlier in the media of revelation, describable in mystical, rational and prophetic persons and movements. The prophetic, as in Israel's election yet judgment, is of special significance, for it is a concrete anticipation of the paradox of Christ's unity with and surrender towards the divine ground and abyss.

Revelation in both its universality and finality has its healing consequences. 'The history of revelation and the history of salvation are the same history'.[63] Wherever miracle and ecstasy take place, transformation occurs. Using the Latin term *salus* as indicative, salvation is the making whole of what has been torn asunder. Thus the Holy Spirit both reveals and heals. And while this experience is always fragmentary in our world of finitude, the religious symbols of 'the vision of God' and 'the Kingdom of God' point to a larger and completed unity of revelation and salvation.

REVELATION AS THE WORD OF GOD

Tillich concludes his section on revelation with an interpretation of another traditional symbol, 'the Word of God'. It provides a natural summary of his position, and also illustrates the attempt at comprehensiveness which marks our four major interlocutors. He summarises the 'six different meanings' as:

> 'God manifest' – manifest in himself, in creation, in the history of revelation, in the final revelation, in the Bible, in the words of the church and her members. 'God manifest' – the mystery of the divine abyss expressing itself through the divine Logos – this is the meaning of the symbol, the 'Word of God'.[64]

Here we find a hint of the 'narrative of revelation' we have been tracing: its origins in the inner being of God, its exfoliation in nature and history, its action in prophetic Israel, its definitive expression in Jesus the Christ, testimony to it in Scripture, appropriation of it in the church and its traditions, and its culmination in the vision and realm of God.

CONTRIBUTIONS

The signs of our times in art and literature, our ultimate concern, our philosophical formulations – the human venture as such and its deepest insights – for Tillich these matters count heavily in the work of theology. Correlation must be made between the questions they pose and the Gospel to be proclaimed. In revelatory terms, such a correlational theology presupposes the disclosure of truth in human experience, the 'World' beyond the historical particularities of Israel and Christ, Bible and Church. As such, Tillich's emphasis accords with the covenant with Noah. We note various respects in which this is so.

ULTIMATE CONCERN

As 'Noahides', human beings in their condition of resistance to the divine purposes are given a dim sense of their larger destiny. The human spirit is restless with the givens, cajoled by an awareness of a goal missed or not yet attained: 'a sense of Deity is indelibly engraven on the human heart...thoroughly fixed as it were in our very bones'.[65] Myriad ways of describing this mark and sensibility have found their way into the history of theology, and 'ultimate concern' is one of them. Tillich recognises that its content is culture-relative, but resists the conclusion that the existence of the awareness is itself a cultural-linguistic creation. And he criticises the 'christomonistic' view that would deny the presence and theological significance of the 'sense ...in our very bones'.

Tillich recognises that ultimate concern can be fused to 'preliminary concerns' and thus become demonic. Human experience is a 'factory for idols' (Calvin), hence the captivity of the sense of the unconditional to a heteronomy that absolutises a finite institution, and/or a self-sufficient finitude that settles for autonomy. Authentic ultimate concern is inseparable from 'the Protestant principle' that refuses to domesticate the infinite.[66]

ONTOLOGICAL REASON

The witness which God leaves does not end with a transcendent restlessness. Inseparable from this sensibility is enough of a perception of the ways of the world for the Story to go forwards. Such content includes a fragmentary discernment of the intellectual, moral and aesthetic conditions of human life. Tillich points to this grasp of truth, goodness and beauty in the language of his system – the 'reason that knows being', a 'subjective reason' that comports with the world's structures of 'objective reason'. Here is a love, *eros*, in quest for 'truth-itself', 'justice-itelf', 'beauty-itself' and 'love-itself'. These correspond essentially to the dimensions of the 'world' that are refrains in Christian theology: rational (cognitive/truth), moral (legal/justice, communal/love) and affective (aesthetic/beauty).[67] We focus here on two aspects of this 'ontological reason', Tillich's situational analysis and his interpretation of the role of philosophy.

SITUATION

Tillich's descriptive and normative judgments about 'the situation' – that the church's message has been articulated over time according to the questions posed in one or another era, and that it must be set forth today in terms of the contemporary situation – contribute to the understanding of *how* common grace imparts itself. Sensitivity to time and place does and must enter into the telling of the Christian Story. Moral, rational and aesthetic monitors of historical context are needed to discern the signs of time and place. Political, social and economic analyses, culturally sensitive philosophy, art and literature are antennae that can discern crucial signals from culture. Interpreters of Christian faith cannot ignore their insights into the forces that work upon our psyches and shape our institutions. With specific reference to the moral edge of cultural dilemmas, the church's works of justice and mercy require an understanding of social, political and economic dynamisms. In the end, the church must make up its own mind about its context (and *not* defer to a cultural magisterium), but it cannot despise the analytic and prophetic voices through which God speaks outside its own household.

PHILOSOPHY

Philosophy as a form of 'ontological reason' is of value to the church in its theological work. As Tillich points out, theology presupposes philosophy in the very use it makes of key terms with a long lineage (history, life, being, etc.), and therefore needs to clarify both its debts to, and disagreements with, inherited traditions. God orders the world and provides means for discerning that order as part of the journey of creation towards its destiny. To the extent that this pilgrimage requires wisdom about those structures *generally* accessible, philosophy will make a contribution to the theological task. Thus a process philosophy that speaks of the spontaneities and mutualities at every level of creation, an existentialist analysis of human finitude and anxiety, a Kantian restraint about the claims of knowledge, a materialist reading of institutional and ideational patterns, can illuminate areas of reality about which faith speaks. Insofar as philosophy is itself inseparable from the flow of history, its ideas may well be influenced by the Christian faith's own penetration of culture, so that the church finds its own features mirrored in aspects of Whiteheadian, Heideggerian, Kantian, Marxist and other commentary. Reason, broken by the fall, cannot provide a philosophical system into which faith must fit itself. Yet by the grace of preservation, 'philosophical fragments' (Kierkegaard) may find a place in the structure of Christian belief in a given time and place.

As Tillich argues, 'reasoning', as attention to empirical data, also serves an important purpose in the human enterprise in general, and within theology in particular. While 'technical reason' has only a delimited role in 'preliminary concerns', it plays its part there in the processes of 'experimental' verification. Such testing is applicable to *penultimate* matters, including aspects of Christian lore that enter this terrain. We need the best resources of the human mind in areas to which it can contribute – from critical scholarship in working with biblical materials or church tradition to assessing proposals for raising the budget of the congregation or projecting scenarios for the mission of the church in the twenty-first century.

The laws of logic are another aspect of reasoning that has a legitimate, though not magisterial, place in human discourse, including discourse about matters of faith. Incoherence counts against theological assertions as well as general propositions. While theological paradox is an exception to this rule, it follows a logic internal to the full range of Christian belief as well as a consistency with the data of faith.

Today, 'rationality' is widely held to be inextricably tied to social location and historical tradition. Christian realism about finitude and sin long ago anticipated these suspicionist projects. However, the covenant with Noah questions any solely intrasystemic rationality, and appeals only to one's 'web of faith', community of common commitment or social location. Indeed, arguments for internal rationality made in the public domain presuppose what they deny – a rationality that goes beyond the self-defined boundaries. Thus Tillich's willingness to relate Christian truth-claims to criteria that are public – both experimental and experiential – makes its witness against today's popular social solipsisms.

PROBLEMS

In Tillich's method of correlation, 'the situation' as defined by creative cultural commentary poses the question to which the church must respond with an answer implied in the Christian message; 'reason' formulates the issue to which 'revelation' speaks. Included in this method and its revelatory presupposition is a recognition of the experiential atmosphere in which the theologian lives as a resident of both church and culture. This environment shapes the way the message is heard by the theologian. Playing such a filtering role, it must be identified by appropriate analytical tools, creative cultural commentary and philosophical conceptuality. Tillich's theological enterprise illustrates how this works as the Christian message that answers the cultural problematic is organised around the affirmation of the New Being that confronts the experience of non-being.

When the 'medium' as interpreted by cultural and philosophical frameworks plays such a key role in the formulation of message itself, what happens to the *critical* function of the Christian message? How is 'revelation' whose content has been described in terms provided by 'reason' free to answer the questions posed by reason? Robert Clyde Johnson has raised this issue in connection with Tillich's contention that the revelation 'event' includes its reception and interpretation. Johnson charges that the independence of the biblical witness to Jesus Christ is undercut, 'the self-interpreting nature of the fact' dissolved.

> The result is a *functional* elimination of the content of the fact as an element in the principle of authority... At the same time, it permits the introduction of ontological and mystical elements that admittedly are not an explicit part of the content of the Biblical witness to the fact.[68]

Thus, on Tillich's reckoning, the event of the Word incarnate and the biblical testimony to it are not authoritative disclosure points in their own right. In their place, a more general revelatory process at work outside these particularities, accessed by the experience of ultimate concern and the insights of an ontological reason, becomes definitive.[69]

How active the philosophical aspect of ontological reason is in this equation is noted by Kenneth Hamilton. He charts it against the backdrop of Kierkegaard's critique of the Hegelian system, showing parallels to a Tillichian system with influences from Parmenides, Plato, Hegel, Schelling and Heidegger. Thus 'the system' reaches the level of a 'primary revelation':

> It deserves to be called primary because it comes straight to man through the divine indwelling of the *logos*. Then there follows a 'secondary revelation', the distinctive feature of this being that it is mediated and symbolic... Tillich in his role of philosopher, outlines what he can know about reality. Then in his role as theologian, he accepts gratefully from his philosophical *alter ego* information about the nature of the Universe which enables him to say... what Christian faith can and cannot mean.[70]

The infilling of Christian language with the existential-cum-philo-sophical content is not an accident of Tillich's system but rather the natural outworking of his epistemology. While the symbols of myth and cult are said to give 'knowledge' of ultimate reality, the word in that context means access to the *mystery* of being-itself. Their purpose is expressive and evocative, not cognitive in its usual meaning. The latter applies only to 'reason' in its various Tillichian senses. The asser-tions of 'revelation' are subject to verification and interpretation by experiential and experimental methods. How this distinction works out can be seen in Tillich's understanding of the revelatory significance of Christ and his treatment of aspects of the doctrine of God.

'Christ' is the norm in Tillich's authority structure and thus the centre of revelation. As noted, the normativity and centrality of Christ have to do with a criterion that Tillich brings to the assessment of the New Testament 'picture of Jesus as the Christ'. Is the event so portrayed both in unity with the ground of being and yet also self-emptying? Tillich's answer is 'Yes'; Jesus is the Christ, for he appears as transparent to being-itself. Tillich's dissociation of 'the picture of Christ' from the 'Jesus of history' has been widely criticised. But there are epistemological issues here also. The 'picture' itself is a selective reading of the New Testament data based upon criteria imported from situational, experiential and philosophical frameworks. Exegetical inquiry and testing by the standards of classical Christology would have their own judgments about the figure of Christ that emerges. While Tillich's procedure is docetic, detached from the Jesus of history, the picture of Jesus painted is Ebionite, the highest species of a universal human genus, and thus reduced in its understanding of the Person of Christ, and exemplarist in its concept of the Work of Christ. Both the latter are at work in Tillich's delineation of Jesus as 'trans-parency' through 'self-emptying'. Here, Johnson's observations on the role of 'sin' and 'grace' in Tillich's theology are apt, for the chapter on the fall in the narrative is the premise of the radical action of God in incarnation and crucifixion:

> He has posed for himself the query: 'Are sin and grace, if taken into an ontological frame of reference, still sin and grace?' This is precisely the question. And it would appear to be quite clear that we must answer that, even though all the required definitive elements may be preserved within the systematic definition, where there is a shift in the order of emphasis that alters the motif, sin ceases to be sin. Then *can* grace be grace?[71]

The *ground* of grace is put into question as well by the elimination of the classical problematic of sin. The Work of Christ as Reconciler of the world in his death on the cross is replaced by the symbolic representation of a self-surrendering finitude. The latter is not simply a modern translation for the 'mythical' language of the former, but rather a substitution of one cognitive claim for another claim on the same epistemological level. It is interesting that George Tavard, the Roman Catholic ecumenist and well-known interpreter of the second Vatican Council, changed his sympathetic view of Tillich's theology to a highly critical one as Tillich's christology became more widely understood.

> Paul Tillich has failed to account for the biblical picture of Jesus
> ... [His view] is not in keeping with the traditional formulations
> of the early Councils. It is incompatible with the theology of
> the Fathers and that of the medieval Doctors. It is irreconcilable
> with the faith of the Protestant Reformers of the sixteenth
> century ...[72]

And the christological issues are related to the historic Christian teaching about human nature, revelation and salvation:

> The notion of faith, the notion of original sin, the notion of rev-
> elation, have been stripped by Tillich of their specifically Christian
> elements and made into universal philosophical concepts.[73]

Markus Barth, observing similarly the effects on Tillich's thought on christology, notes the erosion of Jesus' fleshly reality, especially 'the Jewishness of Jesus':

> In the *Systematic Theology* of Paul Tillich . . . the crucifixion means
> that Jesus sacrifices himself as a specific historical figure – includ-
> ing all that is both symbolical and tied to place and time – in
> favor of the timeless and universal significance of Christ. 'The
> Christ' is now to be understood as the transcendent Ground of
> Being.[74]

The philosophical (and also experiential and cultural) wisdom that have their proper place through the covenant with Noah are misplaced when they exceed their limits and edit out critical chapters of the Story.

The doctrine of God is also a theological locus that reflects the hegemony of philosophical principle. Tillich's treatment of God as 'personal' is a case in point: God 'is not a person, but is not less than personal'.[75] What does this mean?

The biblical narrative we are following is an account of happenings initiated by and responded to by Another, a drama moving over time and space through conflict towards resolution. In Scripture, 'God' is the proper name of the chief character, the Other with whom we have to do. The attributes of deity in Christian theology are those qualities that rise from the narrative. A basic turn in the tale comes in God's special bonding with the Jewish people. Then a decisive deed is done in Jesus. In describing the divine Being and doing, the Christian tradition has recourse to a common stock of words, ideas and images, but uses them with a difference, as converted and baptised within the community of faith and its Book.

The word 'personal' has come to hand in theology as a way to ensure faithfulness to the *relational* Deity of the Story – the Initiator and Responder. But more than that, the narrative asserts that God came among us *as* a human being, a 'person'. Therefore, the initiating and responding quality that distinguishes a 'person' is what God wills to disclose to us about the divine nature, reflected in the three divine Persons and their mysterious unity in the one personal God. What God is at this central disclosive point is what God is at every other point in the narrative. At the defining moment, Jesus Christ, the content as well as the form of deity, is disclosed: a holy but vulnerable Agape. The holy God is transcendent Freedom, but so different from all our common assumptions about what it means to be holy, transcendent and free. God's way of being these things is not in distance but in proximity. God's being we learn in Jesus' being is 'vulnerability'. God is free to be vulnerable to the very terms of our existence – indeed, vulnerable to the 'subject–object' conditions of that world. God is not aloof from the subject–object relationship, in Jesus Christ God *is* a Subject. God is so much for us and with us that God is willing to be made an Object by us. Here is the revelation of what 'personal' *really* entails, all analogies in our human experience being measured by the definitive disclosure in Jesus Christ, the personal 'image of God' by which we understand what that *imago* we are/have means.

Can Tillich's philosophical conceptuality do justice to the biblical testimony to the One who relates to, acts towards and comes among us? Tillich cannot speak of the divine subjectivity. God is 'beyond' all such characterisations, for they fall into the subject–object world, a 'being beside all other beings'. While we must descend to this plane when using religious symbol in the life of myth and cult, *ontological* truth is the province of ontological reason and its one non-symbolic assertion of God as 'the ground and abyss of being':

> Ordinary theism made God a heavenly, complete person who resides above the world and mankind. The protest of atheism against such a highest person is correct. There is no evidence for his existence, nor is he a matter of ultimate concern. God is not God without universal participation. 'Personal God' is a confusing symbol.[76]

The 'ordinary theism' of historic Christian teaching, as it is described by Tillich, is indeed about One who is more than 'the world and mankind', who is free enough to come to us in particular deeds rather than required to perform in 'universal participation', free enough not to be tied to an experience of ultimate concern, vulnerable enough to be denied by atheism, strong enough in weakness to be rejected by the strictures of reason.

Assumptions about revelation at work in the doctrines of God and Christ are related to Tillich's concept of symbol. His formula that a symbol participates in the reality to which it points suggests that Christian language about God gives knowledge of the Subject of the story, God. But such is not the case. The symbol puts us existentially in touch with reality but does not convey any assertions about the nature of the Reality to which the response can be Yes or No ('propositional truth'). In the categories of Janet Martin Soskice's study of metaphor, Tillich's concept of symbol is an example of an 'emotive theory'.[77]

Avery Dulles also employs symbol theory to explicate revelation. Drawing on the thought of Michael Polanyi, Dulles affirms that symbols enable us to 'indwell' reality, invite surrender and have the power to transform us. As such, they are an apt medium for Christian communication. While their power *is* evocative and expressive, symbols are not to be denied cognitive weight:

> Propositional explication . . . is not useless. Christian doctrine sets necessary limits to the kind of significances that can be found in Christian symbols . . . Religious symbols, therefore, imply something about the real order.[78]

Christian doctrine depicts reality, expressing the cognitive content of Christian symbols. In Wilbur Urban's comparable terms, a true religious symbol is dual in nature, including a 'truth of the symbol' with cognitive access to ultimate reality and 'symbolic truth', the power of a symbol to bring us into relationship with ultimate reality.[79]

TILLICHIAN TRAJECTORIES

As noted, Tillich's impact on twentieth-century theology is extensive and his method of correlation, with or without direct influences from Tillich, is widespread. We examine some representive figures and trends that circle about this chapter in the narrative. David Tracy adopts and modifies Tillich's method of correlation, reinterpreting it in a postmodern context. Rosemary Radford Ruether appropriates the method of correlation in her exposition of an 'experiential feminism'.[80] John Cobb formulates a correlational epistemology in a Whiteheadian framework. Current 'pluralist' theologies – those of John Hick, Paul Knitter and Wilfred Cantwell Smith – operate with Noachic assumptions, but we conclude this section with a critical response, rather than an exposition of, the latter to indicate the current state of the conversation.

REVISED CORRELATIONIST PARADIGM: DAVID TRACY

Tracy, a major voice in contemporary Roman Catholic theology,[81] proposes a 'revised correlationist paradigm'. Rather than the 'situation' posing the questions to be answered by 'the message', Tracy speaks of 'the attempt to establish mutually critical correlations between an interpretation of the Christian tradition and an interpretation of contemporary experience'.[82] The revision has to do with a clearer separation of the new perspective from the 'classicist paradigm', devoid as it is of historical consciousness and without the needed hermeneutic of suspicion about the power interests at work in the traditions and readings of each partner. Vis-à-vis Tillich, Tracy wants to make clear the *mutual* fructification and corrigibility of both poles of the correlation.

In sifting and sorting the relative weight of the elements in the correlation, Tracy has spoken more recently about the importance of 'coherence with the "Jesus kerygma" of the original apostolic witness and . . . all biblically sound readings of the common narrative of the great Christian tradition',[83] with this pole of 'appropriateness' to the Christian tradition being accountable to Scripture as *norma non normata*. So understood, the 'new paradigm' does not seem very different from the framework of authority that functions in this work: Christ as centre, Scripture as source, the Great Narrative as its substance, the church catholic and its tradition as resource, and the world of human experience as setting. Indeed, Tracy remarks, 'In one sense, this hermeneutical formulation is simply a rendering explicit and deliberate of the fact which unites all forms of theology'.[84] Yet the outworking of the formulation by Tracy proves to be very different from the priorities and interrelationships of the ecumenical hermeneutic presupposed in this work, and in its revelatory underpinning.

Tracy has enriched contemporary theology by his deployment of Hans-Georg Gadamer's figure of 'conversation', and by the wide range of participants he includes at the table, particularly those historically excluded from it. However, his adaptation of 'the game of conversation' to the encounter with a Christian 'classic' (the 'appropriate' pole of the correlation) has serious consequences for a narrative reading of revelation and its associated conception of authority. Tracy wants to avoid both a naive retrievalist reading – premodern, anti-modern or modern – and a postmodern despair over any contact with the text and thus recourse only to playful self-edification.[85] Conversation with a text begins when the world of preunderstandings and prejudgments which one brings to it is nudged, pushed off balance, provoked, intrigued, questioned. Thus an 'excess of meaning' in the text does its work of resisting the interpretive framework that could easily be imposed upon it.

This 'jarring' and 'jolting' reach a point of special richness as the text's existential questions are heard as one's own questions (for example, universal 'limit questions' like 'finitude or fault . . . meaning and trust') and when one attends to its subject matter as worthy of consideration. At this luminous moment, 'interpretation-as-conversation' happens: 'As a work, the text produces its world of meaning in front of the text as a possible way of being in the world'.[86] The 'world of meaning in front of the text' includes the interpretive responses of the reader as well as the subject matter and questions of the text. Rejected in this phrase is a settling too quickly for the historical critic's 'world in back of the text', the fundamentalist's 'world of the text', or a literary (and 'postliberal') 'world of the text'.

In his own formulation of this process, Tracy adds some features which he believes are missing in Gadamer's analysis, having to do with the needed critical and explanatory tools of interpretation. At some juncture in the interpretive process, both a hermeneutics of suspicion and a hermeneutics of historical-critical and literary-critical retrieval must make their contribution, but be relativised within the overall conversational framework.

While Tracy has not acceded to postmodern scepticism about classic texts, what can be derived from them in his conversational hermeneutic is seriously attenuated. The provocations of the text, refined by critical methods, introduce us to its 'existential questions' housed within the specifics of its 'subject matter'. Yet the determinative content affirmed by classical teaching – and apparently by Tracy also elsewhere as the normativity of the 'Jesus kerygma' and 'common narrative' – does not appear as such in the locus of the text's meaning, 'the world in front of the text'. This latter moment in the conversation emerges as the place of authoritative interpretation. Its fusion of the text's critically-shaped provocations and the reader's interpretive framework constitutes the locus of authority, not an identifiable 'Jesus kerygma' or 'common narrative'. That is, prejudgments shaped by reader experience in its widest sense have entered into the perception of the presumedly regulative Jesus kerygma and common narrative so that the latter can exercise no independently critical role in the conversation. As such, Tracy's version of the method of correlation – modified by his Catholic sensibility concerning the important place of the community in the conversation (the church catholic and its tradition, a wide range of interpretive voices within and beyond them especially those of the marginalised 'other', and the voice as well of the academic disciplines)[87] – is in clear continuity with the Tillichian view of revelation as here expounded. The presence of human experience in its rich and varied sense enters so decisively into the hermeneutical conversation that the integrity of the centre, source and resource of authority is called into question. Put in terms of the narrative of revelation, the chapters on Christ, Scripture, the Church and its tradition are read in the light of the covenant with Noah, rather than the other way around.

EXPERIENTIAL FEMINISM: ROSEMARY RADFORD RUETHER[88]

Rosemary Radford Ruether is the first to have visited and developed the standard theological loci in feminist perspective,[89] and to have clearly articulated the methodological and epistemological implications of an experientially-oriented version of theological feminism. We draw here on two later works that clarify the latter and show its connection with a Tillichian trajectory, referring as she does to her alternative 'method of correlation'.[90]

Earlier associated with Letty Mandeville Russell in a 'prophetic-messianic' hermeneutic of the biblical canon, Ruether subsequently declared that

> Feminist theology must create a new canon . . . Feminist theology demands a new collection of texts to make women's experience visible. Feminist theology cannot be done from the existing base of the Christian Bible.[91]

In *Womenguides*, she has set out to produce a 'working handbook from which a new canon might emerge'.[92] Drawing on goddess traditions, Gnostic writings, streams of Christian interpretation considered heretical or treated as marginal, current feminist writings and other sources that call patriarchy into question, she urges the development of a body of 'women-church'[93] lore that will constitute a new canon. Its emergence will allow women to

> read canonical patriarchal texts in a new light. They lose their normative status and we read them critically in the light of the larger reality that they hide and deny. In the process a new norm emerges on which to construct a new community, a new theology and eventually a new canon. This new norm makes women as subjects the center rather than the margin. Women are empowered to define themselves rather than be defined by others. Women's speech and presence are normative rather than aberrant.[94]

Ruether's frank appeal for a new canon is related to her hermeneutic of suspicion that all inherited texts are written from an interest-laden social location. Something called 'the Word of God' cannot be juxtaposed to human experiences but is itelf their creature, and, in particular, a creature of an androcentric experience that codifies a patriarchal agenda, silencing and finally destroying women.

> Thus the criticism of the tradition in the context of women's experience does not merely add another point of view to the prevailing one. Women's experience explodes as a critical force, exposing classical theology, including its foundations in tradition and Scripture, as shaped by male experience rather than human experience. Women's experience makes the androcentric bias of the original formulations and the ongoing interpretation of the tradition visible, rather than hidden behind the mystification of divine authority.[95]

The authoritative 'women's experience' to which appeal is made is not the general experience of women but rather

> the experience which arises when women become critically aware of their falsifying and alienating experiences imposed on them by a male-dominated culture. Women's experience in this sense is a grace event . . .[96]

As a 'grace event', liberating experience in communities of solidarity (women–identifed males as well as women with raised consciousness) constitutes a 'new revelatory experience'[97] that provides the hermeneutical key for interpreting inherited texts and traditions, and the source for the development of a 'new canon' and new norms. The premise of the concepts of authority and interpretation at work in this perspective is a doctrine of revelation in which human experience, understood as liberated 'women's experience', is the locus of ultimate disclosure. Inherited texts and traditions formed by alienating androcentric experience are reread, judged and displaced by this experiential source of authority with its revelatory warrant. 'Correlation' is now understood not only functionally but also formally as accountability of 'centre', 'source' and 'resource' to the experiential 'setting'. As such, the Story of revelation here being told is halted before its major points of turning.

'Human experience', including the critical consciousness that rightly exposes the finitude and fallenness discernible in all inherited texts and traditions, is not itself exempt from the same finitude and sin. Thus the Narrative goes forward, to definitive disclosures not *of* but *through* human experience. As noted, theological feminism is not reducible to its experiential version. The range of Christian feminism includes growing constituencies of 'ecumenical' and 'evangelical' feminism working increasingly in colleagueship. In both cases, the setting of human experience, particularly the experience of women engaged in the current struggle against the oppression, is the *catalyst* for reinterpreting an authoritative Scripture and enriching and correcting the received tradition, not the occasion for its replacement. As such, the covenant with Noah is a chapter in an ongoing Story.[98]

PROCESS CHRISTOLOGY: JOHN COBB[99]

While Alfred North Whitehead rather than Paul Tillich provides the philosophical conceptuality for the theology of John Cobb, the working method is that of correlation. We examine its outworking in Cobb's christology.

In *Christ in a Pluralistic Age*,[100] Cobb reconceives *logos*, the ancient idea of universal order, in Whiteheadian terms as 'the principle of concretion' and organ of novelty in the universe. Located in deity, Logos becomes 'the primordial nature of God', the envisaging and ordering of the infinite range of potentiality or 'eternal objects'. This Logos, however, is no static display of possibility but the lure towards 'creative transformation', drawing 'actual entities' (the Whiteheadian description of rudimentary being) out of the past and into the future. When the Logos, supplying the actual entity with its 'initial aim', brings to be an occasion that is more than repetition of habitual existence, thus increasing the richness of its experience and the width of its scope of possibility, an event takes place that can be called 'creative transformation'. Its enabler is identified as the 'incarnate Logos'. While the incarnate Logos is active in all becoming, the initial subjective aim supplied by it to actual entities at the level of physical objects is only the re-enactment of the immediate past. It is on the 'level of life', and eminently human life, that the opportunity for novelty happens, although the leap from inorganic to organic is itself a sign of creative transformation. Whenever there is new actualisation of possibility in which the past is appropriated in fresh configuration with novel potentiality, there is 'Christ'. Since this event reaches towards both past occasions and future possibilities, and the God who orders the past and envisages the future, Christians read this dynamic as the love known to them in Jesus Christ.

The historical figure of Jesus has a special relation to 'Christ', the universally incarnate Logos. The incarnate Logos so acts in him as to win a total response to the lure of creative novelty. A self so responding can be said to be constituted by the incarnate Logos:

> There might be someone of whom history has left no record who was constituted as Jesus was, but that is idle speculation. So far as we know, Jesus is unique.[101]

Where this kind of coalescence of the self and Logos with its 'unique cumulative richness and aliveness of experience' occurs, there is produced 'a field of force of truly unusual magnitude, sustained and extended through repeated acts of remembrance'.[102] As this coalescence is the 'Person of Christ', so its effect in human history is the 'Work of Christ', the creative transformation of the prophetic tradition's vision of reality that has passed through the Greco-Roman world into the

West and finally into its present global sphere of influence. Its source is in part the remembered teaching of Jesus and in part Jesus' 'causal efficacy', an experiential 'force-field' which Cobb interprets as a Pauline Christ-mysticism of forgiveness, the release from preoccupation with the past and anxiety about the future.

In these process-grounded reformulations, correlating inherited biblical and doctrinal themes with the philosophical and scientific categories of modernity, the Person of Christ becomes the highest known manifestation of a universal process of creative transformation. The Work of Christ is the effect of such an exemplary life on a segment of human history.

Process philosophy, eclectically appropriated, can illumine aspects of the Person and Work of Christ – the 'proper humanity' of Christ as perfect love, the Work of Christ as example and teacher. However, the reshaping of the christological chapter of the biblical Story by the situational pole has eventuated in the reduction of the Person of Christ to a species of a universal genus, a 'degree christology' in which Christ is only the highest expression of a human potential. And the Work of Christ has been reduced to an 'exemplarism' in which the priestly and royal offices that encounter sin and death play no determinative role.[103] Narratively considered, process Christology remains within Noachic boundaries, drawing on disclosures within human experience, especially in twentieth-century philosophical form, but allowing their control to obscure the subsequent revelatory chapters of action, inspiration and illumination that relativise and reorient our best human wisdom.

PLURALIST PROPOSALS AND PROBLEMS: A MARK HEIM CRITIQUE

While the influence of Tillich is not often cited, various twentieth-century responses to religious pluralism employ the method of correlation, and do so with tendencies noted above, in this case in the interests of 'deparochialising' Christianity and honouring universal religious sensibilities. Notable in the pluralist theological enterprise are the writings of John Hick, Wilfred Cantwell Smith and Paul Knitter.[104] We examine their shared perspective through the eyes of a sympathetic critic, Mark Heim, who in a ground-breaking work, Salvations,[105] brings us to the current state of the argument and tests their proposals by their own criteria, an 'intelligibility' appropriate to the contextual pole of correlation.

The goal of all three pluralist positions is to acknowledge religious truth wherever found, challenge imperial claims to Christian unique-ness and superiority, and ascertain criteria by which both truth and 'salvation' can be detected and affirmed within the religious manifold. Each theologian has his own conception of the third factor, which functions as the measuring rod of the first and the relativising of the second. For Hick, albeit found with varying religious histories and heroes and in diverse metaphorical expressions of commitment, there is a 'common noumenal object beyond their conditioned, conflicting, yet epistemically defensible views'.[106] For Smith, the study of the world's religions and the plunge into the depths of one's own tradition reveal both a 'universal common rationality [and] a universal quality of faith'.[107] In Knitter's current view, with full recognition of the evil that historic religions can perpetrate, validity in religion stands and falls with 'orthopraxis . . . the "kingdom" or earthly peace and justice'.[108]

Do these proposals achieve their purpose of persuasive public argument for honouring the diversity of religions, avoiding religious imperialism and developing a respectful theology of religions? Heim poses critical questions to these popular pluralist theologies. Does the quest for a generic quality in the world's religions not deny the very particularities which a 'thick description' of each displays, and a respectful 'theology of religions' requires? Are not the commonalities discerned by each pluralist in fact the constructs of their own Western Enlightenment, and even Christian, social location? How then, given the reduction of the world religions to a perceived kernel of truth or justice-seeking, are these pluralist proposals themselves not prey to the same imperialism which they deplore, albeit now even more cleverly obscured by appeals to a universal reason? Thus:

> The painstaking attempt to become acquainted with and in some measure to understand the distinctive features of other peoples' faiths – precisely what makes them other – has, literally, no reli-gious meaning. At best it has an exemplary meaning: in learning the particulars of another religion we learn nothing of substance except the formal fact that there *are* other ways. For those with a meta-theory of religion, pluralism is real but superficial. The cultural and historical means are different but the actual religious end – transcending self, or relating to the ultimate – is the same . . . And those who judge religions in terms of social effects clearly want existing pluralism severely winnowed to leave only those variations that instrumentally support full justice as they

understand it . . . the operative definition of this absolute [stem-ming] transparently, exclusively from a modern period and Western context . . . Such principles of 'pluralistic theology' have the odd similarity of denying any pluralism of authentic religious consequence.[109]

What Heim has done in his critique is to expose the incoherence of the pluralist proposals by criteria of logic, evidence and moral argument to which they must on their universalist assumptions also have recourse. Heim can do that, for he holds a doctrine of general revelation, similar to the one here developed, affirming as it does enough preservation of the primal light of truth and goodness to communicate across perspectival boundaries. He does press the motif of general revelation in a maximalist direction, however, arguing for ultimate plural 'salvations', albeit none comparable to that of Christian particularity as disclosed by special revelation.[110]

This final foray into the covenant with Noah is an effort to show how revelatory proposals that read the Grand Narrative essentially, or only from this chapter on universality, can be called to account not only on the basis of a foreshortened Story, but also from within its own framework, recognised here to be accountable to the standards of plausibility.

Narratively framed, Paul Tillich's doctrine of revelation (and sequel theologies in Tillichan idiom) are a study in the covenant with Noah. Tillich's philosophical analysis and cultural commentary presuppose a common grace that legitimates such inquiry and invites theological attention to both the questions posed by a given era and universal human sensibilities. The Word that enlightens everyone by the power of the Spirit sufficient for the Story of alienation and reconciliation to go forwards is the giver of that grace.

While Tillich is right in what he narratively affirms, he is wrong in what he narratively denies. The subsequent chapters of the Story of both reconciliation and revelation are collapsed into the world of philosophical premise, cultural diagnosis and religious a priori. Israel and Jesus Christ, the witness of Scripture and the teaching of the church, become exemplifications of our own defining principles and perceptions. This chapter proves particularly seductive, as Karl Barth will not let us forget. The claims of human experience are imperial. In a four-way conversation on the doctrine of revelation, the voice of Karl Barth must speak of 'Jesus Christ . . . the one Word of God . . .'. But so too must be heard Carl Henry's testimony to the unique in-Spiriting of Scripture and Karl Rahner's affirmation of the Spirit's work of illumination in the church. Thus the 'rainbow' of universal grace points beyond itself and bestirs an ultimate concern for deeds and disclosures yet to be.

NOTES

1. Thus the federal theology of Johannes Cocceius and heirs, anticipated in the thought of John Calvin and Heinrich Bullinger.

2. For a detailed account, see David Novak, *The Image of the Non-Jew in Judaism: An Historical and Constructive Study of the Noahide Laws, Toronto Studies in Theology*, vol. 14 (Toronto: The Edwin Mellen Press, 1983).

3. Citation and discussion in C. H. Dodd, *Natural Law in the Bible* (Guildford: Billings & Sons, 1946). Reprint from *Theology* (May and June 1946). See also John Baillie's discussion, 'The Noachic Covenant', in *The Idea of Revelation in Recent Thought* (New York: Columbia University Press, 1956), pp. 125–33.

4. See Novak, *The Image of the Non-Jew in Judaism*, op. cit., passim.

5. On the relation of the covenant with Noah and the final revelation and reconciliation in Christ, see my development of the theme of 'divine perseverance' in Gabriel Fackre, Ronald Nash and John Sanders, ed. John Sanders, *What About Those Who Have Never Heard? Three Views on the Destiny of the Unevangelized* (Downers Grove, IL: InterVarsity Press, 1995), pp. 56–61, 71–95, 150–5.

6. Thor Hall (ed.), *A Directory of Systematic Theologians in North America* (Waterloo, Canada: Council on the Study of Religion, Wilfred Laurier University, 1977), passim.

7. Paul Tillich, *Systematic Theology*, vol. 1 (Chicago: University of Chicago Press, 1955).

8. Ibid., pp. 16, 13.

9. Ibid., p. 4.

10. Speaking of James Luther Adams, Tillich's translator and interpreter, Tillich said: 'Adams knows Tillich better than Tillich knows Tillich'. For evidence, see Adam's important essay in Paul Tillich, *The Protestant Principle*, trans. with a concluding essay by James Luther Adams (Chicago: University of Chicago Press, 1948). Adams, the writer's teacher and long-time friend, reviewed this section on Tillich, although any errors in the interpretation of Tillich's views on revelation are the writer's alone.

11. Ibid., p. 4.

12. Ibid., p. 5.

13. Ibid., p. 3.

14. Ibid., p. 49.

15. Ibid., p. 49.

16. Ibid., pp. 39, 40.
17. See, for example, Tillich's chapter 'The World Situation', in Henry P. Van Dusen (ed. with an intro.), *The Christian Answer* (New York: Scribner's, 1945).
18. Ibid., p. 43.
19. Ibid., p. 53.
20. Ibid., p. 12.
21. Ibid., p. 46.
22. Ibid., p. 45.
23. Ibid., p. 46.
24. Ibid., p. 46.
25. Ibid., p. 46.
26. Ibid., p. 52.
27. Ibid., p. 20.
28. Ibid., pp. 25, 26.
29. Ibid., p. 14.
30. Ibid., p. 163.
31. Ibid., p. 164.
32. Ibid., p. 49.
33. Ibid., p. 49.
34. Ibid., p. 201.
35. Ibid., p. 35.
36. Ibid., p. 34.
37. Ibid., p. 38.
38. Ibid., p. 40.
39. Ibid., p. 47.
40. Ibid., p. 47.
41. Ibid., p. 47.
42. Ibid., p. 48
43. Ibid., p. 49.
44. Ibid., p. 51.
45. Ibid., p. 105.
46. Ibid., p. 109.
47. Ibid., pp. 278, 279.
48. Ibid., p. 95.
49. Ibid., p. 113.
50. Ibid., p. 117.
51. Ibid., p. 116.
52. Ibid., p. 118.
53. Ibid., p. 126.
54. Ibid., p. 127.
55. Ibid., p. 127.
56. Ibid., pp. 129, 127.
57. Ibid., p. 133.
58. Ibid., p. 133.

59. Ibid., p. 133.

60. Ibid., p. 135.

61., Ibid., p. 136.

62. Ibid., pp. 138, 139.

63. Ibid., p. 144.

64. Ibid., p. 159.

65. John Calvin, *Institutes of the Christian Religion*, trans. Henry Beveridge (Grand Rapids: Eerdmans, 1957), III/3, pp. 44–5.

66. *The Protestant Principle*, op.cit., passim.

67. For exposition of the same, see the writer's *The Christian Story*, vol. 2, op. cit., pp. 133–56.

68. Robert Johnson, *Authority in Protestant Theology* (Philadelphia: The Westminster Press, 1959), p. 139.

69. In his study of Paul Ricoeur's thought, Kevin Vanhoozer tracks the similarities (and differences) between Ricoeur and Tillich, reflecting on the dissolution of Christian particularity: 'Thus for Tillich, as for Ricoeur, the Gospel narratives manifest and transform. The Gospels are for Tillich less like histories and more like expressionist paintings ... The idea that the Gospels' truth is a function of their manifesting essential human possibilities allows Ricoeur to account for the universal aspect of the gospel narratives and so satisfy the exigencies of the philosopher of religion. But it is just here that Ricoeur's [and Tillich's] mediation appears to break down, for in stressing the always-already availability of the Christian possibility, the particularity and contingency of the story of Jesus is overshadowed. The concrete actuality of Jesus, what Frei calls his unsubstitutable history and identity, is in danger of being lost'. Vanhoozer, *Biblical Narrative in the Philosophy of Paul Ricoeur*, op. cit., pp. 231, 237.

70. Kenneth Hamilton, *The System and the Gospel: A Critique of Paul Tillich* (New York: The Macmillan Company, 1963), pp. 63, 80.

71. *Authority in Protestant Theology*, op. cit., p. 122.

72. George H. Tavard, *Paul Tillich and the Christian Message* (New York: Charles Scribner's Sons, 1962), p. 137.

73. Ibid., p. 51.

74. Markus Barth, *Jesus the Jew*, trans. Frederick Prussner (Atlanta: John Knox, 1978), p. 17. Tillich's remarks on the relation of Christianity to world religions bear out these suspicions about the erosion of particularity: Paul Tillich, *The Future of Religions*, ed. Jerald Brauer (New York: Harper & Row, 1966), especially pp. 91–4.

75. Tillich, *Systematic Theology*, op. cit., p. 245.

76. Ibid., p. 245.

77. See Janet Martin Soskice, *Metaphor and Religious Language* (Oxford: Clarendon Press, 1985), pp. 26–31.

78. Dulles, *Models of Revelation*, op. cit., p. 143.

79. Wilbur Urban, *Language and Reality* (New York: Macmillan, 1939), p. 443ff.

80. Other forms of feminism vis-à-vis the issue of revelation can be identified as 'evangelical feminism' and 'ecumenical feminism', following a broader typology of contemporary systematic theology as in the writer's 'The Revival of Systematic Theology', *Interpretation* 49:3 (July 1995), 229–41.

81. On his high visibility in the wider culture and as well in theological academia, see Eugene Kennedy, 'A Dissenting Voice: Catholic Theologian David Tracy', *New York Times Magazine*, (9 November 1986).

82. David Tracy, 'Hermeneutical Reflections in the New Paradigm', in Hans Kung and David Tracy (eds), *Paradigm Change in Theology: A Symposium for the Future*, trans. Margaret Kohl (New York: Crossroad, 1989), p. 35.

83. David Tracy, 'On Reading the Scriptures Theologically', in Bruce D. Marshall (ed.), *Theology and Dialogue: Essays in Conversation with George Lindbeck* (Notre Dame: University of Notre Dame Press, 1990), p. 36.

84. Tracy, *Paradigm Change in Theology*, op.cit., p. 462.

85. The following section is an adaptation of the writer's more extended analysis of Tracy's thought in *Ecumenical Faith in Evangelical Perspective* (Grand Rapids: Eerdmans, 1993), pp. 217–20.

86. Tracy, *Paradigm Change in Theology*, op. cit., p. 50.

87. Tracy's use of typology is an indication of the width of the table of conversation, as in the taxonomy: academic/fundamental theology, systematic theology/church theology, practical/political theology, in *The Analogical Imagination: Christian Theology and the Culture of Pluralism* (New York: Crossroad, 1981), pp. 3–98, and 'modernity, anti-modernity and postmodernity' in 'Naming the Present', *On the Threshold of the Third Millennium*, Concillium, Special Issue, ed. Philip Hillyer (London: SCM Press, 1990), pp. 66–85.

88. The following material is an adaptation of a section from the writer's *The Christian Story*, vol. 2, op. cit., pp. 109–12.

89. Rosemary Radford Ruether, *Sexism and God-Talk: Toward a Feminist Theology* (Boston: Beacon Press, 1983).

90. Rosemary Radford Ruether, 'Feminist Interpretation: A Method of Correlation', in Letty M. Russell (ed.), *Feminist Interpretation of the Bible* (Philadelphia: Westminster Press, 1985), pp. 111–24.

91. Rosemary Radford Ruether, *Womenguides: Readings Toward a Feminist Theology* (Boston: Beacon Press, 1985), pp. ix–x.

92. Ibid., p. ix.

93. Rosemary Radford Ruether, *Women-Church: Theology and Practice of Feminist Liturgical Communities* (San Francisco: Harper & Row, 1985).

94. Ibid., p. xi.

95. Ruether, 'Feminist Interpretation', op. cit., p. 113.

96. Ibid., p. 114.

97. Ibid., p. 112.

98. For the cultivation of such an alliance, see the development within the journal *Daughters of Sarah*. A recent attempt to articulate an alternative to a generalised experiential feminism by an evangelical feminism committed to the struggle against patriarchy, including that for inclusive language, is Aida Besancon Spenser, Donna F. G. Hailson, Catherine Clark Kroeger and William David Spenser, *The Goddess Revival* (Grand Rapids: Baker Books, 1995). The writings of Roberta Bondi (*To Pray is to Love, To Love as God Loves* and *Memories of God*) reflect the ecumenical feminist engagement with Scripture and tradition, as illustrated by the representative article that struggles with traditional language for God, 'Be Not Afraid: Praying to God the Father', *Modern Theology* 9:3 (July 1993), 235–48.

99. The materials for this section are drawn from the writer's research in *The Christian Story*, vol. 2, op. cit., pp. 136–40.

100. John Cobb, *Christ in a Pluralistic Age* (Philadelphia: Westminster Press, 1975).

101. Ibid., p. 142.

102. Ibid., p. 145.

103. For an exposition of the three-fold office of Christ and attendant reductionisms, see the writer's *The Christian Story*, vol. 1, 3rd edn (Grand Rapids: Eerdmans, 1996), pp. 123–47.

104. See, especially, John Hick's development from the early work *The Center of Christianity* (New York: Harper & Row, 1968) through his widely-read *The Myth of the God Incarnate* (Philadelphia: Westminster Press, 1977) to the more recent *An Interpretation of Religion* (New Haven: Yale University Press, 1989); Wilfred Cantwell Smith, *The Meaning and End of Religion* (New York: Macmillan, 1964), *Faith and Belief* (Princeton: Princeton University Press, 1979) and *Towards a World Theology* (Maryknoll: Orbis Press, 1981); Paul Knitter, *No Other Name?* (Maryknoll: Orbis Books, 1985); and on both Knitter and Hick, essays in John Hick and Paul Knitter (eds), *The Myth of Christian Uniqueness* (Maryknoll: Orbis Press, 1987).

105. S. Mark Heim, *Salvations: Truth and Difference in Religion* (Maryknoll: Orbis Books, 1995).

106. Ibid., p. 24.

107. Ibid., p. 55.

108. Ibid., p. 77.

109. Ibid., pp. 7, 92, 7.

110. Ibid., pp. 158–229.

PART II

Special Revelation

4

THE COVENANT WITH ISRAEL: ELECTIVE ACTION

The universal light of preservation keeps life livable, but sets up a yearning for something more. What will it take to release the captive from bondage and give clarity to dimmed vision? Two-thirds of Scripture have to do with 'covenant' in a *particular* sense, the first particular *action* in the narrative of both reconciliation and revelation: *the covenant with Israel*:

> When Abram was ninety-nine years old, the Lord appeared to Abram, and said to him, 'I am God Almighty; walk before me, and be blameless. And I will make my covenant between me and you . . . No longer shall your name be Abram, but your name shall be Abraham, for I have made you the ancestor of a multitude of nations . . .' (Gen. 17:1–2, 5)
>
> I bore you up on eagles' wings and brought you to myself . . . Now, therefore, if you obey my voice and keep my covenant, you shall be my treasured possession of all the peoples. . . . So Moses went down to the people and told them. Then God spoke all these words: I am the Lord thy God who brought you out of the land of Egypt, out of the house of slavery; you shall have no other gods before me . . . (Exodus 19:4, 5, 25, 20:1–3)
>
> The law indeed was given through Moses . . . (John 1:17) . . . Abraham believed God, and it was reckoned to him as righteousness . . . For this reason it depends on faith, in order that the

> promise may rest on grace and be guaranteed to all his descendants, not only to the adherents of the law but also those who share the faith of Abraham (for he is the father of all of us, as it is written 'I have made you father of many nations') . . . the gifts and the calling of God are irrevocable. (Romans 4:3, 16–17; 11:29)

'God's history with Israel' is essential to the Great Narrative because it is the entry point into a fallen world of both deliverance and disclosure. The bonding with Israel is the expression among us of who God is and what God does, pointing back to the primal Life Together that God is, and forwards to the reconciliation to be realised.

> I will take you as my people and I will be your God. (Exodus 6:7)

Israel is the biblical showcase of 'covenant', the trustworthy promise of life together and expectation of response in kind. From Israel's book, we know that the God of Israel is the Promise-keeper; the covenant with Israel exegetes the covenant with Noah and behind that the covenant with creation itself – the election of the world to partnership with God. And deepest of all, the *shalom* which God purposes for the world disclosed to the eye of the prophet points to the very *Shalom* that God is. The covenant which God makes with this people is a paradigm of the Covenant God, the triune Life Together, in the call of world the promise of divine faithfulness to it, and finally the bonding that God secures in Jesus Christ, our 'peace' (Eph. 2:14) and its completion in the last chapter of the Story when God is 'all and in all'.

To this people is revealed the holy love of God, the mercy and the wrath, the commandments, the clear vision of the prophet: 'To them belong the adoption, the glory, the covenants, the giving of the law, the worship and the promises' (Rom. 9:4). Christians hold these things to be true because they believe that God's electing deed in Israel is, at one and the same time, an act of divine disclosure witnessed to in the Scripture of the two Testaments. A doctrine of revelation must take up *why* that Scripture is deemed trustworthy, and that is the subject of 'inspiration' explored in Chapter 6. At the heart of the Why? is the *that* of disclosive action in the Israel of the Old Testament and the Christ of the New. Therefore, in both this chapter on Israel and the following one, on Jesus Christ, the focus will be on the 'thatness' of the revelatory deed and the conversation between those who either assert it or deny it. The *what* of these chapters – the nature and purposes of the God disclosed in election and Incarnation: 'Israelology', 'Christology', 'soteriology' – is presupposed, as all doctrine is interrelated, but must be the formal subject of other works in this series that go beyond the prolegomenal issues of authority, interpretation and revelation.

THE SCANDAL OF ISRAEL'S PARTICULARITY

The assertion of Israel's special election flies in the face of the assumptions of a fallen world. The history of anti-Semitism and anti-Judaism is testimony to the offence given. The horror of the Holocaust is a measure of what humanity is capable of in rejecting the electing love of God and the vision of *shalom*. In defining microcosm, the slaughter of 'Jesus the Jew' tells the story of human hate for the scandal of particularity and its witness to Life Together.[1]

The particularist witness is predictably offensive to modernity's ahistorical and relativist premises – 'foolishness to the Greeks'. What might not be expected is the failure of traditional Christianity to honour its own texts and testimonies to the importance of this chapter in the narrative. Noting the church's historic ambivalence, Hendrikus Berkhof says:

> In some respects she is intensely concerned about the Old Testament; think of the important place Israel has in her instruction or the Psalms in her liturgy. In other respects she seems to forget Israel almost completely and not need her at all. This is especially the case in creedal statements and systematic theology handbooks. An example is the structure of the Apostles Creed: the confession jumps directly from the Creator to Christ . . . In the study of faith . . . usually . . . one proceeds directly from the doctrine of sin to Christology. There is hardly any room and interest for God's history with Israel.[2]

As judgment begins with our own household, we must remind ourselves of the Christian history of active as well as passive denial of this chapter of the Story, from Marcionite excision of the God of Abraham, Isaac and Jacob through Luther's 'two abominable pamphlets' (*Jews and Their Lies* and *The Shem Hamphoras and the Lineage of Christ*)[3] to 'the German Christians'[4] and the still pervasive supersessionist mentality in the churches, the view that the covenant with the Jewish people ended at the coming of Jesus Christ. The blood on our hands is not unrelated to the eraser which they hold.

There are many ways to enter the twentieth-century Christian conversation about the necessity of this chapter in the Story of both reconciliation and revelation. We choose here the debate about the *continuing* place of Israel in Christian faith. Its proponents make the strongest case for the existence of this chapter. At the same time, some of its advocates succumb to the temptation to diminish other chapters or reduce the Story to the one at hand. Thus the retrieval of this phase of revelation draws on the *anti*-supersession advocacies of our time, their relation to the Holocaust, the continuing and growing virulence of anti-Semitism and anti-Judaism and the emergence of the state of Israel.[5] The God of history with the common grace of preservation has, through these current *human* and *cultural* experiences, forced us to look again at our own texts and discover what has been censored. Because such a diversity of points of view exists in this still largely uncharted territory, a range of anti-supersession perspectives will be noted (here identified as *anti-supersession*, with *anti-supersessionism* reserved for the reductionist *ism*). Anti-supersession is the belief that with Israel God 'has commanded his covenant forever' (Psalm 111:9). 'Israel' is understood as *the Jewish people*. While land claims may be entailed, the covenant promise is not seen, as such, to include them.[6]

Anti-supersession has juxtaposed itself to the *supersessionism* that has been associated with historic Christian teaching, one that has taken various forms.[7] A current spectrum of the same includes: (1) a retributive replacement view which holds that the disobedience of Israel provoked the divine 'hate', the replacement of Israel by the Christian church, the result of Israel's disobedience being the suffering of its people over time;[8] (2) a non-retributive replacement view that rejects the idea of divine punishment but finds no place for the continuing role of Israel, stressing the singularity of the Person and Work of Christ, and holding the conversion of Jews necessary for their salvation;[9] (3) a modified replacement view which stresses the place of the Hebrew Scriptures in Christian faith, actively struggles against anti-Semitism and anti-Judaism, seeks dialogue with the Jewish people and endorses the right of Jews to their homeland, while at the same time seeing no continuing role for Jews in the plan of salvation and requiring their conversion for salvation;[10] (4) the messianic replacement view of Messianic Judaism ('Jews for Jesus') which maintains the continuing validity of many aspects of Judaism, often including its land claims and incorporating some of its ancient practices into worship and piety, while at the same time actively evangelising Jews for Jesus Christ;[11] (5) a christological election view in which the people of Israel are, with the Christian church, part of the one community of those elected for service, with the hardening of Israel's heart making possible the mission to the Gentiles, an interlude on the way to the End 'when all Israel will be saved'.[12]

In disagreement with all of the foregoing, anti-supersession runs the gamut from conservative evangelical to radical pluralist points of view. In each case, the noetic as well as the soteric role of the Jewish people is underscored by the declaration of a permanent place for Israel in Christian faith. These perspectives include the following.

Dispensationalism

As set forth originally by John Nelson Darby (1800–82), widely disseminated through the Scofield Reference Bible (1902–09) and popularised in the writings of Hal Lindsey and many current television evangelists, dispensationalism finds a continuing place for the Jewish people in human history and beyond, while espousing a very traditional, particularist theology. In the present sixth period of God's dispensations, Jews return to the Promised Land, succeeded by the climactic events of the rapture of believers, the tribulation, the arrival of the anti-Christ, Armageddon, the millennium. The birth of the state of Israel in 1948 is portentous, warranting a Christian Zionism, one that anticipates the full restoration of its ancestral lands in the coming 1,000-year reign, although the destiny of Jews in the eternal Kingdom to follow depends on their conversion to Christ.[13]

One People View

Markus Barth has carried forwards in anti-supersession form Karl Barth's 'christological election' view. Christians are seen as naturalised citizens of the Israel of God with Jesus the only Jew raised from the dead, enacting and disclosing justification and sanctification for all people. As one people with Israel, Christians have no need to convert Jews, but rather must live out a penitence for their historic hates and inflicted hurts, and be in solidarity with Jews in their suffering and their struggle to establish a safe space in the state of Israel after Auschwitz, even as Israel's claim to the land is conditional, requiring faithfulness to the biblical vision of justice with its implications for fair treatment of the Palestinian people.[14]

Paradoxical View

'God's covenant with the Jewish people has not been rescinded or abrogated by God but remains in full force', declares a 1987 General

Synod resolution of the United Church of Christ.[15] On its heels, a theological panel appointed to review its controversial resolution reaffirmed the stand but added:

> In the same breath in which Paul affirmed God's unswerving covenant with the Jews, he also declared 'faith comes from what is heard, and what is heard comes by the preaching of Christ' (Romans 10:17) . . .We cannot be who we are without this belief in the singular deed God has done to redeem all the world in the life, death, and resurrection of Jesus Christ.[16]

In a similar vein, the 1987 Presbyterian Church, USA Study Document on Jewish–Christian relations set before the General Assembly an anti-supersession position to which, after floor debate, was added the clarification: 'At the same time we can never forget that we stand in a covenant established by Jesus Christ (Hebrews 8) and that faithfulness to that covenant requires us to call *all* women and men to faith in Jesus Christ'.[17] This appeal to paradox – in which two mutually exclusive propositions are asserted but not explained, because so warranted by biblical testimony and Christian faith – appears more and more in official church statements. Land issues may also be involved with the affirmation of the state of Israel, but concern also for the rights of the Palestinian people, and now the celebration of Israel–PLO agreements on the West Bank and the Gaza Strip.

The Eschatological View

In this view, the 'faith of Abraham' saves (Romans 4:16). That faith is possible for Jews *after* Christ as well as before. As the gift of the triune God, the source of saving faith is in the reconciliation won by Jesus Christ. Drawing on 1 Peter 3:19–20 and 4:6, and on an ancient tradition about Christ descending to the dead (Apostles Creed) to preach to Old Testament believers, this view asserts a comparable encounter with all those of Abrahamic faith, affording revelation of its source in the triune God. Thus Paul's call for all to confess Christ (Romans 10:9–13), in the same discourse in which he speaks of the irrevocable covenant with Israel, is affirmed eschatologically.[18] This view does not single out Jews for evangelism, but neither does it exclude them from the church's mandate to share its message. It affirms the state of Israel on moral grounds, after Auschwitz, and as a keeper of the vision of *shalom*, holding it thereby accountable also to its own standards in its relation to the Palestinian people.[19]

Double Covenant View

God calls Jews from the beginning to live by Abrahamic faith, to be obedient to the Law and to be a light to the nations. God comes in Jesus the Jew, and in a 'provisional act' hardens Israel's heart in order that the church may carry out the mission to the Gentiles. Jews and Christians, each with their covenants, are 'partners in waiting' for the glory of the Lord yet to be manifest. Christians are not required to convert Jews, for the eschatological promise has been made that 'all Israel will be saved'. The truth-claims of each also await eschatological verification. Short of the end, Christians must be in solidarity with suffering Jews, and Jews in turn keep faith with their prophetic heritage, especially so as a state in their relations with the Palestinian people.[20]

Midrashic View

Historic Christian claims to the finality and deity of Christ and the authority of Christian Scripture and tradition, as reviewed through the lens of 'Israel's God' and the world's Holocaust hate, must be questioned and reformulated. God's defining revelation runs from the ancient action of God among the Hebrew people through its post-*Christum* history, including the anti-Semitism and anti-Judaism spawned by the church and its imperial claims, the Holocaust, and the creation of the state of Israel. The charter to which Christians must turn for understanding Israel's God is the Hebrew Bible, defined as 'Scripture', with the New Testament as 'Apostolic Writings' and thus 'midrash'. As the revelatory history of Israel's God continues to the present state of Israel, there is a theological warrant for its land claims, albeit with due regard for the poor and the stranger and thus its responsibilities towards the Palestinian people.[21]

Pluralist View

As all religions are human expressions of a common sensibility of, or hunger for, ultimate meaning, no one faith can lay claim to defining truth or salvation. As different species of this genus, Christians and Jews have their own separate heroes, texts and histories, right for each of them, not to be imposed by one on the other. The history of Christianity's role in anti-Semitism, anti-Judaism and the Holocaust, on the one hand, and the genocide carried out by Israel's occupation

111

of another land in biblical times and its violation of Palestinian rights in our day, on the other, demonstrates the evil of ignoring the relativity of religious truth-claims. The moral norm intrinsic to the human commonalities calls each tradition to abandon its hegemonic behaviour, and all to seek justice, a stance that can play out for pluralists either as support of the state of Israel after the Holocaust or for the Palestinian cause as victims of the state of Israel's policies.[22]

Cultural-linguistic View

With religions understood as language systems and doctrine as rules of their communities' speech, both Judaism and Christianity have *distinct* stories to tell, not reducible to varying species of a common genus. Depending on whether religious world-views are held to make propositional truth-claims or not, however, this perspective could be ranged alongside the pluralist viewpoint that 'we all have stories to tell', each giving the community its identity, but none claiming correspondence with ultimate Reality, or found elsewhere on the spectrum making such claims but seeking to hold together the particularities of Israel's call and that of Christ and the church as in the paradoxical, eschatological and double-covenant views.[23]

CONTRIBUTIONS

Anti-supersession is a 'wake-up call' for traditional Christianity. It retrieves from Scripture a chapter of the Story missing or muted in its historic creeds, theologies, liturgies and hymnody. We are only at the beginning of the effort to reclaim the election of Israel in its full meaning.

Its impact on the narrative of revelation is two-fold. It restores the *past* chapter to the role that it deserves in the economy of revelation, and it presses Christians to consider the *present* epistemological significance of the covenant with Israel.

Past

Narratively considered, standard views of revelation, whatever their focus, assert the presence of past disclosure: general revelation or its equivalents and/or revelation in Christ and/or the inspiration of Scripture and/or the illumination of the church and the believer.

112

These revelatory 'covenants' continue; what took place then is communicated to us now. By affirming the *continuing* covenant of God with Israel, anti-supersession locates it alongside other present revelatory claims with their corresponding sources in God's past deeds. As such, it reminds the church of the missing past chapter in its Grand Narrative, for no leap can be made from creation, fall and the covenant with Noah to the new covenant in Christ. A disclosure is made in the narrative of revelation, as a deed is done in the narrative of reconciliation, ones to be reflected in both the doctrine of revelation and the doctrine of reconciliation.

The retroactive import of anti-supersession is its reclamation of the revelatory significance of the defining deeds of God in the biblical history of Israel. What the God of Israel *did* among this people is what God there *disclosed*. The Word is spoken *in* these events as well as *about* these events.

We know of these events, so organised and interpreted, through the sacred writings of the Hebrew people. As such, this covenant chapter includes *words* as well as deeds. Our attention to the events as of a piece with the Christian metanarrative presupposes a trust in the words. As John Baillie puts it:

> We must therefore say that the receiving is as necessary to a completed act of revelation as the giving. It is only insofar as the action of God in history is understood as God means it to be understood that revelation has taken place at all (quoting Archbishop Temple): 'the intercourse of mind and event' or 'the coincidence of event and interpretation'.[24]

Why should we trust these words of Scripture? The canonisation of the Hebrew Bible as the Christian Old Testament presupposes the trustworthiness of these writings as witness to the God of the Jewish and Christian peoples. They are 'prophetic' in the same sense that the New Testament is 'apostolic' – a trustworthy 'speaking for God'. In the Christian revelatory framework, this 'prophetic-apostolic testimony' is a gift of the Holy Spirit. The discussion of this feature of the chapter on the covenant with Israel – 'the God who speaks (as well as) shows'[25] – will be postponed until Chapter 6, on inspiration. However, underscored here is the revelatory significance of reportage and interpretation about the meaning of the events as well as the occurrence of the events themselves.

Present

The emphasis of anti-supersession on the continuing covenant with the Jewish people sharply poses the question of the present as well as the past significance of its election. What does it mean for the doctrine of revelation that 'the gifts' of Israel are not abrogated?

If the election of Israel is irrevocable, functioning in some way in this time between the Times of the coming of Christ and the consummation of all things, then the gifts given in the past chapter must continue in the present one, albeit in the setting of the New Age of reconciliation and revelation that has arrived in Jesus Christ. The events in Israel's continuing history are on a trajectory that comes from its past. Thus the Jewish people have borne witness over time to the righteousness of God that claims us, in turn, for 'doing justice, loving mercy and walking humbly' (Amos). In the midst of its own rebellion and failures – that stretch from the foot of ancient Mt Sinai to the modern Golan Heights – they know about, and are known for, their stewardship of the vision of *shalom* – righteousness, justice, peace. At their most faithful, Jews are found in the front lines of today's social struggles for justice and peace.[26] That continuing role is of a piece with the call of Israel to be a 'light to the nations'. When faithful to their covenant, the Jewish people are a conscience to the human community. As such, they shed continuing revelatory light on the purposes of God.

Again, continuing the Old Testament trajectory, this people of God knows pain in its deepest form. The suffering of Israel has been a mark of its life for the past 2,000 years. But here the discontinuities as well as continuities enter. The witness of the Hebrew Scriptures is that suffering was inextricable from rebellion. But the testimony of history since is that their continuing suffering – from the pogroms carried out by Christians to the neo-pagan assaults of the Holocaust – are witness to the depth of *our own* human sin, not witness to the judgment of God on the Jews. Here is a revelatory Word spoken to the human heart about its capacities for evil, one that confirms the New Testament declaration that 'no-one is righteous, not even one' (Romans 3:10) and overturns the 'blame the victim' mentality. The latter is the last retreat of human self-righteousness, in this case, reading Jewish suffering not as our own grievous fault but as the victims' curse.

Is there a correlation between the stewardship of *shalom* and the suffering of the Jewish people? If the suffering of 'Jesus the Jew' who *is* Shalom is a clue, then this correlation cannot be easily dismissed.

Love and justice do 'heap burning coals' on their enemies (cf. Romans 12:20). But the little light given to us on the mission of the Jewish people in this time between the Times is not sufficient to make such definitive judgments. The light to the nations that Israel gives is its continuing witness to *shalom*, and her suffering as a judgment on our sin and call to our repentance.

Another kind of continuing light to the nations is the intellectual gift which Jews bring to the understanding of Christian faith itself. In the late twentieth century, Jewish scholarship on the figure of the historical Jesus has been of special importance. Those who share in the Jewish tradition out of which Jesus lived and spoke have been able to show to the Christian believer aspects of the human and historical nature of the Person of Christ professed in classical Christian doctrine, making welcome the extensive current research on Jesus by Jewish biblical scholars.[27]

The raised awareness of Christians about their complicity in the 'teaching of contempt' for Jews has come not only from the events themselves – the Holocaust, most of all – but also from the intellectual challenge by Jews to face honestly the connection between its traditional supersession doctrine and its history of anti-Semitism and anti-Judaism. Jewish thinkers such as Michael Wyschogrod and Eugene Borowitz have not only read deeply and critically in Christian texts and traditions but also been a constant presence in Jewish–Christian dialogue, respecting Christian particularity yet reminding the church of both its tragic supersession legacy and the possibilities of an anti-supersession reading of its own texts.[28]

PROBLEMS

The advances made in the Christian doctrines of reconciliation and revelation by the recovery of the unabrogated covenant with Israel carry with them the same problems met at every turn in the narrative. Its lustre is mesmerising, and other light recedes from view. This chapter becomes so compelling that the rest of the Story is muted or left untold. The espousal of anti-supersession, as such, does not constitute that closure, but the points of view at the end of the spectrum do succumb to the reductionist temptation.

In Paul van Buren's 'midrashic view', the Trinity, the Person of Christ as both divine and human, the unique reconciling and revealing work of Christ, and salvation by grace through faith in Christ are all rejected as supersessionist. The defining acts of both reconciliation and revelation are relocated to Israel's history, past and present. Defining interpretation as well as decisive events are also reconceived with the Hebrew Bible becoming the pivotal text – 'Scripture' – and the New Testament only commentary thereon. Thus the succeeding chapters of the Christian narrative of revelation – Christ, Church (Scripture and tradition), salvation, consummation – fall away.

The pluralist view represents a second form of reductionism. In this case, the christological centralities also disappear, but so does the unique chapter on the covenant with Israel. Singular Jewish as well as Christian truth-claims are denied alongside those of all other religious traditions. Each is seen to be a creature of social history whose times and circumstances give particular expression to a universal religious quest, one identified by the pluralist conceptuality. As the validity of each religious claim must be judged by standards (moral, philosophical, religious, aesthetic) accessible to all, this pluralist view makes assumptions similar to those who end the narrative with Noah's covenant: human beings are given powers to discern something of the good, true and holy. Yes, the covenant with Noah promises a common grace. No, this chapter does not close the Tale. The depth of the fall and the lengths to which God must go to overcome its noetic (and soteric) effects is not understood by those who settle for a foreshortened journey.

Both the midrashic and pluralist views have vocal advocates in Christian–Jewish dialogue. Isaac Rottenberg, a long-time participant, has shown how the abandonment by either Christians or Jews of their particularist commitments actually weakens the dialogue as well as rejects aspects of the faith integral to both Christian and Jewish identity.[29] The covenant with Israel is 'forever' (Psalm 111:19). But it is also a stage on the way.

To what end? The pillar of fire points forwards, with the promise of another and greater light.

> Then his father Zechariah was filled with the Holy Spirit and spoke this prophecy ... 'By the tender mercy of our God, the dawn from on high will break upon us, to give light to those who sit in darkness and in the shadow of death, to guide our feet on the way of peace'. (Luke 1:67, 78–9)

NOTES

1. See Markus Barth, *Jesus the Jew*, op. cit., passim.

2. Hendrikus Berkhof, *Christian Faith: An Introduction to the Study of the Faith*, rev. edn, trans. Sierd Woudstra (Grand Rapids: Eerdmans, 1985), p. 225.

3. Ibid., p. 14. See also Eric Gritsch and Marc Tannenbaum, *Luther and the Jews* (New York: Lutheran Council in the USA, 1983).

4. See Arthur Cochrane, *The Church's Confession Under Hitler* (Philadelphia: Westminster Press, 1962).

5. A showcase of the new sensibility can be found in the record of church statements approximating or reflecting the conviction that the covenant with Israel *continues* after the coming of Christ, with commensurate acts of repentance for Christian failure to respect the role of the Jewish people in the purposes of God: World Council of Churches, *The Theology of the Churches and the Jewish People: Statements by the World Council of Churches and its Member Churches* (Geneva: WCC Publications, 1988). Closer to home is the writer's participation in the anti-supersessionist studies of the United Church of Christ, as in *New Conversations* 12:3 (Summer 1990), with the writer's essays, 'Perspectives on the Covenants of Israel and Christ', pp. 35–44, and 'Israel's Continuing Covenant and God's Deed in Christ', pp. 25–7.

6. On the relation of land to covenant, see Paul K. Jewett, *Election and Predestination* (Grand Rapids: Eerdmans, 1985), pp. 30–44.

7. For details, see the writer's 'The Place of Israel in Christian Faith', in *Ecumenical Faith in Evangelical Perspective*, op. cit., pp. 147–53.

8. See Charles D. Provan, *The Church Is Israel Now: The Transfer of Conditional Privilege* (Vallecito, CA: Ross House Books, 1987); and Jerry Falwell, *Listen America!* (Garden City: Doubleday, 1980), pp. 93–8.

9. As in traditional systematics works, for example Louis Berkhof, *Systematic Theology*, 4th rev. and enlarged (Grand Rapids: Eerdmans, 1982), pp. 698–700.

10. See Consultation on the Gospel and the Jewish People, *The Willowbank Declaration on the Christian Gospel and the Jewish People* (Wheaton, IL: World Evangelical Fellowship, 1989).

11. See Daniel Juster, *Jewish Roots: A Foundation of Biblical Theology for Messianic Judaism* (Rockville, MD: Davar Publishing Co., 1986).

12. See Karl Barth, *Church Dogmatics*, II/2, trans. G. W. Bromiley and T. F. Torrance (Edinburgh: T. & T. Clark, 1957), pp. 195–305, and also IV/1, pp. 20–35 and IV/2, pp. 761–6, 768–71.

13. For a visual portrayal of the dispensationalist scenario, see Charles Taylor, *The Destiny Chart: Today in Bible Prophecy* (1978). For a review of the practical import of political dispensationalism, see Grace Halsell, *Prophecy and Politics: Militant Evangelists on the Road to Nuclear War* (Westport, CT: Lawrence Hill & Co., 1986).

14. See Markus Barth, *Jesus the Jew*, op. cit., p. 94. The One People view has its roots in the theology of Heinrich Bullinger. For its exposition and related themes in Reformed theology, see Alan P. Sell (ed.), *Reformed Theology and the Jewish People* (Geneva: World Alliance of Reformed Churches, 1986), p. 8ff. and passim.

15. See the issue of the UCC's *New Conversations* devoted to the panel's statement (widely reported in an AP wire service story) and its interpretation, vol. 12, no. 3 (Summer 1990).

16. Jewish–Christian Theological Panel, United Church of Christ, 'Message to the Churches', *New Conversations* 12:3 (Summer 1990), 6.

17. 1987 General Assembly, Presbyterian Church, USA, *A Theological Understanding of the Relationship between Christians and Jews* (A Paper Commended to the Church for Study and Reflection), p. 9.

18. This view has its counterpart among orthodox Jews who hold that Christians may be saved before God by their Noachic faith, but must acknowledge its source in the God of Abraham, Isaac and Jacob (viz. the writings of Michael Wyschogrod).

19. For an exposition of this view based on an exegesis of Romans 9–11, see the writer's *Ecumenical Faith in Evangelical Perspective*, op. cit., pp. 162–7.

20. See the section 'Christology in Jewish–Christian Dialogue', in Jürgen Moltmann, *The Way of Jesus Christ: Christology in Messianic Dimensions*, trans. Margaret Kohl (San Francisco: HarperSanFrancisco, 1990), pp. 28–37.

21. Paul van Buren has developed these views in great detail in his three-volume series, *Discerning the Way: A Theology of the Jewish Christian Reality* (New York: Seabury, 1980), *A Christian Theology of the People of Israel*, Part 2 (New York: Seabury, 1983) and *A Theology of the Jewish Christian Reality* (San Francisco: Harper & Row, 1987). This series, out of print, was reprinted by The University Press of America in 1995.

22. The writings of John Hick, Wilfred Cantwell Smith and Paul Knitter develop in one way or another this 'common core' view, applicable to all world religions, Judaism included. For a searching analysis and critique of the pluralist position of these three writers, see Mark Heim, *Salvations*, op. cit., pp. 13–126. Krister Stendahl carries the pluralist premise into Jewish–Christian theological issues. See his interpretation of religious traditions as metaphorical 'love talk', not metaphysical truth-claims, in Gerald H. Anderson and Thomas F. Stransky, *Christ's Lordship and Religious Pluralism* (Maryknoll, NY: Orbis Books, 1981), pp. 13–15.

23. George Lindbeck, known for giving definitive expression to a cultural-linguistic understanding of doctrine in *The Nature of Doctrine*, falls into the latter category, and on this subject holds a One People view. On his propositional commitments, see Bruce Marshall, 'Aquinas as a Post-Liberal Theologian', *Thomist* 53:3 (1989), and on Jewish–Christian

theological issues see Lindbeck's essay 'The Story-Shaped Church: Critical Exegesis and Theological Interpretation', in Garrett Green (ed.), *Scriptural Authority and Narrative Interpretation* (Philadelpia: Fortress, 1987), pp. 161–78.

24. John Baillie, *The Idea of Revelation in Recent Thought* (New York: Columbia University Press, 1956), pp. 64–5.

25. The subtitle of Carl Henry's series, *God, Revelation and Authority*, argues for the place of inspiration as well as action in a doctrine of revelation.

26. Reinhold Niebuhr regularly observed that Jews were at the foreground of movements for social change in the North American struggles of the day.

27. For example, see the studies by Geza Vermes, *The Religion of Jesus the Jew* (Minneapolis: Fortress Press, 1993); Arthur E. Zannoni (ed.), *Jews and Christians Speak of Jesus* (Minneapolis: Fortress Press, 1993); James H. Chadsworth (ed.), *Jesus' Jewishness*, American Interfaith Institute (New York: Crossroad, 1991); Trude Weis-Rosmarin (ed. with intro.), *Jewish Expression on Jesus* (New York: KTVA Publishing House, 1977); Pinchas Lapide, *Israelis, Jews and Jesus*, trans. Peter Heinegg (Garden City, NY: Doubleday, 1979); Jacob Neusner, *A Rabbi Talks about Jesus: An Intermillennial, Interfaith Exchange* (New York: Doubleday, 1993); D. Cohn-Shembok, *Rabbinic Perspectives on the New Testament* (Lewiston, NY: E. Mellen Press, 1990).

28. See the writings of Michael Wyschogrod, especially *The Body of Faith* (New York: Seabury Press, 1983) and the recent representative essay, 'Incarnation', *Pro Ecclesia* 2:2 (Spring 1993), 208–15. On the work of Eugene B. Borowitz, see his ground-breaking *Contemporary Christologies: A Jewish Response* (New York: Paulist Press, 1980) and the recent *Renewing the Covenant: Theology for the Postmodern Jew* (Philadelphia: The Jewish Publication Society, 1991).

29. See Isaac C. Rottenberg, *The Turbulent Triangle: Christians–Jews–Israel* (Hawley, PA: Red Mountain Associates, 1989), and *Jewish Christians in an Age of Christian–Jewish Dialogue* (Lord's Valley, PA: privately printed, 1995). See also Jürgen Moltmann's messianic christology, especially 'Christology in Jewish–Christian Dialogue', in *The Way of Jesus Christ: Christology in Messianic Dimensions*, trans. Margaret Kohl (San Francisco: HarperSanFrancisco, 1990), pp. 28–37.

5

JESUS CHRIST: INCARNATE ACTION

'How beautiful are the feet of those who bring good news!' (Rom. 10:15). The gospel is *news*. News of what? Beautiful feet bringing news of the long-hoped-for 'way of peace' onto which yet other feet shall tread. And this is a news *story* that reaches back into history and beyond to eternity itself:

> Long ago God spoke to our ancestors in many and various ways by the prophets, but in these last days he spoke to us by a son, whom he appointed heir of all things, through whom he also created the worlds. He is the reflection of God's glory and the exact imprint of God's very being, and he sustains all things by his powerful word. (Hebrews 1:1–3)

In Jesus Christ, the hoped-for dawn comes, the very 'glory' of God now among us:

> the Word became flesh and lived among us, and we have seen his glory, the glory as of a father's only son, full of grace and truth. (John 1:14)

The embodied Word is about the new turn taken in the Great Story. The plot has moved from the triune God's call of the world to life together, to the world's rebel cry of 'No!', to God's covenantal promises – universal in Noah, particular in Israel, always long-suffering under our continuing hostility. Only God, first-hand, enfleshed, can turn the tide. So comes Emmanuel, God with us. And the struggle is on in a life and a death, and finally a victory won in a resurrection and ascension. To what end?

> in Christ God was reconciling the world to himself, not counting their trespasses against them. (2 Cor. 5:19)

'Life Together' has come among us in Christ to move the world from alienation to *reconciliation*. In the language of the Church, the coming is set forth in a doctrine of Incarnation, and the struggle and victory that overcomes separation by at-one-ment is expressed in a doctrine of Atonement.

In the rich imagery of Hebrews and John, where there is Life, there is also Light: 'What has come into being in him was life, and the life was the light of all people' (John 1:4). Life and Light, reconciliation and revelation – a decisive deed done, a defining disclosure made.

> For it is God who said, 'Let light shine out of darkness', who has shone in our hearts to give the light of the knowledge of God in the face of Jesus Christ. (2 Cor. 4:6)

The incarnation of the Word *is* 'the light . . . the knowledge of God', towards which the rainbow points and the pillar of fire moves. Jesus Christ is the central chapter in the narrative of both reconciliation and revelation, the 'truth' as well as 'the way' and 'the life' (John 14:6).[1]

These are awesome claims, with a multitude of varying interpretations in the history of Christian thought on where and how the deed was done and the disclosure made in Jesus Christ. Indeed, they run parallel to one another in doctrinal debates. If the thirty-nine-plus theories of atonement were distilled into major types, four would come into prominence, corresponding to stages in the Jesus story at the centre of the overarching Narrative:[2] an exemplarist type in which the deed of reconciliation takes place in the life and teachings of Jesus of Nazareth; a substitutionary type in which the deed is done on Calvary; a conflict and victory type in which resurrection is the decisive event; an incarnational type in which incarnation *is* atonement

Theories of christological revelation follow the same course – Galilee, Calvary, Easter, Bethlehem. Exemplarist views find the disclosure in Jesus' life and teachings, substitutionary ones at Golgotha, conflict and victory views at Easter, and incarnational ones at Bethlehem.

While not reaching ecumenical consensus, an inclusive framework for understanding the atonement has taken shape in doctrinal history, challenging the perennial reductionist temptations: the *munus triplex*, the 'three-fold office of Christ'. Prophetic, priestly and royal roles witness to the Work of Christ in Galilee, Calvary and Easter, with Bethlehem as undergirding, the incarnate Person who does the three-fold work. Is there a counterpart to this full-orbed soteric view of reconciliation in an inclusive noetic view of revelation? Our quest here in the micro-story of revelation in Christ reflects the same search for fullness in the overarching narrative of revelation. Where better to look in that quest for catholicity than to the most searching twentieth-century restatement of the three-fold office?

KARL BARTH

The doctrine of revelation as found in volume 4 of Barth's *Church Dogmatics* is set forth within the framework of the three-fold office of Christ. Barth is known as both 'the theologian of christological con-centration' and 'the theologian of revelation'. The two are conjoined in his terse trinitarian description of God as 'Revealer, Revelation, Revealedness', with Jesus Christ the middle term. As the theologian for whom the singular deed in Jesus Christ is the sole locus of the disclosure of the triune God, he is the natural interlocutor for this chapter of the narrative, especially so as his view is articulated in the framework of the triple ministry of Christ.

Commentators on Barth's thought on revelation often turn to the initial volumes of his *Church Dogmatics*. Reference has been made in Chapter 3 to aspects of this earlier work. However, our basic resource here is *Church Dogmatics* IV/3, first part, in which the doctrine of revelation is interpreted in terms of the *munus triplex*, and specifically the *prophetic* office of Christ. In this exposition, Barth clarifies earlier ambiguities, speaks to his critics, and introduces some new themes. In the latter case, attention will be given to his concept of 'free communications' and 'parables of the kingdom' in the world beyond the 'Bible' and the 'Church'. And throughout, note will be taken of the impact on the doctrine of revelation of Barth's stress on the *divine sovereignty*.

For Barth, revelation has to do

> with Jesus Christ Himself in His prophetic office and work, as He confesses and makes Himself known as the humiliated Son of God and the exalted Son of Man, and therefore as the Mediator between God and man, and therefore as the One who restores

fellowship between them and accomplishes the justification and sanctification of man.[3]

God's reconciling deed in Christ – the priestly work of humiliation – receiving the judgment on sin, and the royal work of exaltation, victorious over death and giving life to humanity – must be *made known* to the world. In Christ, 'reconciliation is also revelation'.[4] Accordingly, the gifts of true *prophecy* are given in Christ – 'light', 'glory', 'truth'.

OBJECTIVE AND SUBJECTIVE REVELATION

Barth is known for his 'dynamic' understanding of revelation, the *happening* of the Word as that Word reaches the hearer.

> For me the Word of God is a *happening*, not a thing. Therefore the Bible must *become* the Word of God, and it does so through the work of the Spirit.[5]

The *address* to us, received through grace by us, is a critical accent in Barth's teaching, bound up with a wariness of all attempts to deny the freedom of God, as in the identification of the Word with the words of the biblical text. But this emphasis does not stand alone: the fundamental *fact* of revelation is the first-century *act* of revelation in the life, death, resurrection and ascension of Jesus Christ. Revelation does not depend on its subjective reception. God's reconciling deed in Jesus Christ is, *as such*, revelation.

> For as it takes place in its perfection, and with no need of supplement, it also expresses, discloses, mediates and reveals itself . . . It displays itself. It proclaims itself . . . No matter what the result may be or what may be achieved or effected, it displays and proclaims itself as truth . . . Its donation sovereignly precedes all reception on our part . . . it is not dark and dumb but perspicuous and vocal, that it may and will therefore be received, but is independent of our actual reception . . . reconciliation is indeed revelation . . . In itself it is the basis of knowledge even when it does not correspond to the knowledge of a single man . . . It is out-going and self-communicative, even before it attains its goal in the creaturely world . . . This objectivity of even its revelatory character must be emphasized so expressly because misunderstanding can so easily creep in . . . it is necessary to hold fast not only to the objectivity of reconciliation . . . but also to the

123

objectivity of its character as revelation, to the *a priori* nature of its light in face of all human illumination and knowledge . . .[6]

The objectivity of revelation, therefore, is Jesus of Nazareth, born, teaching, preaching, healing, serving, suffering, dying, rising – the Word of God incarnate.

Barth's stress on the objectivity of revelation is yet another way of underscoring the 'scandal of particularity' so central to his theology. He does not want revelation to be confused with anything else, in this case with our *reception* of it, even with the enlightening work of the Holy Spirit that enables us to hear the Word. Here, and here only in the enfleshed Word, the free God discloses who God is. Neither the freedom *from* nor the freedom *for* us can be taken in tow by our subjectivity, as is done by the modernism that traces all things to our general experience, or the pietism that grounds faith in our religious experience:

> Jesus Christ is *the* light of life. To underline the 'the' is to say that He is the one and only light of life. Positively, this means that He is the light of life in all its fulness, in perfect adequacy; and negatively, it means that there is no other light of life . . . outside and alongside the light which He is. Everything which we have to say concerning the prophetic office of Jesus Christ rests on this emphasis . . . 'Jesus Christ as attested to us in Holy Scripture is the one Word of God whom we must hear'.[7]

The repetition of this note in IV/3/1 is a response to those who appropriated his earlier stress on the *moment* of the Word's action in existentialist terms,[8] and to those who accused him of a new form of 'liberal' subjectivism.[9] These criticisms may have a point to make, and we shall investigate the evangelical charges against Barth, but their validity does not lie in the association of Barth with experiential reductionisms.

Barth's determination to stress the historical event of Christ as self-disclosing – 'self-attestation' – is reminiscent of high-school physics debates that pose the question: does a tree falling in a forest and heard by no-one make a sound? For Barth, the descent of the Word incarnate is a divine Sound whether or not there is a human receiver attuned by the Holy Spirit to its vibrations. The triune God *hears* as well as utters the divine Speech, establishing it as a Word, freeing it from all dependency on us to validate it as such. The 'objectivity' of the Word made flesh in Jesus Christ, therefore, constitutes the primal meaning of the prophetic office of Christ:

What takes place in the existence of Jesus Christ as the true Son of God who is also the true Son of Man is that God Himself is present in person and speaks this Word which cannot be co-ordinated or compared with any human word. It is for this reason and in this sense that Jesus is the one and only Word of God. He is not the only word, nor even the only good word. But He is the only Word which, because it is spoken directly by God himself, is good as God is, has the authority and power of God and is to be heard as God Himself. He is the only Word which all human words, even the best, can only directly or indirectly attest but not repeat or replace or rival, so that their own goodness and authority are to be measured by whether or not, and with what fidelity, they are witnesses of this one Word . . . There is only one Prophet who speaks the Word of God as He is Himself this Word, and this One is called and is Jesus.[10]

Here is the heart of Barth's theology of revelation, Jesus Christ, the 'one and only Word of God', spoken as preceding 'all reception on our part', reconciliation *as* revelation.

THE TRAJECTORY OF REVELATION

Barth's christological concentration cannot be separated from the entire sweep of the drama of God's deeds. He tracks the revelatory reconciliation in the historical event of Jesus Christ back to its origins in the inner-trinitarian Life, and then follows the course of the elect-ing Love there present forwards into the covenant with creation, the call and expectation of Israel, to the Word enfleshed – and from there again to the witness of Scripture, the recollective life and tradition of the church and finally to the full light of eschatological radiance. The echoes of a narrative interpretation of Christian doctrine can be heard in this encompassing epistemology.

TRIUNE SELF-REVELATION

The description of the Trinity as Revealer, Revelation, Revealedness indicates the grounding of the doctrine of revelation in the divine Life Together. Thus Barth's initial treatment of revelation is part of his early discussion of the Trinity in I/1.[11] The act of Self-disclosure in Jesus Christ is an expression of the character of God as intrinsically self-disclosive. What God does in the missions of the economic Trinity is who God

125

is in the immanent Trinity. While there are reaches of mystery in the divine being, God does not tell us

> one thing in history while being something else in eternity. His secondary objectivity is fully true, for it has its correspondence and basis in His primary objectivity[12]

God *as* the Word incarnate *is* God the self-revealing One. Whether Barth is consistent in the application of this assertion of the primal self-disclosivity (found in his fertile idea of the social nature of the *imago Dei* as well as here) is a matter of debate. Critics find modalistic tendencies in his thought which would preclude the revelatory coinherence of the Persons suggested by the 'primary objectivity' of revelation in the inner-trinitarian Being.[13] We shall return to this question.

LITTLE LIGHTS, FREE COMMUNICATIONS AND PARABLES OF THE KINGDOM

As noted in Chapter 3, on the Noachic covenant, Barth categorically rejects 'natural theology' or whatever he considers its equivalent, such as the Reformed tradition's 'general revelation', or Emil Brunner's 'point of contact'. Jesus Christ alone is 'Revelation'. Yet in IV/3/1, a line of argument appears that has prompted some to think that Barth has altered his views. The language employed is surprising, as in his allusion to 'other revelations'.[14] However, his argument is subtle and requires careful scrutiny.

There is only one true Light, defining Revelation and sole Prophet: Jesus Christ. Yet

> we recognize that the fact that Jesus Christ is the one Word of God does not mean that in the Bible, the Church and the world there are not other words which are quite notable in their way, other lights which are quite clear and other revelations which are quite real.[15]

With specific reference to 'world',

> Nor is it impossible that words of this kind should be uttered outside this circle [of Bible and Church] if the whole world of creation and history is the realm of the lordship of God at whose right hand Jesus Christ is seated, so that He exercises authority in this outer as well as the inner sphere and is free to attest Himself or to cause Himself to be attested in it.[16]

Barth describes these 'little lights' in the Night as 'free communications' of the sovereign God in the events of human history, and a luminosity in the constancies of nature as well, including the natural condition of human beings. Such illuminations do not give the true Light found alone in Jesus Christ. Further, all such flickerings must be measured by that final Radiance. But these truths, 'revelations', are 'worth something' and we must 'take note of them'.[17]

Modest indicators are to be seen in nature:

> The creaturely world . . . the cosmos, the nature given to man in his sphere and the nature of this sphere, has also as such its own lights and truths and therefore its own speech and words. That the world was and is and will be, and what and how it was and is and will be, thanks to the faithfulness of its Creator, is declared and attested by it and may thus be perceived and heard and considered . . . Like its persistence, its self-witness and lights are not extinguished by the corruption of the relationship between God and man . . . However corrupt man may be, they illumine him, and . . . he does not cease to see and understand them.[18]

Barth calls these the 'constants' in nature that sustain and order creation and prevent it from falling into chaos. They include the 'natural laws' accessible to scientific inquiry, and also the patterns of human behaviour discerned by the sociologist and psychologist, the regularities of history and the rhythms and beauties of life attested by the arts as well as by the sciences.

These patterns have been adduced by others as evidence for a 'natural theology'. Not so for Barth:

> They do not strike him from the eternity of God, but merely as self-attestations of His creation, as part of its dialogue with itself. Nor do they strike him personally, as directed to him, but only with a universal application and in relation to qualities which he shares with men of every time and place. They enlighten him concerning himself, i.e., his possibilities, situation and environment. But they do not illumine his heart and therefore himself . . . He lives with them, but he might live equally well without them. For he does not live by them; neither by the rhythm of the creaturely world, however powerful; nor by the revelations of its regularity and freedom and certainly not by the declaration of its immanent mystery. Of what avail is it to man to know these things? He has

certainly to take note of them ... [But] they carry neither real threat nor real promise. For they speak neither of real judgment and loss nor of real grace and salvation.[19]

'Revelation' in its true sense is of a different order. The penultimate value of these disclosures can never be confused with the ultimacy of God's singular act in Jesus Christ.

There are yet other lights in the world around us, 'parables of the kingdom', not the 'constants' of nature but the unforeseen 'free communications' of God that take place in human history. In this 'wider field' we behold 'the capacity of Jesus Christ to raise up of the stones, children of Abraham'.[20] These

> world-occurrences ... illumine, accentuate or explain the biblical witness in a particular time and situation, thus confirming it in the deepest sense by helping to make it sure and concretely evident and certain.[21]

Thus 'Jesus Christ can raise up extraordinary witnesses to speak true words of this very different order'.[22] These witnesses can take the form of movements that are actively hostile to Christ, for 'even from the mouth of Balaam the well-known voice of the good Shepherd may sound'.[23] Nothing is forbidden to God as an instrument of the divine Word.

Barth tells us he is not going to give any examples for fear of violating the event-character of free communications. However, he comes close to it now and then in descriptions that sound like the graced encounters with human 'limit-situations' of Karl Rahner, to be examined in a subsequent chapter:

> We may think of the lack of fear in face of death which Christians to their shame often display far less readily than non-Christians near and far. We may think of the warm readiness to understand and forgive which is not so frequently encountered in the Evangelical world just because it has too good a knowledge of good and evil and in spite of its acknowledgment that justification is by faith alone. Especially we may think of a humanity which does not ask or weigh too long with whom we are dealing in others, but in which we find a simple solidarity with them and unreservedly take up their case. Are not all these phenomena which with striking frequency are found *extra muros ecclesiae* in circles where little or nothing is obviously known of

the Bible and Church proclamation except perhaps by very devious ways and in attenuated forms? Is nothing to be learned from these phenomena? However alien their forms, is not their language that of true words, the language of 'parables of the kingdom of heaven'?[24]

While openness to these parables of the kingdom is urged by Barth, they cannot be conjoined to Christ, as a second principle, and certainly not taken as the interpretive key to the Gospel:

> As the One Word of God, He can bring Himself into the closest conjunction with such words . . . [Yet] there is no legitimate place for projects in the planning and devising of which Jesus Christ can be given a particular niche in co-ordination with those of other events, powers, forms and truths . . . As the one Word of God He wholly escapes every conceivable synthesis envisaged in them . . . Sooner or later they will make an open bid for sole dominion – the prophecy of Jesus Christ asks to be excused and avoids any such incorporation . . . No man can serve both the one Word of God called Jesus Christ and other divine words.[25]

In a given time and place, candidacy for the status of 'free communication' must be rigorously scrutinised in the light of the one Word of God. Barth discusses four tests to which it must be put:

> First . . . we must always ask concerning its agreement with this witness of Scripture . . . If it is a true word, its message will harmonise at some point with the whole context of the biblical message as centrally determined and characterized by Jesus Christ . . . With certain qualifications we must also consider the relationship of these other words to the dogmas and confessions of the Church as a criterion of their truth [albeit as] the secondary authority of the fathers and brethren of the Church . . . As a further criterion . . . we may refer to the fruits which such true words have borne and seem to bear in the outside world . . . In world-occurrence as such all cats are not grey, but the Church can distinguish, if not the good from the bad, at least the better from the worse . . . We return to surer ground when we maintain that other words may be recognized as true words by what they signify for the life of the community itself . . . of affirmation and criticism, of address and claim, of summons to faith and a call to repentance.[26]

The tests and their priorities anticipate the stages on the trajectory we are tracing and the priorities among them.

In both the constants of creation and the free communications of God in history, the world shows itself to the eye of faith as the theatre of the divine glory. But let not those lights discerned there be mistaken for the one true Light.

SCRIPTURE AS PRIMARY WITNESS TO THE LIGHT

How do we know this one true Light, Jesus Christ? In Barth's initial dogmatic exposition of the 'three forms of the Word of God' (I/1), an extended answer is given to the warrant for the first form of the Word, the witness of Scripture. He summarises it in these words:

> The Bible constitutes itself as canon. It is the canon because it has imposed itself as such on the Church and invariably does so. The Church's recollection of God's past revelation has computed that the Bible is her object, because as a matter of fact, this and no other object is the promise of future divine revelation . . . The Bible is the canon just because it is so. But it is so because it imposes itself as such . . . The prophetic and apostolic Word is the word, the witness, the proclamation and the preaching of Jesus Christ . . . Holy Scripture is the word of men who longed for, expected, hoped for this 'Immanuel', and finally saw, heard, and handled it in Jesus Christ. It declares, attests, and proclaims it . . . Thus it is in virtue of this its content that Scripture imposes itself.[27]

The Scripture is the prophetic-apostolic testimony to Jesus Christ, promised and recollected. And thus the Bible is the concrete medium by which the Church recalls God's revelation in the past, is called to expect revelation in the future, and is thereby challenged, empowered and guided to proclaim it now.[28]

In these earlier formulations, Barth speaks with less inhibition about 'future revelation' as the actualisation of the Word in its reception by the believer or the believing community through the power of the Holy Spirit (interestingly, not the 'future' as the eschatological disclosure at End). Thus we hear of the Bible 'becoming' God's Word:

> It takes place as an event, when and where the word of the Bible becomes God's Word . . . when and where John's finger points not in vain but really pointedly, and when and where by means of its word we also succeed in seeing and hearing what he saw and heard.[29]

This remains a critical aspect of Barth's doctrine of revelation in IV/3/1, the Word spoken to you and me in the here and now. As noted, because of the misunderstanding of this as yet one more subtle captivity of the free Word to religious experience (reception), he subsequently stresses the revelatory self-sufficiency of the historic event of Jesus Christ.

The Word that comes to us *now* comes through Scripture, the 'Word written'. Yet, for all its unique role in the revelatory process, Scripture must not be confused with the incarnate Word.

> The Bible ... is not itself and in itself God's past revelation ... the Biblical witnesses point beyond themselves ... We do the Bible a poor honor, and one unwelcome to itself, when we directly identify it with this something else, with revelation itself.[30]

The words of Scripture are human words, subject to error in all about which they speak, theology and ethics as well as science and history (a point that Barth's inerrantist critics are quick to challenge). Its words *are* trustworthy when they witness to Jesus Christ, expected and recollected.

The stress upon the humanity of Scripture is underscored in IV/3/1 when the Bible is placed on a continuum with other human witnesses. The one Word of God, the Prophet, Jesus Christ, cannot be confused with the words of any human witness. But

> As the one Word of God, He can bring Himself into the closest conjunction with such words ... He has actually entered into a union of this kind with the biblical prophets and apostles, and it is the prayer and promise in and by which His community exists that He will not refuse but be willing to enter into a similar union with it. Nor can any prevent Him entering into such a union with men outside of the sphere of the Bible and the Church, and with the words of these men.[31]

THE CHURCH

Basic to Barth's understanding of revelation is

> the fundamental distinction of the written word of the prophets and apostles above all other human words spoken later in the church and needing to be spoken today.[32]

Yet the freedom of God and the promises of God are such that we have a right to hope for 'His free revelation of grace' in the Christian community as well, albeit always expository of and accountable to 'the written Word of God'. Indeed, the change of the name of Barth's opus from *Christian Dogmatics* to *Church Dogmatics* witnesses to the role of the church and its tradition in his theology, and its implied revelatory underpinning. Indeed, in an earlier formulation, Barth speaks of the church as the third term in the 'threefold form of the Word': the Word revealed, the Word written and the Word proclaimed.

How does the church enter the revelatory trajectory?

> The Holy Spirit is simply but most distinctly the renewing power of the breath of His mouth which as such is the breath of the sovereign God and victorious truth. It is the power in which His Word, God's Word, the Word of truth, is not only in Him, but when and where He wills goes out also to us men . . . thus establishing communication between Him and us and initiating a history of mutual giving and receiving.[33]

The life of the church is the locus of this giving and receiving. Here the Word has 'happened', and ever again will happen. Evidences of it include sedimentations in 'the dogmas and confessions of the Church'. Respect for these deposits is a matter of 'honouring our fathers and mothers'. Yet the Word lives among the sisters and brothers as well. To the *present* as well as the past church comes the promise of the Spirit. In both cases, Barth stresses the role of the whole people of God, and thus the epistemological ministry of the laity, as the proper locus for hearing the Word, as against a special magisterium.

But caution is in order in claiming too much for the specifics of these ecclesial happenings. As with the Bible and with the world at large, the freedom of God must be respected.

> All well-meant but capricious conjunction of Jesus Christ with something else, whether it be Mary, the Church, the fate worked out in general and individual history, or a presupposed human self-understanding, etc., all these imply a control over Him to which none of us has any right . . .[34]

The promise lies in the *hope for* the Word, not in confidence about its continuing presence:

> Is not perhaps the surest test of genuine Christianity and Church life whether the men united in it exist wholly in this expectation

and therefore not at all in a supposed present possession of the glorious presence of their Lord?[35]

This wariness about any claims to the 'present possession' of Christ recurs at many points in Barth's thought, and has its consequences all along the trajectory we are tracing. For now we underscore the determination to assert that all human attestations to the Word of the Prophet of God are *broken* human witnesses to Truth. In Scripture there is surety of the bonding, in the Church there is the hope and prayer for the Spirit's illumination of the community of faith, and in the world there is the possibility of free communications with no locale to be anticipated or, in principle, excluded.

ESCHATOLOGICAL RADIANCE

The finality and clarity of God's self-disclosure awaits us at the End. What has been given to us in the darkness of human history – the Word of God as communicated through biblical, ecclesial and secular media – comes to full light at the return of Christ,

> His total presence, action and revelation which will conclude and fulfil time and history, all times and all histories . . . The theme of Christian hope, to the extent that it is not yet fulfilled nor cannot be so long as time endures, is the revelation of the fact that neither formally nor materially, theoretically nor practically, can the one Word of God be transcended . . . The inclusion of the eschatological element, then, does not imply any restriction, but the final expansion and deepening, of our statement that Jesus Christ is the one Word of God.[36]

Barth expresses the same confidence that we shall ultimately see 'face to face' in a tribute to friends and colleagues who have died. Even now, there 'shines on them the eternal light in which we, *adhuc peregrinantes*, shall some day need no more dogmatics'.[37]

CONTRIBUTIONS

Of the major theologians discussed in this work, Karl Barth makes the greatest contribution to a narrative understanding of the doctrine of revelation. His 'christological concentration' secures the centre of the Story. And no chapter is lost from view.

As noted, a line can be traced from the inner-trinitarian life of the triune God as Revealer through the 'free communications' within a universal Noachic covenant to the promissory covenant with Israel, to the centrepoint of disclosure in Jesus Christ, and from there to an authoritative Scripture 'engendered' by the Spirit, a community and believer illumined by the same Spirit, to an End when the light of God is 'all in all'. We review Barth's reading of the 'overarching story' with emphases proportionate to his contributions.

Jesus Christ

The twentieth-century church, too ready to take up the proposals and premises of its surrounding culture, has a Word it needs to hear. In his own imagery, the tower rope which Barth stumbled upon rang a bell too long silent. It called the church into a sanctuary with one centre: 'Jesus Christ . . . is the one Word of God whom we have to hear' (Barmen Declaration). The struggle against a demonic blood-and-soil philosophy made for a sharper hearing of that one Word. But culture has its softer voices today, no less seductive, that make listening for that bell no less necessary.[38]

In narrative terms, Barth will never let us forget the Centre of the Story. 'Christological concentration' means *christocentricity*. In the historical event of Jesus Christ, an utterly new deed is done, and a defining Word spoken. Life overcomes death and an ultimate Light pierces a penultimate Night. Reconciliation *is* Revelation. With the defeat of alienation, 'error' joins sin, evil and death as foes that have met their match in the Person and Work of Christ.

In the structure of Barth's thought, 'revelation' *is* Jesus Christ and brooks no contenders. His earlier language was sometimes interpreted as a fusion of this historical event with the moment of its reception, the ever-new 'becoming' of the Word of God. But his later writing seeks to avoid misunderstandings that bind the Word to the appropriation process. As Barth is so often misunderstood on this, we have to keep before us his insistence that

> There is human knowledge, and a theology of reconciliation, because reconciliation in itself is not only real but true, proving itself true in the enlightening work of the Holy Spirit, but first true as well as real in itself, as disclosure, declaration and impartation. This is the basis of certainty and clarity when it is a matter of the knowledge of Jesus Christ and His work through the work of the Holy Spirit.[39]

The 'basis' is the enfleshment of the Word, whose place in the narrative of revelation is established by both the speaking and hearing of the same by the Father through the power of the Spirit.

The centrality of Jesus Christ could obscure the role of Israel in the narrative of both reconciliation and revelation, as it does in the unabashedly supersessionist theologies to which earlier allusion was made. Not so in either Karl Barth's soteriology or epistemology. No understanding of Christ is possible without the trajectory of promise constituted by the special covenant with the Jewish people and the testimony to it in the Old Testament. In Israel, the first particular deed of God is done and particular disclosure given, although note must be taken that Barth's promise-fulfilment framework does not do full justice to the anti-supersessionist import of Romans 9–11.[40]

The Bible

'Jesus Christ, *attested by Holy Scripture*, is the one Word of God whom we have to hear' (Barmen Declaration). The One we hear, trust and obey is not the creature of our pious feelings, our speculative genius, our doctrinal deposits. Scripture is the sole trustworthy *source* of our knowledge of the Word of God, Jesus Christ; *sola Scriptura*, so understood, is inextricable from *solus Christus*. Christ finds us when we enter into 'the strange new world of the Bible'. He does so because 'revelation engenders the Scripture which attests it'.[41] Barth practises what he teaches by his detailed and profound theological exegesis, letting Scripture speak its own Word. So understood, stated and practised, Barth points to what the in-Spiriting of Scripture has meant in classical Christian teaching on the authority of Scripture, narratively described here as a chapter on 'inspiration'.

Further, the way that Barth relates Scripture and Christ yields insight about the interpretation as well as the authority of the Bible. For Barth, Scripture is understood when it is interpreted by Christ. 'Then beginning with Moses and the prophets, he interpreted to them all things about himself in all the scriptures' (Luke 24:27). As with Luther, Scripture speaks its Word when it 'preaches Christ'. Barth's christological reading of the Bible is rich and varied.[42] Here we refer to the hermeneutical significance of Jesus Christ as the interpretive framework for understanding whatever appears in the canon and as the criterion for determining what is and is not the 'pattern of teaching' for which Scripture is given to the church.[43] In the first instance, the christological chapter itself comes into sharp profile, the Old Testament expectation and the New Testament recollection giving content to 'Jesus Christ'. In the second instance, the substance of Scripture, the Grand Narrative, is brought into bold relief by the deed done by God in Christ. To see Christ as the *Centre* is to say that Scripture is purposed for the *Story*, one that leads to and away from this turning point.

Church

The Christian community has been promised the Holy Spirit, the 'renewing power of the breath of his mouth', which 'where and when He wills goes out also to us'.[44] As the locus of the 'Word proclaimed', the church meets the Word incarnate through preaching and teaching based on the Word written, ever and again, by the gift of the Spirit. The historical moment of 'illumination' in the narrative of revelation, in the ecclesial form to be discussed, is here given its due.

Barth's accent on the 'becoming' of the Word is personal as well as corporate. The Word proclaimed is *pro me* as well as *pro nobis*. Within the Christian community, the believer, 'where and when He wills' it, is addressed and so receives the Word by the inner testimony of the Holy Spirit. This is the event of 'divine–human encounter' prominent in the earlier writings of Barth, and characteristic of 'neo-orthodox' views of revelation that juxtaposed 'personal' to 'propositional' revelation.[45] In the narrative terms of this work, the 'happening' of the Word 'for me' is an aspect of the soteriological chapter of revelation.

For Barth, only in the End is the divine Radiance total and God 'all in all'. The Light given 'in part', and on occasion – in Scripture and to the Church corporate and personal – now shines fully and unremittingly. Here is the eschatological chapter with the gift of illumination given as totally as it can be for eschatological eyes.

World

In IV/3/1 we noted that 'the Bible, the Church and the world' were linked as loci of 'other words . . . other lights'.[46] Against the long background of his battles against natural theology, Barth is yet able to speak in his later years of 'free communications' and 'parables of the Kingdom' possible in a history outside of *Heilsgeschichte*. And he finds meaningful patterns in nature that make and keep life human and the cosmos ordered. While the latter do not have the parabolic significance of the former, both can be understood as related to the promises of the Noachic covenant and thus to yet another chapter in the narrative of revelation, albeit never understood by its own lights, always to be interpreted *christologically*.

As the richness of Barth's thought unfolds, the shape of the narrative emerges. A measure of his greatness is the fullness of the Story told.

PROBLEMS

Karl Barth taught a generation to be wary of theologies that take deity captive in forms of human manufacture. God is Sovereign. We learn what the freedom of God means in the one place God has chosen to be free for us and among us, Jesus Christ, as this Word is given to us in the witness of Scripture. The problems with Barth's epistemology arise when he departs from his own biblical standard for understanding that freedom of God for and among us. This might be described as the influence of an 'actualism' with philosophical roots in existentialist philosophy[47] Yet actualism has more to do with Barth's ecclesial tradition than his philosophical borrowings. While determinedly challenging the control of the Word by 'principles' of our own making, two such refrains from the Reformed tradition have a significant impact on Barth's doctrine of revelation: the *divine sovereignty* and the *internal testimony of the Holy Spirit*. These accents in both Reformed theology and piety are critical components of any full-orbed understanding of Christian faith and life. They are gifts given by the Reformed tradition to the church catholic. When functioning as arbitrating *principles* that exclude other critical accents, however, they claim more than their due.

The entrance of Reformed accents into the doctrine of revelation is related to Barth's determination to protect the decisiveness of this chapter of the Story. Only here in Jesus Christ is God free *for* us and among us. Sovereignty is earthed in Christ alone. Any claim to continuity of the divine presence other than the incarnate Word imperils that particularity.

As noted in the previous section on Barth's contributions, 'Bible', 'Church' and 'World' take their place in the revelatory narrative. They do so for Barth as epistemic 'articles of hope', rather than 'articles of faith'.[48] While the promise is there of a Word to be spoken, the actual address 'happens' only 'when and where He wills' it to be so – by the act of divine freedom working through the internal testimony of the Holy Spirit. The occasionalist nature of this assertion has to do with the confluence of the protective teachings of divine sovereignty and the internal testimony of the Spirit. While the high God is free to

137

stoop low anywhere, the divine freedom is protected, for no assurance can be given that the 'media' – Bible, Church, World – are in their respective ways always and everywhere bearers of the knowledge of God. The outworking of these principles can be seen in each of the three arenas taken up by Barth in IV/3/1. Before examining them, however, we must ask what is obscured by these accents when they become determining principles.

The theological dialogue encouraged by the twentieth-century ecumenical movement has forced participants to see the partiality and corrigibility of their own traditions. Such a learning from the bilateral Reformed–Lutheran conversations of the last forty years sheds light on the issue at hand.[49] Based on the formula of 'mutual affirmation and admonition', one Lutheran–Reformed dialogue asserts that the Lutheran accent – *finitum capax infiniti* – and the Reformed emphasis – *finitum non capax infiniti* – must be understood as complementary not contradictory.[50] The Reformed *non capax* witnesses to the divine *sovereignty* over us, and the Lutheran *capax* to the divine *solidarity* with us. Each accent is faithful to an aspect of Christian faith and also constitutes a 'no trespassing sign' warning the other of the dangers of exclusive focus on its identifying feature. Note is taken of how both the strengths and delimitations of the respective themes have played out in Lutheran–Reformed eucharistic controversies, with Reformed self-critically acknowledging the dangers of *only* sovereignty in a Zwinglian 'memorialism' that eliminates the real Presence, and Lutherans self-critically acknowledging that the stress on solidarity alone invites a too-simple fusion of the singularity of the Incarnation with the sacramental Presence.[51]

An ecumenical understanding of the narrative of revelation will strive to appropriate the epistemological implications of both the Reformed *non capax* and the Lutheran *capax*. Barth's own ecumenical commitments prompt him to do just that vis-à-vis these formulas when he specifically qualifies Reformed sovereignty in a comment on the meaning of faith:

> In faith men have an actual experience of the Word of God; and no *finitum non capax infiniti*, nor *peccator non capax verbi divini* ought now to prevent us from taking this affirmation seriously, with all its consequences.[52]

While lodged in an earlier discussion of revelation whose subjectivist tenor prompted the later emphasis on the objectivity of the Word noted here, this assertion reflects the companion Reformed stress on the actualisation of the Word by the inner testimony of the Spirit. The *capax* is a happening of faith, 'an experience', the occasional nature of which is a sign of, and also a protection of, the divine initiative.

The sovereignty principle that controls such a reading of *capax* becomes clear in his refrain: 'all well-meant but capricious conjunction of Jesus Christ with something else, whether it be Mary, the Church ...'[53] As such, Barth makes the needed Reformed witness to the divine sovereignty. In epistemology as well as in ecclesiology, sacramentology etc., there can be no undialectical insistence on 'the continuation of the Incarnation'. The once-happenedness of Jesus Christ – perfect in deity and in humanity – is not replicated in the church. However, Barth goes on to interpret this discontinuity as requiring the denial of the 'present possession of the glorious presence' of Jesus Christ. At work here is the actualist premise that continues to mark Barth's thought, even after his repudiation of Kierkegaardian subjectivity and later clarifications about the objectivity of revelation in the enflesh-ment of the Word. Its persistence has to do with the exercise of a *non capax* veto over the witness of both Scripture and the classic Christian tradition. While it is Christ who 'possesses' the church, not the other way around, a sign of that ownership is the 'glorious presence' of Christ in the midst of his people: 'For where two or three are gathered in my name, I am there among them' (Matt. 18:20).

Christ's *promise* of solidarity calls into question undialectical views of divine sovereignty that fail to honour the Yes as well as the No of continuity between Christ and the church. The eucharistic controver-sies in which memorialist conceptions that distance Christ from the Lord's Supper are rightly challenged by a doctrine of the real Presence are a case in point.[54] In the same vein, a doctrine of revelation in which the promise of uninterrupted *epistemic* presence is denied in order to protect the divine sovereignty must be challenged. The dialectic of presence and absence is at work in epistemology as it is in ecclesiology. Barth is right in what he affirms but wrong in what he denies.

Dietrich Bonhoeffer early identified Barth's 'act' view of revelation and its consequences, connecting it to traditions that stressed the divine transcendence and the 'contingency of revelation' (Duns Scotus, William of Occam), and viewing it with characteristically Lutheran eyes:

> Revelation is interpreted purely in terms of act. It is something happening to receptive man, but within God's freedom to sus-pend the connection at any moment. How could it be otherwise,

> since it is 'God's pleasure, majestically free' (Barth) which initiates the connection and remains its master . . . However this attempt is bound to come to grief against the fact that (according to Barth) no 'historical' moment is *capax infiniti*, so that the empirical action of man – 'belief', 'obedience' – becomes at most a pointer to God's activity and can never, *in* its historicality, be faith and obedience themselves . . . [For Bonhoeffer] God is *there*, which is to say . . . 'haveable', graspable in his Word within the Church.[55]

The promise of the divine 'haveability' – *capax infiniti* – cannot be excluded by *non capax infiniti* deployed as a controlling 'principle'. The effects of the latter show up in three areas.

BIBLE

Barth bases the authority of the Bible on its 'direct witness' to the Word of God, Jesus Christ. Scripture is the megaphone through which the free Word of the majestic God is spoken when and where so willed. The warrant for Scripture's authority is relocated from traditional notions that imply 'possession' to occasions actualised in the freedom of God, reflecting the conjunction of the sovereignty–internal testimony partnership. The mysterious unpredictability of conviction and conversion by the internal work of the Holy Spirit is relocated from its place in the Reformed tradition of *attesting* personally truth established on other grounds, to *testing* – that is, *establishing* – the truth of Scripture itself. Scripture is revelatory because it is revealing. Its authority rests on the dead letter coming to be, as God wills it to be the 'living' Word of God.

The motif of sovereignty functions here rightly to challenge the domestication of Deity in and by a sacred book. The target that it strikes is a doctrine of verbal inspiration/inerrancy in which the perfections of the divine knowledge are attributed to the biblical 'autographs', a point of view to be subsequently discussed. Barth brings his teaching of divine sovereignty to bear to challenge this fusion. Further, the Holy Spirit does attest the truth of Scripture in mysterious and unpredictable ways, *convicting* and *convincing* by an internal testimony. Where the grace of 'inspiration' is received by the grace of 'illumination', Scripture's latent truth become patent to the believer and the believing community.

While necessary to protect Scripture from bibliolatry, the accent on divine sovereignty-cum-internal-testimony is not a sufficient warrant for the authority of Scripture. Standing alone, it precludes the promise of a trustworthy epistemic presence 'in, with and under' the Word written. Barth's occasionalist understanding of biblical authority, ironically, opens him to the same charge which he mounts against the anthropocentrism of theology since Schleiermacher. Thus Carl Henry accuses him of allowing 'subjectivity' to determine the status of Scripture:

> Karl Barth's interpretation of the Bible as an instrumentality through which God sporadically communicates his paradoxical Word . . . redefines the doctrine of inspiration dynamically and connects it with the psyche of the believer.[56]

While this charge does not do justice to Barth's assertion of the objectivity of revelation in Jesus Christ as witnessed to by Scripture, it succeeds in relating Barth's actualism to the subjectivity associated with the Reformed doctrine of the internal testimony of the Holy Spirit (and also the lingering early influence of Kierkegaard, from whom Barth later declared himself free).[57] And, as shall be argued, Henry makes a contribution to the narrative of revelation by drawing attention to a needed chapter on 'inspiration', one that has not been redefined in actualist terms.

Geoffrey Bromiley, Barth's English translator, also has an evangelical ear for the absence of a defensible doctrine of biblical authority. In discussing 'the problem areas' in Barth's thought, he says:

> One must also wonder whether it is not a mistake to stress the present ministry of the Spirit in the use of scripture at the expense of the once-for-all work of the Spirit in its authorship. Barth would later resist a similar imbalance in the matter of reconciliation. Is there not also a need for rethinking in the matter of inspiration?[58]

While the historic doctrine of the inspiration of Scripture requires restatement in the light of critical scholarship, it is an effort to express the divine solidarity vis-à-vis this medium of revelation. The Holy Spirit graced the prophetic–apostolic testimony in such a manner as to render reliable its telling of the biblical Story. As such, the authority of the Bible is warranted, not by a pneumatological actualism, but by a trustworthy work of the Holy Spirit in its authorial communities. In Christian context, this means a dialectical relation between Incarnation and inspiration, rejecting both the too-simple continuities of inerrancy and the too-simple discontinuities of occasionalism. As has often been pointed out, Karl Barth's practice is better than his theory, for his extensive and intensive exegesis of Scripture suggests a deeper and more sustained warrant for biblical authority than that of a hermeneutic controlled by principles from a crucial but not exhaustive theological tradition.[59]

CHURCH

As with the Bible, so with the church, for Barth the knowledge of God is given only as by divine initiative. The third form of the Word, the 'Word proclaimed' in the church, 'always and will always be – man's word'.[60] But it can 'become' something else when God so chooses.

> It is, namely, when and where God pleases, God's own Word. Upon the promise of this divine good pleasure it makes its venture in obedience. Upon that depends the claim and the expectation.[61]

Revelation as 'illumination' is promised as a gift of God's 'good plea-sure', always to be hoped for, but never assured as a presence within the Body of Christ.[62]

We have already alluded to the importance of the Yes and No dialectic and the sovereignty/solidarity partnership in the relation of Christ to the Church. Again, Barth's warnings against idolatry are telling, especially so, when creedal and confessional lore are absolutised, or divine infallibility is conferred on a corporate or personal magisterium, or the words of the preacher are thought to be coterminous with the divine Word. Of importance, as well, is the expectancy of church proclamation becoming ever and again the living Word, as in the openness to fresh and different hearings of the same in new and dif-ferent contexts. But once again, as the Body of Christ is more than an unpredictable 'happening', so the wisdom of the Body can be count-ed upon in the continuities of its teaching. Because of it, the church functions as a reliable 'resource' to understanding the biblical 'source'; Christ keeps his promise to be noetically, as well as soterically, among his people.

> I am with you always, to the end of the age. (Matt. 28:20)

The knowledge of God given to the church, for all its fragility, devel-opment and corrigibility, is grounded in the solidarity of God with us as well as the sovereignty of God over us. Again, there are discontinuities between Christ and the illumination of the church, but also continuities, the dialectic of divine presence and distance. And again Barth's astute and detailed inquiry into the historic church teaching – its creeds, confessions and catechisms – reflects a trust in the continuing epistemic work of the Holy Spirit in the church belied by his theory. Indeed, his judgment that the biblical canon is authoritative because it represents a valid decision of the church, and the possibility of other books being added to the canon by the decision of the church ecumenical, suggest a 'possession' of lasting truth in the church by the power of the Spirit that his theory explicitly denies.[63]

THE WORLD

The volume which we have been using is notable for the attention given by Barth to the 'free communications' in the world beyond the church, the Scripture and the events of 'holy history'. Although this refrain appears to be a departure from Barth's earlier 'Nein!' to Brunner, such is not the case. He is as firm as ever in his 'christocentric concentration'. But, it must be said, so are orthodox defenders of 'general revelation' no less firm in their assertion of the centrality of God's disclosure in Jesus Christ. For them also, the grace of preservation is the work of the Word, known only to be what it is by the light of Jesus Christ.

The difference between classical christocentricity and Barth's view of the 'free communications' and 'little lights' in the world lies in *how* Christ's disclosive action *extra muros ecclesiae* is understood. For Barth, once again, the actualist premise born from the principled use of divine sovereignty and inner testimony is at work. The 'parables' of secular grace are unforeseen 'happenings' in which a human phenomenon becomes the occasion for a 'free communication'. The distinctiveness of these events consists

> 1) in the fact that they come to the Church in a specific time and situation, and are to be heard in these circumstances, but in other times and situations their scope and significance are an open question to be answered only in the course of its history . . . 2) in the fact that, assuming they are received at all, their reception is never in practice an affair of the whole community and all its members, but they are usually regarded as authoritative only by certain smaller or larger sections and occasionally only by a few individuals. These two characteristics make it quite evident that the right use of these free communications of the Lord can never be regarded as other than extraordinary . . . They cannot be

regarded and proclaimed as a source and norm of knowledge which is valid for all times, in all places, and for all.[64]

Does this way of describing disclosures in 'the outer circle' cohere with the constancies of the covenant with Noah? Barth concedes that there is a pattern of biblical teaching that promises that kind of revelatory light, albeit not the 'chief line of the biblical message'.[65] However, a chapter so much part of the *storyline* declaring the constancies of an epistemic grace must not be censored. The rainbow is the biblical sign of a covenant Love that will not let us go forwards in the Story without rudimentary knowledge of the purposes of God required for that journey. Such knowledge includes an awareness of the elemental norms of life together and intimations of the Source and Goal of the world's pilgrimage.

The covenant with Noah is the assurance of modest revelatory constancies. But why not also Barth's 'free communications', the unexpected and unpredictable given in unique personal and cultural moments? God is free enough to be with us in both commonalities *and* occasions, being captive to the principles of neither discontinuity nor continuity. There is a dialectic in the disclosive work of the Spirit in the world as well as in Scripture and the church.

Whether the universal *offer* of knowledge given to the world by the common grace of God is accepted or rejected depends on the presence of faith. Grace *knows* by faith, as grace *saves* by faith. Thus Paul's pointed commentary in Romans about the reception of the universal disclosures of God in a fallen world. On the one hand, for all the world's inhabitants since its beginnings, 'what can be known about God is plain to them, because God has shown it to them' (Romans 1:19). On the other hand, there are those who

> by their wickedness suppress the truth . . . because they exchanged the truth about God for a lie and worshipped and served the creature rather than the Creator . . . God gave them up to a debased mind . . . filled with every kind of wickedness, evil, covetousness, malice. Full of envy, murder, strife . . . gossips, slanderers, God-haters . . . rebellious towards parents, foolish, faithless . . . (Romans 1:18, 25, 29, 30, 31)

Paul is not referring here to humanity as such (not all are 'full of murder . . . rebellious towards their parents'), but to 'those who by their wickedness suppress the truth'. There are others, such as 'the

Gentiles who do not possess the law [but] do instinctively what the law requires' (Romans 2:14). But in this discussion of the measure of light given to all, the focus is on those who 'became futile in their thinking . . . their senseless minds . . . darkened' (Romans 1:21). From one point of view, they 'know' about God and the law – a 'knowledge of acquaintance'. Yet in the deeper meaning of 'know' – the 'knowledge of friendship' – they are innocent of understanding.

Paul refers to those who have obscured the light given to them as the 'faithless'. As gifts of grace are received only in faith, so the common grace that gives the light of the Noachic covenant requires a 'common faith'.

As common grace sustains the world in its journey towards salvific events yet to come, so the response of common faith commensurate with the 'grace of preservation' does not save souls. It can make one responsive to the mandates of God, but not 'righteous' before the majesty of God (Romans 3:10). It does not save, but it does sustain.[66] The offer of true knowledge, sustaining knowledge, is made to all, but it reaches beyond acquaintance to friendship only by the presence of this rudimentary meaning of faith, a portent in commonality anticipating the particularities of Abrahamic faith and its heirs in Christ (Romans 4:3–5:21).

Barth's recognition of the 'little lights' of God in the world *extra muros* bears testimony to the covenant with Noah in the narrative of revelation. The promise to sustain the world by a common noetic grace, however, is a promise kept always and everywhere, not only now and then.

CAPAX/NON CAPAX: AN EXCURSUS

Wolfhart Pannenberg, as christocentric as Barth in his own narrative of *reconciliation* with the resurrection of Jesus Christ from the dead as the decisive turning point, develops a doctrine of *revelation* juxtaposed throughout his multi-volume systematics with the position of Barth.[67] The epistemological differences appear at two critical points: the status of truth-claims short of the *eschaton*, and the role of reason in the verification process before the End.

We shall give attention to the first point, Pannenberg's eschatological contribution to the doctrine of revelation, in Chapter 9, on Consummation. Suffice it to say here that the truth of assertions about God is the *goal* rather than the presupposition of theological inquiry, and doctrines are *hypotheses* yet to be confirmed eschatologically. While Christian claims of Jesus Christ as the 'proleptic revelation' of the One who is to come are integral to faith,

> decisions regarding their truth rest with God himself. It will finally be made with the fulfilment of the kingdom of God in God's creation. It is provisionally made in human hearts by the convincing ministry of the Holy Spirit.[68]

In the second case, the departure from Barth is dramatic, for Pannenberg holds that he 'remains imprisoned in the religious subjectivism from which Barth wished to free himself'.[69] Barth does so by failing to adjudicate doctrinal truth-claims by the public tests of a universal rationality. While statements of doctrine must conform to Scripture and cohere among themselves, their status as 'true' has to be demonstrated in relation to the

> nontheological knowledge of humanity, the world, and history, and especially of what the statements of philosophy that deal with the question of reality have to say about these themes, in the dogmatic presentation of humanity, the world, and history in the light of the Christ revelation. Here again it is a matter of the universal coherence and therefore the truth of Christian doctrine.[70]

We place the Pannenberg critique of Barth under the present rubric because it reflects the little-noted Lutheran/Reformed *capax/non capax* differences between the two theologians as much as it does the standard distinctions made between them on the role of reason. For Pannenberg, 'God is the one all-embracing theme of theology', and when we speak of God we 'must speak also of the world and humanity'.[71] As God of the world, on the way to final Self-disclosure at its End, the integrity of all that precedes that finale must be honoured as the medium in, with and under which God moves. In contrast to traditions that distance the Infinite from this finitude and its own categories, the palpable and intellgible must be respected for what they are, and, of necessity, must be coherent with the One to whom they belong and the 'proleptic revelation' thereof in Jesus Christ. As the Reformed accent on the divine sovereignty plays a role in Barth's doctrine of revelation, so here too, the Lutheran theme of divine solidarity – the capacity of the finite for the Infinite – expresses itself in Pannenberg's epistemological counterpoint. Human reason is not distanced from Deity but is a fit medium for the One who is to come. A similar case can be made for the presence of the *capax* in Pannenberg's 'retroactive' view of the divinity of Christ. The humanity of Christ – the finite – must be protected from both a Nestorian separation of the natures and a monophysite fusion of them. The integrity of the humanity is assured, for it is Jesus' resurrection from the dead that not only discloses but also establishes his divinity, making that humanity retroactively a bearer of 'the Infinite'.[72]

We shall return to Pannenberg's theology of revelation in Chapter 9, on eschatology, noting again the influence of his ecclesial tradition.

CONCLUSION

All that is said in this work about revelation is finally traceable to the Word that God spoke to us in the historical event of Jesus Christ. This central chapter of the Story determines what we read in all the others. Here, the defining action of God is at one and the same time the defining revelation of God, the ultimate deed of God *as* the ultimate disclosure of God. Karl Barth, the twentieth century's 'theologian of revelation' and 'theologian of christological concentration', has taught a generation about the Centre on which the whole Tale turns. He has pointed as well to a longer narrative of revelation in this volume of his dogmatics.

Solus Christus as the turning point of the Story does not preclude the freedom of God promising a trustworthy Presence throughout, derivative and dialectical. Barth's caution that no principles of our own making should obstruct attention to that one Word, as attested by Scripture, must be applied to his own doctrine of revelation. Where deployment of divine sovereignty and inner testimony obscure the biblical witness to the length and breadth of the narrative of revelation, a No must join the Yes.

On what authority do we say that Jesus Christ is the centre of the narrative of reconciliation and revelation? In the thought of Karl Barth, and throughout this work, we have turned to the 'Bible' definitively and the 'Church' derivatively as witness to the Word come among us. But why so? The Where of authority – Scripture and tradition – presses us to the Why of revelation. In the history of the doctrine of revelation, certain traditions are associated with their confluence. In the twentieth century, evangelical thought has fixed up the epistemic warrant for biblical authority, and Roman Catholic thought the epistemic warrant for ecclesial authority. In the next two chapters, we engage major representatives of each tradition: Carl Henry in the exposition of the *inspiration* of Scripture, and Karl Rahner for the exploration of the *illumination* of the church.

NOTES

1. On the interrelationship of the three claims made in John 14:6, see the writer's *The Christian Story*, vol. 2, op. cit., pp. 254–340.
2. For analysis of these types, see the writer's *The Christian Story*, vol. 1, op. cit., pp. 118–51.
3. Barth, IV/3/1, p. 180.
4. Ibid., p. 165.
5. Barth in John Godsey (recorder and editor), *Karl Barth's Table Talk* (Richmond: John Knox Press, n.d.), p. 26.
6. Barth IV/3/1, pp. 8, 10–11.
7. Ibid., p. 86.
8. As in CD, I/2, p. 518. While he sought to correct in IV/3/1 the subjectivist impressions left by his earlier emphasis on the appropriative act, he did not describe the 'happening' and 'becoming' of the Word stressed earlier in terms of the work of the Holy Spirit. Responding to a student's question as to why the Holy Spirit does not 'appear more explicitly in the section on the "revealed Word"' in CD I, Barth says that in 1932

   > I wanted to place a strong emphasis on the objective side of revelation: Jesus Christ. If I had made much of the Holy Spirit, I am afraid I would have led back to subjectivism, which I wanted to overcome. (Barth in Godsey, *Karl Barth's Table Talk*, op. cit., p. 27)

   The 'objectivity' thought to be to the fore, however, was so shaped by actualist assumptions that it was open to the charge of subjectivism that had to be repudiated in the volume under consideration.
9. So Carl Henry, *GRA* IV, pp. 196–200, 270–1 and passim.
10. Barth IV/3/1, pp. 98, 99.
11. I/1, pp. 339–560.
12. *Church Dogmatics*, II/1 op. cit., p. 16. On our knowledge of God as grounded in God's self-knowledge, see George Hunsinger, *How to Read Karl Barth: The Shape of His Theology* (New York: Oxford University Press, 1991), pp. 76–9.
13. As in Jürgen Moltmann, *The Trinity and the Kingdom: The Doctrine of God*, trans. Margaret Kohl (San Francisco: Harper & Row, 1981), pp. 139–44.
14. IV/3/1, p. 97.
15. Ibid.
16. Ibid.
17. Ibid., p. 155.
18. Ibid., p. 139.

19. Ibid., pp. 155, 156.
20. Ibid., p. 118.
21. Ibid., p. 115.
22. Ibid., p. 118.
23. Ibid., p. 119.
24. Ibid., p. 125.
25. Ibid., pp. 101, 102.
26. Ibid., pp. 126–8.
27. *Church Dogmatics*, I/1, pp. 120–1.
28. Ibid., pp. 124–5.
29. Ibid., p. 127. 'John's finger' is Barth's frequent reference to John the Baptist's pointing to Christ in a famous Grünewald altarpiece.
30. Ibid., p. 126.
31. *Church Dogmatics*, IV/3/1, op. cit., p. 101.
32. *Church Dogmatics*, I/1, p. 115.
33. *Church Dogmatics*, IV/3/1 op. cit., p. 42.
34. Ibid., p. 101.
35. Ibid., p. 322.
36. Ibid., p. 103.
37. Ibid., p. xiii.
38. See David Wells, *No Place for Truth* (Grand Rapids: Eerdmans, 1993) for an evangelical critique of evangelicalism's captivity to the narcissisms of the day, one that echoes Barth's indictment of culture-Protestantism. For mainline church parallels, note the rising neo-confessional movements in North America described in the writer's 'Culture-Protestantism and Confessing Christ', *Theology News and Notes*, Fuller Theological Seminary, vol. 41, no. 3 (October 1994), 19–23.
39. Barth, *Church Dogmatics*, IV/3/1 op. cit., p. 11.
40. As argued in Fackre, 'The Place of Israel in Christian Faith', *Ecumenical Faith in Evangelical Perspective*, op. cit., pp. 152, 162–7. See also the evaluation of Katherine Sonderegger, *That Jesus Christ Was Born a Jew: Karl Barth's 'Doctrine of Israel'* (State College: Pennsylvania State University Press, 1992).
41. *Church Dogmatics*, op. cit., I/1, p. 129.
42. The writer traces seven strands in *The Christian Story*, vol. 2, op. cit., pp. 79–82.
43. See *CD* IV/3/1, pp. 32, 39, 44–6, 49–53, 86–103, and *CD* I/1, pp. 121–3, *CD* I/2, p. 817, *CD* II/1, p. 18ff., *CD* II/2, pp. 52–3.
44. *CD* IV/3/1, p. 421.
45. See, for example, Emil Brunner, *Revelation and Reason*, trans. Olive Wyon (Philadelphia: Westminster Press, 1946); and John Baillie, *The Idea of Revelation*, op. cit.
46. IV/3/1, p. 97, and the section as a whole, pp. 96–103.
47. For a discussion of the role of 'actualism' in Barth's theology – its understandings and misunderstandings – see George Hunsinger, *How to Read*

Karl Barth: The Shape of His Theology (New York: Oxford University Press, 1991), pp. 30–2, 107–9, 112–14, 148–9, 226–8, 230–1, 271–2; Dietrich Bonhoeffer, *Act and Being*, pp. 78–91; Hugh Ross Mackintosh, *Types of Modern Theology: Schleiermacher to Barth* (London: Nisbet and Co., 1937), pp. 314–16; Herbert Hartwell, *The Theology of Karl Barth: An Introduction* (Philadelphia: Westminster Press, 1964), pp. 32–7, 143–7.

48. The distinction between 'hope' and 'faith' is drawn from Barth's views on universalism. *Apokatastasis* is a matter of hope not doctrine because the ultimate Future is in the hands of the sovereign God. Hope for universal salvation is warranted by the saving deed done for all by God in Christ, but with the eschatological reserve appropriate to the divine freedom, so articulated in IV/3/1, pp. 477–8.

49. See, for example, James Andrews and Joseph Burgess (eds), *Invitation to Action* (Philadelphia: Fortress Press, 1984), which includes a discussion of the European conversation and its resulting consensus document, *The Leuenberg Agreement*, as well as reports of the North American dialogue.

50. As in Keith F. Nickle and Timothy F. Lull (eds), *A Common Calling* (Minneapolis: Augsburg Fortress, 1993), pp. 39–40, 65–6.

51. Ibid., pp. 40–50.

52. *CD* I/1, p. 250.

53. Barth, *Church Dogmatics*, op. cit., p. 101.

54. The Mercersburg theology and its mentors, John Williamson Nevin and Phillip Schaff, represent a Reformed tradition that seeks to maintain the broken but real continuity between Christ and the church and thus the real Presence of Christ in the eucharist. See Charles Yrigoyen Jr and George H. Bricker (eds), *Catholic and Reformed: Selected Theological Writings of John Williamson Nevin* (Pittsburgh: The Pickwick Press, 1978), and Charles Yrigoyen Jr and George H. Bricker (eds), *Reformed and Catholic: Selected Historical and Theological Writings of Philip Schaff* (Pittsburgh: The Pickwick Press, 1979). Barth, true to his sovereignty principle, holds to a memorialist view of the eucharist. (Note his interesting exchange with a student on this point in Godsey, *Karl Barth's Table Talk*, op. cit., pp. 22–3.)

55. Dietrich Bonhoeffer, *Act and Being*, trans. Bernard Noble, intro. Ernst Wolf (New York: Harper & Brothers, 1961), pp. 81, 83, 90–1.

56. Henry, *God, Revelation and Authority*, op. cit., p. 148.

57. Kierkegaard, rightly resisting the volatilising of 'the individual' in Hegelian speculation, Danish Christendom and the bourgeois society of the nineteenth century, formulated his protest in the starkest of terms: 'Truth is subjectivity . . . Faith is the objective uncertainty, with the repulsion of the absurd, held fast in the passion of inwardness, which in the relation of inwardness intensified to its highest . . . Christianity is spirit; spirit is inwardness; inwardness is subjectivity; subjectivity is essentially passion, and at its maximum an infinite, personally interested passion for one's own happiness'. Søren Kierkegaard, *Concluding*

Unscientific Postscript To Philosophical Fragments, ed. and trans. with notes, Howard V. Hong and Edna H. Hong, vol. I: Text (Princeton: Princeton University Press, 1992), pp. 189, 611, 33 and passim.

58. Geoffrey Bromiley, *Historical Theology: An Introduction* (Grand Rapids: Eerdmans, 1978), pp. 420–1.

59. For an effort to retain 'the evangelical insistence on the proper relation of human to divine' in Scripture while taking into account Barth's stress on 'the decision and action of the Holy Spirit', see Gregory G. Bolich, *Karl Barth and Evangelicalism* (Downers Grove, IL: InterVarsity Press, 1980), pp. 195–207.

60. *CD* I/1, p. 79.

61. Ibid.

62. Barth's 'event' ecclesiology was influential in the World Council of Churches' missiology of the 1960s, especially in its study, *The Church for Others*. One result was a sharp critique made of the local congregation for failing to hear the Word that propelled it to be a 'church for others', and the judgment that the Word was active instead outside the walls of the church in secular movements for social change. For a survey of the literature of the debate between actualist ecclesiologies and those that stressed the promise of Christ's presence through Word and sacrament *in spite of* the congregations' failures, not *because of* its responsiveness, see Gabriel Fackre, 'The Crisis of the Congregation', in D. B. Robertson (ed.), *Voluntary Associations: A Study of Groups in Free Societies*, (Richmond: John Knox Press, 1966), pp. 275–98.

63. Godsey, *Karl Barth's Table Talk*, op. cit., p. 27.

64. *CD*, IV/3/1, p. 133.

65. *CD*, II/1, pp. 109, 112.

66. As Cruden's *Concordance* lists two meanings of 'salvation' – salvation from sin and salvation from misery – a case can be made that common grace *saves* from suffering, sickness, misery, pain, injustice. Here is salvation in 'horizontal' terms, in contrast to the 'vertical' relationship, salvation *coram Deo*. See the writer's discussion of the historical graces of redemption in 'The Scandals of Particularity and Universality', *Mid-Stream* 22:1 (January 1983), 46–51. Mark Heim builds on this distinction, proposing in the context of the debates on religious pluralism multiple eschatological as well as historical salvations (and revelations) commensurate with the ends of varied religious traditions, while maintaining at the same time the primacy of Christian revelation and salvation. See S. Mark Heim, *Salvations*, op. cit., pp. 129–229 and passim.

67. Wolfhart Pannenberg, *Systematic Theology*, vols 1 and 2, trans. Geoffrey W. Bromiley (Grand Rapids: Eerdmans, 1991, 1994).

68. Ibid., vol. 1, p. 56.

69. Ibid., p. 47.

70. Ibid., p. 49.

71. Ibid., p. 59.

72. As in Pannenberg, vol. 2, op. cit., pp. 303–4, 325–96 and earlier, Wolfhart Pannenberg, *Jesus–God and Man*, trans. Lewis L. Wilkins and Duane A. Priebe (Philadelphia: Westminster Press, 1964), pp. 135–41.

6

SCRIPTURE: INSPIRATION

We have been following the thread of the Story as it develops within the Christian canon. *Why* the Bible as 'source' of the narrative? The answer, often cited as *locus classicus* within Scripture itself, is:

> All scripture is inspired of God and is useful for teaching, for reproof, and for training in righteousness, so that everyone who belongs to God may be proficient, equipped for every good work. (2 Timothy 3:16)

Scripture – 'inspired' – *theopneustos*, the very 'breath of God' forming the Word here uttered. So declares the evangelical voice to which we now listen.

While identified here as a 'chapter', unlike others in the narrative we are tracing, Scripture is a phase of revelation associated with the deeds of God done with Israel and in Jesus Christ, 'prophetic' testimony to the former and 'apostolic' witness to the latter. Narratively construed, the gift of inspiration could be explored in Chapter 7, on the church, for there the enlightening work of the Holy Spirit is done in the church apostolic warranting Scripture as the authoritative testimony to the determinative actions of God in Israel and Jesus Christ. However, the importance of the Bible as the source of the Story itself, and the necessary distinction between the *inspiration* of the prophetic –apostolic testimony and the *illumination* of the post-apostolic community, merits this separate treatment.

In twentieth-century theology, the status of Scripture has been the absorbing interest of the evangelical community. While marginalised and regularly misunderstood in the larger church, evangelicals are stewards of this phase of the narrative of revelation.[1] James Orr puts it in a straightforward way in commenting on the 'deeds of God':

> attention is increasingly concentrated on revelation as something distinctively *historical* . . . But we have now found that the line between revelation and its record is becoming very thin, and that, in another true sense, the *record*, in the fullness of its contents, *is itself for us the revelation.*[2]

To investigate the role of 'the record' in the narrative of revelation, we turn to the century's most influential evangelical thinker, Carl Henry. The placing of Henry alongside Barth, Tillich and Rahner, however, has to do not only with the importance of this Scripture chapter in the revelation story, but also with the need to challenge an academic hauteur that regularly excludes the evangelical from the wider table of theological conversation.[3]

'Evangelicalism' is a movement shaped by pietism, the Great Awakenings, revivalism, the fundamentalist-modernist controversies, and their current repristinations and revisions. Common to its diverse expressions is the interiorisation and radicalisation of the formal and material principles of the Reformation: the authority of Scripture and justification by faith. The Bible becomes an intimate devotional companion read through either an inerrantist or infallibilist hermeneutic.[4] Justification becomes an intense initial appropriation of salvation by grace through faith, a 'born again' experience. Scripture and faith so intensified are inextricable from evangelical piety, morality and evangelistic passion. Within the commonalities are varieties of evangelicalism that include militant fundamentalists drawing lines of combat at hyper-inerrancy (with its own internal divisions between political and apolitical, apocalyptic and non-apocalyptic fundamentalism), 'old evangelicals' who stress mass evangelism, 'new evangelicals' who find a place for rational apologetic and social ethics, 'charismatic evangelicals', 'justice and peace evangelicals' with a social agenda very different from political fundamentalists, 'ecumenical evangelicals', and most recently 'post-evangelicals'.[5]

CARL HENRY

The six-volume *God, Revelation and Authority* is a magisterial treatment in evangelical idiom of the doctrine of revelation. Volume 4 is the heart of Henry's investigation of the inspiration of Scripture and its correlate, the concept of biblical 'inerrancy'.[6] Henry contends that the traditional grounding of biblical theology in a doctrine of inspiration has receded before the rise of critical scholarship, or has been transmuted into experiential or existential categories:

> Few Christian tenets are now more misunderstood and more misrepresented than the doctrine of the inspiration of Holy Scripture . . . As Klaus Runia notes . . . 'While the liberal subjectivizes and relativizes inspiration, the neo-orthodox actualizes it'.[7]

What then is 'inspiration'? This lost chord in the doctrine of revelation is

> a supernatural influence upon divinely chosen prophets and apostles whereby the Spirit of God assures the truth and trustworthiness of their oral and written proclamation. Historic evangelical Christianity considers the Bible the essential textbook because, in view of this quality, it inscripturates divinely revealed truth in verbal form.[8]

Clustered here are critical refrains in Henry's argument: 'plenary verbal inspiration', 'the autographs', 'inerrancy'.[9] Allusion to the last (inerrancy) will be made here, but the focus will be on its revelatory underpinnings in the Spirit's work of prophetic and apostolic disclosure through the words of the original biblical documents. Or, in terms that Henry employs to sharpen the distinction between his view and that of Karl Barth, the Bible is God's own 'epistemic Word'.

The confidence in 'divinely revealed truth in verbal form' is warranted by the testimony of Scripture itself. Scripture is inspired because Scripture states it so to be. Yes, the inner testimony of the Holy Spirit convinces Christians of the same, as asserted in the Westminster Confession, but the case for trustworthiness is made, finally, by the Bible's own self-declaration.[10] However, Henry, as a 'new evangelical' with apologetic intent, also holds that reason can corroborate the status of inspiration, for 'evangelicals apply to the Bible the same logical tests that they apply to modern writers'.[11] (Hence the detailed rational polemic Henry carries on in all his writings, with special reference to the 'law of non-contradiction'.)

Biblical testimony to its verbal inspiration is found in the passage earlier cited, 2 Timothy 3:16–17. But a stretch of other texts held to echo the same inspiration/inerrancy claim are also brought to the fore:

- 'no prophecy ever came by human will, but men and women moved by the Holy Spirit spoke from God'. (2 Peter 1:20–1)
- 'the scripture cannot be annulled . . .'. (John 10:35)
- 'the Jews were entrusted with the oracles of God'. (Romans 3:2) (on the 'oracles' of God, see also Acts 7:38, Heb. 5:12, 1 Peter 4:11)
- 'You received the word with joy inspired by the Holy Spirit . . . the word of the Lord has sounded forth from you . . .'. (1 Thess. 1:7–8)
- 'I solemnly command you by the Lord that this letter be read to all of them'. (1 Thess. 5:27)

Further, Jesus' many allusions to authoritative Hebrew Scripture are cited as part of Henry's textual case for biblical inspiration: Matt. 11:10, 12:3, 19:4, 21:13, 16, 22:31, 26:24, 31; Mark 2:25, 9:12–13, 11:17, 12:10, 26, 14:21, 27; Luke 6:3, 7:27, 19:46. Thus,

> Not only does Jesus adduce what is written in Scripture as law, but also explicitly adds: 'and the scripture cannot be broken' (John 10:55 KJV). He attaches divine authority to Scripture as an inviolable whole. The authority of Scripture, he avers, cannot be undone or annulled, for it is indestructible.[12]

A key term in the 2 Timothy passage is *theopneustos*. Henry understands it to mean that the words of the original writings are themselves 'breathed out'.

> There is a marked difference between the notion that God 'breathed into' the biblical writings, and the biblical declaration that God 'breathed out' the writings; the former merely approximates the Scriptures to revelation, whereas the latter identifies Scripture with revelation.[13]

The spiration of authors' minds or ideas (as held by evangelical and other theologians whom Henry criticises) is far short of biblical words that are 'God-breathed'. So understood, Timothy's assertion has to do with the deliverance of sentences that convey information, *verbal* inspiration. Verbal inspiration is 'plenary', as the Spirit's out-breathing of words ranges throughout the whole canon, and thus 'the entire corpus of Scripture is an authoritative document'[14] and 'inspiration extends to the whole – not merely to the ideas but to the words also'.[15] Further, propositions about *history* and *nature* that are the environment for the outworking of the divine plan are also guarded from error by the Holy Spirit, a belief that marks the advocates of inerrancy, distinguishing them from proponents of 'infallibility' who hold only to the trustworthiness of Scripture's *doctrinal* and *moral* assertions.[16]

While defending verbal inspiration, Henry distinguishes it carefully from a 'mechanical' view:

> *The biblical-evangelical view denies* . . . that the Holy Scriptures are a product of a mechanical divine dictation . . . Neither the Bible nor standard evangelical works teach this extreme view.[17]

The words are not dictated, but *are* 'superintended'. As human media, they bear the marks of the authors' time and place. Yet, they are protected from error in all about which they speak:

> Already a century ago, A. A. Hodge and B. B. Warfield insisted on a necessary differentiation between scriptural inspiration and verbal dictation . . . The evangelical view of inspiration does not assert that prophets and apostles were infallible, nor that in their own learning they were exempt from limitations imposed by the cultural horizon of their day . . . The original manuscripts have a theopneustic quality because of their divinely given rational and verbal content and because of the Spirit's superintendence of the prophets and apostles in the process of writing . . .[18]

The inspired documents in question are the 'autographs'. These

> original writings or prophetic-apostolic autographs alone are error-free . . . The sacred writers were guided by the Spirit of God in writing the original manuscripts in a way that resulted in their errorless transmission of the message God desired them to communicate to mankind.[19]

We do not have these primordial sources, however (as yet – Henry allows for their retrieval someday), and cannot identify the claims of verbal inspiration with the present working texts.

> No informed Christian contends for the inerrancy of the present existing copies of the prophetic-apostolic autographs, far less for the inerrancy of many translations and versions . . .[20]

Because of the purity of the originals, it is important to get as close as we can to them. 'Textual criticism', therefore, becomes a tool for seeking approximations of the inspired writings. However, even with copies short of the originals, the Holy Spirit watches over the transmission process to ensure the 'infallibility' of Scripture, that is, its total reliability in matters of faith and morals. With acknowledgement of both the continuing theological trustworthiness of Scripture yet also the humanity of the existing texts, Henry holds a moderate 'trajectory' view of inerrancy rather than a conservative 'transmissive' view that would demand the harmonisation and validation of disputed sections of current texts.[21]

While errors in matters of science and history in the received texts are possible, to date only a tiny portion seem to Henry to be subject to factual error. Further, as archaeological research proceeds apace and more ancient copies are discovered, more and more of the formerly alleged mistakes in geography and history are found to be the fault of a later hand.

Students of Scripture are admonished to make modest use of 'historical criticism' as well as textual criticism. Historical criticism probes the contingencies of time, circumstance and authorship. However, Henry holds that much of the current use of these tools reflects Enlightenment prejudices. In a chapter on 'The Uses and Abuses of Historical Criticism', Henry admonishes the evangelical who 'rejects the method outright' to reconsider, cautioning that

> The ready temptation of believers to leap over issues such as the progressive character of divine disclosure, and the problems of communication in a changing historical milieu, underscores the propriety of many of the questions posed by criticism.[22]

He then provides ten rules for a modest use of historical-critical inquiry which counsel attention to past context, yet take into account Scripture's own self-testimony and wariness about the presuppositions brought to the investigation by the historical critic.[23]

Henry holds that because the second Person of the Trinity is *Logos*, God is, by nature, rational. Reflecting that rationality, inspiration is *propositional*. A proposition is an 'expression of anything which is capable of being believed, doubted or denied; a verbal expression which is either true or false'.[24] Assertions in Scripture of this sort, about states of affairs, have a fixed transcultural meaning discernible through grammatical-historical inquiry. The authors are not so conditioned by their time, nor readers by theirs, that intelligible 'information' and 'abiding instruction' cannot be communicated by God to us.[25]

While acknowledging the figural nature of some biblical language, Henry rejects the 'doctrine of analogy' vis-à-vis propositions, arguing that

158

only univocal assertions protect us from equivocation . . . All man needs in order to know God as he truly is, is God's intelligible disclosure and rational concepts that qualify man – on the basis of the *imago Dei* – to comprehend the content of God's logically ordered revelation. Unless man has epistemological means adequate for factual truth about God as he truly is, the inevitable outcome of the quest for religious knowledge is equivocation and skepticism.[26]

Propositional revelation, so understood, is set against both 'modernist' and 'neo-orthodox' perspectives that are indicted as subjectivism. In each case, Henry holds, Scripture functions only expressively and evocatively, making no cognitive truth-claims, withholding assertions about reality that have abiding truth.

Henry engages a number of twentieth-century writers who fall into a 'modernist' camp held to reduce Scripture to performative utterances that make no ontological truth-claims. A broadly-conceived neo-orthodox movement, with purportedly anti-modernist views, however, is also charged with subjectivism. His sharpest criticism, in this regard, is aimed at Karl Barth:

> Karl Barth's interpretation of the Bible as an instrumentality through which God sporadically communicates his paradoxical Word . . . redefines the doctrine of inspiration dynamically and connects it with the psyche of the believer . . . Scripture for Barth is a fallible witness through which God personally encounters the trusting reader or hearer . . . For Barth, Scripture is not truly the Word of God, but becomes the Word of God only in some mysterious divine confrontation. The Bible plays only an instrumental role in relation to revelation; it is the framework through which God's voice may be heard.[27]

Henry's two main charges against Barth have to do with the complementary themes of inerrancy and inspiration: for Barth, Scripture contains errors, not only in science and history but also in doctrine and morals; and inspiration has been relocated from the autographs to the occasion of encounter between the Word of God, Jesus Christ and the believer. In contrast, Henry asserts the trustworthiness of Scripture in anything about which it speaks (doctrine, morals, science, history – the theory of 'inerrancy' albeit a moderate form of it, given the latitude of interpretation that Henry allows in matters of science and history, as in Scripture's account of the world's beginnings),[28] and the verbal inspiration of the autographs.

HENRY AND THE STORY

While the focus of Carl Henry's doctrine of revelation falls on the inspiration of Scripture and its defence against those who seek either to eliminate or to compromise it, the context in which his case is made is a wider and longer view of the Holy Spirit's revelatory activity. Hence the elements of the larger narrative of revelation are discernible in Henry as they are also in our other major interlocutors.

While the fall has shattered the human capacity to discern the truth, needing the verbally-inspired and inerrant autographs of univocal propositional truth, some light is given outside this luminous moment. Without explicit reference to the covenant with Noah, Henry speaks about the grace of noetic preservation as the 'sullied', but not destroyed, image of God in human beings allowing for elements of reliability:

> Mankind everywhere has an elementary knowledge of what is ultimate and abiding, of God's reality, and of final answerability to and judgment by him (Rom. 1:20, 32). In and through human reason and conscience, the human race has an ineradicable perception of the eternal, sovereign deity.[29]

Indeed, human reason remains intact enough to require its laws of logic as a test of the claims of special revelation itself. While authentic faith rises from the work of the Holy Spirit in the believer, and Scripture's authority rests on its own self-testimony, their consonance with reason means that Christian truth-claims must cohere with our rational processes; for, as noted, 'evangelicals apply to the Bible the same logical tests that they apply to modern writers'.[30]

Other parts of the narrative of revelation also appear. Jesus Christ, as the redemptive Life at the centre of God's drama, is the final Light of God. Inspired Scripture has faithfully preserved his testimony. As such, his own assertion of the trustworthiness of the Bible is a principal warrant for its inspiration and inerrancy, the reconstructions of the 'historical Jesus' by biblical critics to the contrary notwithstanding. This, of course, means that the New Testament's Jesus when quoting Scripture validates Scripture as verbally inspired.

And the narrative goes on, in and past the Scripture's inspiration, to the Christian believer's eye of faith, opened by the Holy Spirit, to read the Scripture aright. Thus in the believer the illumination of the mind accompanies the conversion of the soul.

> The Reformed view . . . is that the Spirit convinces readers of the Bible of its truth and elicits from them the believing response that links them experientially with the saving grace of God in Christ . . . The Bible does not use the specific term *illumination*; it does, however, refer to that special activity of the Holy Spirit by which man can recognize that what Scripture teaches is true, and can accept and appropriate its teaching.[31]

The church corporate as well as personal is given the same gift of illumination, as it was able to recognise the epistemic Word in the process of the canonisation of Scripture.

And the narrative goes forwards to its culmination. Only in the *eschaton* will the fullness of God's revelatory glory shine forth. So, in the last sentence of our working volume, Henry speaks of the End when

> face to face (cf. Gen. 32:30; Num. 12:8; 2 Cor. 3:18), our heavenly Father will unveil intimacies of love and knowledge hitherto unknown, and reserved for those who love him.[32]

The place of 'the overarching story' in Henry's theology is succinctly stated in his summary of

> the message and meaning of the book, namely the living sovereign God stands at the beginning of the universe – man and the worlds – as Creator and Governor, and at the end of history as final Judge; that he made mankind in his likeness for moral rectitude and spiritual fellowship and service; that human revolt precipitated disastrous consequences for humanity and the cosmos; that the manifested mercy of God, extended first to the Hebrews, proffers the only prospect of salvation; that the divine promise of deliverance, disclosed in the course of Hebrew redemptive history to the prophets, finds its fulfillment in Jesus of Nazareth; that the incarnation, the crucifixion and resurrection of the Logos of God marks the beginning of the new and final age; that the church is a new society of regenerate persons of all races and nations over whom Christ presently rules; that the history of mankind has a dual track, issuing in final and irreversible doom for the impenitent and in eternal blessing for the righteous; that Christ will return in awesome vindication of the holy will of God, to judge

men and nations, and will in the resurrection of the dead conform the people of God to his moral image; that the benefits of
redemption will embrace all creation in a final subordination of
evil and of the wicked, and in the eternal vindication of righteousness.[33]

Here is the story of reconciliation told in evangelical voice, with its
intertwined narrative of revelation. The accent falls on the prophetic
—apostolic authorship of the autographs of Scripture because it secures
our knowledge of these plans and acts of the Creator and Redeemer
in a time when the inspiration of that authorship is ignored or denied.

CONTRIBUTIONS

From proof-texting to detailed exegetical inquiry in matters of doctrine, to a devotional intimacy with the text in the life of piety, the
authority of Scripture is a passionate evangelical commitment. But
why should the Bible have this status? Taking up a much-neglected
theme in contemporary theology, Carl Henry gives the evangelical
answer: inspiration. As such, he makes an evangelical contribution to
the understanding of the narrative of revelation.

Since the Enlightenment and the rise of critical scholarship, the
warrants for Christian belief have moved away from Scripture to some
dimension of human experience, or reconceived in terms of ecclesial,
existential or eschatological terms.[34] While each such chapter in the
narrative of revelation has a bearing on the status and interpretation of
Scripture, they do not constitute the central basis for the Bible as the
source of Christian teaching. That warrant lies in this chapter of the
Story, the giving of a gift of understanding by the Holy Spirit to
'prophet and apostle'. The 'inspiration of Scripture', therefore, finds its
place in the narrative.[35]

As all ultimate loyalties are rooted in a 'leap of faith', so the doctrine
of inspiration presupposes a primal decision: the Yes to the living Word
by the inner testimony of the Holy Spirit. The believer, brought to
Jesus Christ by that Word spoken and received through the power of
the Spirit, is led into the Great Narrative found only in this Book. To
be drawn to Christ is to be drawn into the Story, into its 'source' text,
and into its 'resource' community. The authenticity of the encounter
with the Word, Jesus Christ, is inseparable, therefore, from the trustworthiness of Scripture. To know Christ is to know the benefits he gives

to us in the inspiration of the tale told in this Text. (We shall explore the entry point of conviction in Chapter 8, on personal illumination.)

The convincing work of the Holy Spirit in the heart of the believer does not happen in a vacuum. The Word is heard and the Story believed in the context of the Christian community. The authority of Scripture is reinforced and its Story validated by its reading and hearing in the church. From the early Fathers through the Reformers to the present church ecumenical, the Christian community has held itself accountable to Scripture on the assumption of its unique inspiration. Henry takes note of the same, tracing evidences of a working doctrine of inspiration from Clement of Rome and Polycarp to Calvin and Luther and beyond.[36] A case has also been made by Roman Catholic theologians that its 'Tradition' is an exfoliation of uniquely-inspired Scripture rather than an addition to it, and thus dogmatic declarations must be rooted in Scripture.[37] We shall turn to these matters in Chapter 7, on ecclesial illumination.

Finally, the authority of Scripture rests on its own self-testimony. The convictions of the heart may prove deceptive and the judgments of the community in error. The evangelical search for that self-witness is an important contribution. The citation of 2 Timothy 3:16–17 and other random texts as internal evidence, however, is not sufficient for a narrative reading of revelation. The sequel to the central deed and disclosure in Jesus Christ is the descent of the Spirit on the day of Pentecost. Here, the Spirit gives light as well as fire, knowledge joined to power. We shall examine that account in Chapter 7, on the church. Here, we note that a gift of discernment is given to the apostolic community to bear witness to 'God's deeds of power' (Acts 2:11). In the succeeding homily by Peter, the highlights of the Grand Narrative are recited (Acts 2:17–36 and again in Acts 3:11–26). Thus, given to the church is the light to understand and the power to tell the Story. Within this chapter on the church, the place of epistemological privilege is given to the apostles. Here is the originative in-Spiriting of which all subsequent church testimony is exegetical – the inspiration that is foundational for the illumination.

The fugitive self-testimony to the inspiration of Scripture to which Henry points is to be read as instantiation of this pneumatological chapter rather than as unframed proof-texts. Because the Holy Spirit opened the eyes of this community of seers at this point in the narrative of revelation, an apostle is able to say that 'all scripture is inspired by God and is useful for teaching' (2 Timothy 3:16). The narrative grounding of inspiration will also have its implications for the inter-pretation of Scripture. The *scopus* of Scripture is the Story, 'God's deeds of power'. Inspiration has to do with 'teaching' the Tale that gives it coherence.

To grant the apostles normative teaching authority has implications for the status of the Old Testament in Christian Scripture. In the Acts' account of the descent of the Spirit on the first Christians, Peter's telling of the Story includes the covenant chapter and cites Hebrew Scripture (Acts 2:16–21, 25–31, Acts 3:18–25). And throughout the New Testament, the covenant with Israel and its texts are integral to the Christian story. In the much-cited 2 Timothy 3:15–16, the refer-ences to 'the sacred writings' and 'all scripture' as 'inspired by God' have to do with the scripture of the Hebrew people. So, too, Jesus' frequent citation of the same as authoritative. For Christians, the authority of Scripture, therefore, includes the 'prophets' as well as 'the apostles'. Pentecost does not constitute them as inspired, but recognises them as inspired.

Henry makes a contribution to an understanding of the place of *words* in the inspiration of Scripture. Twentieth-century studies on the relation of language to meaning and truth should give pause to the standard dismissal of theories of 'verbal inspiration'. From the arguments of Max Black and other students of metaphor that figural language is not ornamental but integral to communicating truth, to Clifford Geertz's reflections on culture and language as the matrix of experience rather than simply its expression, the 'verbal' is commanding new attention.[38] While metaphor study and cultural anthropology do not constitute a new theological magisterium, they are human wisdom that can (by the common grace of the Noachic covenant) shed light on the Scripture's own self-testimony. Words do count.

Austin Farrer makes a case for the noetic work of the Spirit in Scripture through its 'master images'.[39] 'Kingdom of God', 'Word of God', 'Lamb of God', 'Father, Son and Spirit', the 'sacrifice of Christ' – in each case, some aspect of human experience is taken up and transfigured by its biblical usage. Carrying forward Christ's own image-filled self-understanding,

> The interpretive work of the Apostles must be understood as participation in the mind of Christ, through the Holy Ghost; they are the members, upon whom inflows the life of the Head ... The great images interpreted the events in Christ's ministry, death and resurrection, and the events interpreted the images; the

interplay of the two is revelation . . . The several distinct images grew together into fresh unities, opened out in new detail, attracted to themselves and assimilated further image-material: all this within the life of a generation. This is the way inspiration worked. The stuff of inspiration is living images.[40]

Farrer's 1946 Bampton lectures are natural elaborations of the use of figural language by one of its master practitioners, interestingly, from a very different church tradition, suggesting the ecumenical nature of such insights. So John Bunyan:

Solidity indeed becomes the Pen
Of him that writeth Divine to men;
But must I needs want solidness, because
by Metaphors I speak? Were not God's Laws,
His Gospel-Laws in olden times held forth
by Types, Shadows and Metaphors? Yet loth
Will any sober man be to find fault
With them, lest he be found to assault
The highest Wisdom. No, he rather stoops,
And seeks to find out what by Pins and Loops,
By Calves, and Sheep, By Heifers, and by Rams,
By Birds, and Herbs, and by the blood of Lambs,
God speaketh to him. And happy is he
That finds the light and grace that in them be . . .
Dark Figures, Allegories? Yet there springs
From that same Book that lustre, and those rays
Of light, that turns the darkest nights to days.[41]

Both Bunyan and Farrer are forerunners of a vast literature on the role and meaning of image, symbol, analogy, metaphor, simile and story in both Scripture and Christian theology. Bolder than most, they each link the figural language of the Bible to the doctrine of inspiration itself – 'From that same Book that lustre, and those rays . . .'. We continue here that epistemological claim, drawing also on current thought on this literary genre.[42]

Important as are the distinctions among metaphor, simile, image, analogy, symbol and story – as species of a genus, strong and weak comparisons, verbal or visual or both, extension or delimitation of one or the other, etc. – they appear as a family within Scripture. In all cases, evocative words are taken from common experience to express the uncommon, the ordinary the extraordinary, the immanent pointing to the transcendent. They mirror a Reality other than themselves, inviting an imaginative leap from the tangible to the intangible.

Throughout this work, we have drawn on one master image, 'story'. In the present context, a story can be described as 'an extended metaphor' (Soskice). Storytelling is *imaginative*, a purposeful parade of images. Specific images within the biblical narratives give us glimpses of the chief Character. The God of Abraham, Isaac and Jacob is disclosed when second Isaiah says in simile that 'The Lord goes forth like a soldier, like a warrior he stirs up his fury' (Isaiah 42:13), but in the same breath declares that God can 'cry out like a woman in labour . . . gasp and pant' (Isaiah 42:14). Who Christ is (the Person) comes forcefully home in the affirmation that 'the Word' became 'flesh'. What Christ did (the Work) touches a cognitive chord when we sing 'the Lamb of God takes away the sins of the world'. Every one of the chapters of the Great Narrative can be described in an image with experiential associations relocated theologically: creation, fall, covenant, the person and work of Christ, the nature and mission of the church, salvation, consummation.

But the disclosive power of biblical stories goes beyond individual to storied images. In these micro-narratives, the character of God is revealed.[43] The God of Jesus Christ, God *as* Jesus Christ, is known by us through the stories told in the New Testament:

> The church identifies Jesus by telling a story in which he figures as the central character; like any human being, Jesus can be identified adequately only by narrative means. The narrative that identifies Jesus, which the church has in the canonical form of four mutually enriching versions, begins with the first-born son of Mary, renders his words and deeds in the midst of his disciples and the multitudes in Galilee and Jerusalem, turns on a dramatic and voluntary transition from doing to suffering in the garden of Gethsemane, and culminates in his crucifixion and utterly involuntary transition from death to resurrection and exaltation.[44]

Yes, the Jesus stories are the heart of the matter, but not without their context, the 'overarching' canonical Story from creation to consummation of which it is the Centre. The relation of the latter to 'inspiration' will be taken up in the subsequent discussion of the 'teaching' referred to in 2 Timothy 3:16.

Why are 'image', 'metaphor', 'simile' and 'story' so omnipresent in Scripture (and tradition)? The Gospel is addressed to the whole person. Ultimate truth invites total commitment, engaging every dimension of the self. Faith, as response to the Good News, is *fiducia* and *assensus*, the trust of the heart and the assent of the will, as well as *notitia*, the knowledge of the mind. The recovery of the place of symbol and story, metaphor and image in contemporary literary studies and theology has its progenitors in Scripture and the classical heritage of liturgy, sacrament, hymnody, creed and confession.

As full-orbed faith includes 'knowledge of the mind', any recovery of the power of metaphor and story that excludes the validity of *reference* – states of affairs, historical or transcendent, critical to the Great Narrative – must be judged reductionist. Acknowledging the importance of the expressive and evocative, Vanhoozer asserts:

> While I believe that poetic texts can transform our existence within certain limits, is not the message of the Gospel that the very limits of human existence have somehow been stretched? Surely the New Testament authors believe that the possiblity created by the Christ event is *sui generis*: the necessary conditions for its being genuine include historical acts and events.[45]

The importance of reference in biblical imagery raises the question of the role of propositions.

Henry does not take his theory of verbal inspiration in the direction of Austin Farrer's images, nor is he sympathetic with current versions of 'narrative theology', the writer's included.[46] His view of verbal inspiration, however, is linked to a legitimate concern, the place of propositions in the inspiration of Scripture. Do biblical 'images' and Scripture's 'overarching story' correspond to states of affairs, human and divine? Does Scripture make cognitive truth-claims of this sort?

Revelation cannot be reduced to the personal or social power of metaphor and story, nor to a community story whose only function is to distinguish the church from the ways and wisdom of the world. Scripture *does* meet us at the level of affect, putting us in touch with dimensions of being untouched by didactic modes of discourse, and *does* constitute the unique language world of the Christian community. But its meaning is not exhausted by its evocative and expressive power, or its definition of communal boundaries. The story that Scripture tells, and the master images which it employs, are eloquent of the 'truth of the symbol' as well as 'symbolic truth', as Wilbur Urban, an early twentieth-century philosopher of language, anticipating current debates, expressed it.[47] Biblical symbol, in whatever form, depicts Reality as well as drawing us into relationship with it. It discloses states of affairs, the way things are with both God and the world. However expressed in imagery and the language of story, fundamental assertions about reality – propositions – are made that invite the response of 'Yes' or 'No': God created the world, the world fell away from God's invitation, God sustains it in spite of its rebellion, Israel is called into special covenant, God comes among us in Jesus Christ to reconcile the world, and so on. In each chapter, figurally portrayed, are embedded propositional 'truths of the symbol'. Propositions, so understood, are 'that which is expressed in a statement, as opposed to the way it is expressed'.[48] John Baillie is right in his concern that Farrer's images not be too simply juxtaposed to propositions, for 'images and propositional truths are inextricably intermingled'.[49] On the other hand, Karl Barth is right in contrasting the speaking of the Word in the Person of Jesus Christ as '*Deus dixit*' with the '*Paulus dixit*' of biblical words,[50] thereby challenging theories of inspiration which identify one with the other, most blatantly, oracular/dictation views. Henry, however, is right in defending propositional content and in refusing to draw Barth's sharp line between *Deus dixit* and *Paulus dixit*, for assertions are made in the latter ('propositions expressed in a statement . . .') that are in continuity with the Word spoken in Jesus Christ. Henry's continuities have their own problems, to be noted, but at this point he bears witness to the propositional dimension of the narrative of revelation. Because these assertions come to us in the symbolic form of image and story – 'symbolic truth' that moves the heart and seeks the commitment of the wil – they are better described as 'affirmations' than by the bloodless term 'proposition'.

The 'plenary' aspect of inspiration and the related theme of 'inerrancy' make their contribution also to a doctrine of revelation. Each points to the revelatory significance of Scripture in its totality, and rejects a 'pick and choose' hermeneutic or a 'Reader's Digest Bible', both scissoring out portions that do not fit one's own framework. While Henry's deployment of the plenary and inerrancy theories will be challenged, their contribution lies in their purpose (seen in the practice of their advocates) to prepare readers to listen to the Bible 'in all its parts' for 'some Word from the Lord'. Barth's dynamic understanding of the Bible as the 'becoming' of the Word is here germane. To appropriate the contribution of inerrancy is to stand ready to find in the entirety of the Bible some illumination, including those parts of it that cannot be reconciled with its overarching message. Who is to say that at some point and in some place a Word cannot be spoken by words that seem transitory or even morally offensive? A feminist hermeneutic which sees even 'texts of terror' as of value is instructive, as is the use of historical-critical scholarship which attempts to show the contextuality of passages that do not accord with what appears to be the manifest meaning of the Story.[51]

While focusing on the specifics of inspiration, Henry does not deny the other loci of disclosure, and in fact speaks about the 'central message' in narrative fashion. As noted, he traces both the deeds and disclosures of the triune God from creation and preservation to the covenant with Israel, the centrepoint in the Person and Work of Christ, the inspiration of Scripture, the illumination of believer and the finality of eschatological Light. Here, Henry connects with the ecumenical conversation and its concern for the full narrative of both reconciliation and revelation.[52]

PROBLEMS

As a representative evangelical voice, Henry illustrates the weaknesses as well as the strengths of that sub-community in the church's dialogue on revelation. The 'intensification' that marks the new birth and new life experience of evangelicals is echoed in his doctrine of biblical inspiration. The born-again Christian knows that a line has been crossed from death to life, from sin to salvation. The sense of the decisiveness of this transition, however, makes more difficult the awareness of the persistence of sin in the life of the believer. Thus the evangelical temptation in the political arena as well as the soteriological realm to divide the world up between 'us and them', the attraction of apocalyptic eschatology and the allure of 'perfectionist' views of sanctification. While the latter do not apply to Henry, a striking parallel to these appears in his views of verbal inspiration and inerrancy.

The full narrative of *reconciliation* concludes with a chapter on the *eschaton*. In subjective soteriology, the justification of the sinner is the presence of the End now as pardon and the sanctification of the sinner as power. Still on a journey towards the Last Things, however, the Christian life with all its graces is *simul iustus et peccator*. Sin persists in the life of the saint. Salvation is a foretaste of things to come; we await the Banquet yet to be.

The full narrative of *revelation* concludes with the same eschatological chapter. Short of the End, the glass of vision is 'stained glass' with its disclosive but darkened and diffuse colours and images. The same eschatological reserve appropriate to soteriology is required of epistemology.

The evangelical experience tempts closure of the distance between the Now and the Not Yet. Its result is the tendency to obscure the *simul iustus et peccator* in soteriology and thus the attendant naivety about, and hauteur of, the 'righteous'.[53] The counterpart in epistemology is the temptation to overlook or understate the mirror dimmed and the glass darkened: Scripture is held to shine now with a light reserved only for a Day yet to be. The theory of the verbal inspiration of inerrant autographs and univocal propositions reflects this eschatological pressure on evangelical epistemology.

To hold that the original writings of Scripture in *all* their parts and on *all* their subject matter are so superintended by the Holy Spirit as to constitute them with an unqualified inerrancy is to confuse the present Dawn with the final Day. Oracular views of inspiration are the purest form of epistemological apocalyptic. Henry rejects them. But his formal argument for verbal inspiration and his mediating view on inerrancy accept the same premise that the autographs have an eschatological validity.

The eschatological nature of verbal inspiration appears in Henry's construal of biblical propositions. His contribution to the understanding of the doctrine is the defence of the revelatory significance of biblical assertions about the real order of things, human and divine. But his understanding of them as 'sentences' protected from error by the Holy Spirit affiliates the human words themselves with the clarity of Light reserved alone for the End. The only sentenced 'timeless truth' spoken to us and heard by us is, by definition, *beyond* time, and thus not in history but at its End.

The same failure to honour the distinction between the ultimate and the penultimate leads Henry to make inordinate claims for the univocal nature of biblical assertions. He is rightly concerned about points of view that interpret *analogy* to mean 'likeness' to, but not 'coincidence with', the truth, thereby emptying language of its capacity to identify a referent in Reality. However, the concept of analogy in theological usage is designed to protect just that referent but to acknowledge the limitations of finitude under which all human discourse about God labours. Put narratively, the concept of analogy is an attempt to ensure the integrity of the eschatological chapter of the Christian story, to maintain the reserve appropriate to all knowledge-claims short of the Finale.

Within Henry's own presuppositions, there is a corrective principle to the claims to the timelessness of propositions: his theory of 'progressive revelation'.[54] While it cannot be transferred without serious qualification to post-biblical articulations, the 'ever-new light and truth breaking from God's holy Word' is 'progressive illumination'. Indeed, both within and without Scripture, such unfolding reflects the narrative character of God's self-disclosure. The Holy Spirit gives the Christian community the power of discernment as each new historical context poses questions that draw out fresh understandings of the church's biblical charter. No privileged magisterium has control of this growing understanding, as the wisdom of the Body is given by the Spirit to the church catholic. By its grace, the community is granted the ability to discern the signs of the times and speak a Word to each new context, one that enriches its doctrinal lore. The discernment is always accountable to inspired Scripture, as it witnesses to the incarnate Word.

While Henry cannot be charged with the identification of a detailed time-bound theological formulation with inspiration, the stress on revealed 'timeless truths' lends itself to that kind of mistake. For example, the penal substitutionary theory of the atonement regularly reaches this level of authority in evangelical preaching and teaching. However, this view of the atonement is a human construct rising out of New Testament stories of Christ's death and apostolic metaphors of interpretation of that death. The formulation of the meaning of the crucifixion in penal terms is a doctrinal inference born of a time and place in the church's life. It does not exhaust the meaning of the cross and has been subject to reformulation and enlargement, as in the three-fold office of Christ.[55] Further, it is subject to subsequent reformulation as the Holy Spirit in new contexts along the trajectory of its biblical purpose and subsequent ecumenical elucidation. Doctrine develops over time and place. As such, doctrine is timely, not timeless.

The humanity of biblical propositions is reflected again in the form in which they are given. Evocative image and compelling story are the 'way' in which a proposition is embodied. These media are gifts of the Holy Spirit, but gifts given *in via*, appropriate to a finite human receiver from whom commitment of heart and will as well as mind is sought. This side of the eternal Realm, biblical image and story – 'of the earth, earthy' – make contact with human beings – also of the earth, earthy. Thus symbol/image/story, understood as the inseparability of affective 'symbolic truth' and propositional 'truth of the symbol', is the fitting vehicle of the inspiration phase of a narrative still on its way in this world. As noted earlier, propositions, so inextricable from their evocative home in symbol, are therefore better described as 'affirmations'.[56]

A narrative assessment of Henry's view of revelation will ask if other chapters are also given their due. The status assigned to the inspiration of Scripture raises questions about the integrity of the christological centre of the Story. Indeed, the temptation to collapse the eschatological into verbal inspiration recurs in the relationship of the incarnate Word to the epistemic Word. Narratively described, the continuity between the Word enfleshed and the inspiration of Scripture is so accented as to exclude the discontinuity that marks revelatory moments derivative from and subsidiary to the revelation of God in Jesus Christ. The 'one Word of God' is not replicated by, but 'attested by', Holy Scripture (Barmen). The undialectical continuity between the unique deed of God in Christ and Scripture resembles the doctrine of an ecclesial 'continuation of the incarnation' in Catholic traditions. In each case, two chapters of the story have been fused and thus confused: incarnation and inspiration in the first, and incarnation and illumination in the second.[57] Thus the problems associated with the collapse of eschatology into inspiration (sentence propositionality, inerrancy, univocity) reappear when viewed from the angle of Christology. The perfections of the Person are assigned to the imperfections of the human media of inspiration.

The importance of biblical narrative reaches into the key passage that grounds Henry's doctrine of revelation, 2 Timothy 3:16. Its interpretation requires a reading in the context of the letter as a whole with its refrain of Paul as 'herald' of the 'gospel', the gospel as 'sound teaching' and 'sound doctrine' with 'Jesus Christ, raised from the dead, a descendent of David' (2 Timothy 2:8) at its centre, the worshipping church and its call to faithfulness, and the promise of 'the heavenly kingdom' and the Author and Finisher to whom 'be the glory forever and ever. Amen' (2 Timothy 4:18). When so situated, the 'for' of 3:16 assumes its rightful place in the understanding of the verse 'all scripture is inspired for *teaching*' that will issue in 'training in righteousness', the teaching of the gospel so necessary for a faithful church under siege from unsound teaching and its pernicious fruits – 'lovers of themselves, lovers of money, boasters, arrogant, abusive . . .' (3:2).

The 'teaching', the 'gospel', the 'sound doctrine' for which scripture is inspired is the *Story*. The breath of God is given to prophet and apostle to speak *this* Word. Scripture is inspired to *that end*, for the purpose of witness to the Grand Narrative and the One who is its Alpha and Omega. The narrative we have been tracing throughout this study is the *scopos* of Scripture, its aim, direction and goal. By the gift of illumination, the church returns ever and again to this inspired Story, bearing witness to it in 'articles by which it stands or falls' discernable in the earliest baptismal rules of faith, the ecumenical creeds, the historic confessions and catechisms, its eucharistic prayers, the standard loci of its systematics and contemporary statements of faith. Swinburne, identifying this 'propositional' core, says:

> The original propositional revelation was the teaching of God to the Israelites of the centuries BC about himself and his dealings with them and other nations, culminating in the teaching of Jesus Christ, including his teaching about the significance of his actions, and the teaching of the apostles about the significance of those actions. This is the virtually unanimous claim of Christians over two millenniums . . .[58]

All four of our major interlocutors are drawn in one way or another to this formative 'teaching', including Henry at a critical juncture of his exposition,[59] as well as in the overall structure of his thought. While functionally otherwise, Henry formally argues for the autographal inerrancy of Scripture on every subject about which it speaks, the weight of which claim this passage – about the 'teaching' at the heart of the canon – will not bear. Thus the canon is for the telling of the Story, and its ever-fresh retelling with new implications and applications:

> The role of the canon as scripture of the church and vehicle for its actualization through the Spirit is to provide an opening and a check to continually new figurative applications of its apostolic content as it extends the original meaning to the changing circumstances of the community of faith . . . an extension of the one story of God's purpose in Jesus Christ.[60]

The 'story of God's purpose in Jesus Christ' appears throughout the canon in the imagery that befits a plot with characters moving over time and place through conflict towards resolution. Sentences are integral to the Tale told, hence the witness of Henry to the importance of the verbal. Yet it is the verbal imaginatively formed and narratively configured that is in-Spirited, communicating the pattern of teaching to which the church returns ever and again for its fundamental identity.

The relation of epistemology to ecclesiology in Henry's story of revelation also invites comment. The critical distinction between the apostolic and post-apostolic stages espoused by Henry rightly honours the distinction between inspiration and illumination and thus the legitimate evangelical concern for the accountability of church tradition to Holy Scripture. However, the epistemological role of the church is regularly muted in evangelical thought. Henry does cite the early church fathers and the Reformers when amassing evidence for his theory of inspiration and inerrancy. Further, what he identifies as the revealed propositions of Scripture – from the ecumenical doctrine of the Trinity to the evangelical theory of penal substitution – are, in fact, formulations of the church in both Catholic and Reformation traditions. And the Scripture to which Henry makes final appeal is itself the fruit of an ecclesial canonisation process. Thus the church *functions* both explicitly and implicitly in his understandings of revelation and authority. But no epistemological grounds are given for this presence, and no careful delineation of the interrelationships of the ecclesial work of the Spirit in inspiration and illumination is undertaken. Playing a part in these omissions is both the inordinate role given to biblical inspiration and the delimitation of the Spirit's noetic work in the church to that of the individual believer who comes to faith when the biblical Word is enlivened by the internal work of the Holy Spirit.[61]

A standard issue in the doctrine of revelation is the relation of reason to revelation, narratively considered; the place of the covenant with Noah. Henry's stress on the role of reason implies a 'high' view of the state of the *imago* sustained by the covenantal grace of preservation after the fall, at least with respect to the rational faculty. However, when Henry maintains that even biblical assertions must pass the test of humanity's universal capacity, the Noachic covenant is given a status out of proportion to its chapter in the narrative. While reason is certainly not designated by Henry as the 'source' of authority – for definitive knowledge of God comes only through inspired Scripture – it is assigned the role of adjudicating all truth-claims, those of Scripture included. In principle, if Scripture's claims do not pass muster before the canons of reason, they are failed propositions, although none such are discovered. In fact, Henry does use the standards of reason to determine what Scripture can and cannot say, for 'paradoxes' are ruled out as a violation of the principle of non-contradiction. Once again, the similarity to the framework of traditional Catholic theology is notable. In this case, it is not an ecclesial teaching office that interprets Scripture authoritatively, but a universal rational capacity is so designated. In both cases, the radical character of the fall is not given its due. Fallen reason is under the regency of Jesus Christ, accountable to, not arbiter of, the Word.

Reason, while damaged, is not destroyed by the fall, preserved as it is by the promises of God in a state trustworthy enough for the world to make its way forwards. In relation to the subsequent chapters, it is healthy enough to elucidate the biblical testimony to the deeds of God done in Israel and Jesus Christ. Such 'faith seeking understanding' will meet and acknowledge the paradoxes of the election of Israel, the incarnation of the Word and the intellectually inscrutable divine–human antinomies found everywhere: Scripture, church, sacrament, grace and faith. It will be able to *explore* but not *explain* them. They will not conform to the law of non-contradiction, but will cohere with the narrative in its fullness, and also show tangents of human meaning, plausible but not finally accountable to our faculties. Reason, by the grace of preservation in the Christian story, is bashful not bold.

The evangelical voice, often muted or missing in the ecumenical conversation, makes its most important contribution in this phase of the revelation narrative. Carl Henry's detailed defence of the inspiration of Scripture is such a word to be reckoned with. Ecumenical and academic theology that excludes the evangelical presence in the conversation impoverishes itself. Yet inspiration, while part of the revelation story, is neither the whole nor the heart of it, and must find its derivative place under the Word enfleshed and its relative place before the Word eschatological. Thus the need for mutual affirmation and admonition from ecumenical conversation partners.

NOTES

1. See the writer's argument in *Ecumenical Faith in Evangelical Perspective* (Grand Rapids: Eerdmans, 1993), passim.
2. James Orr, *Revelation and Inspiration* (New York: Charles Scribner's Sons, 1910), pp. 67, 159.
3. Thus the irony of David Tracy's appeal in *Plurality and Ambiguity: Hermeneutics, Religion, Hope* (San Francisco: Harper & Row, 1987) for 'interpretation-as-conversation' across the theological spectrum, but recognising no evangelical viewpoint. An exception to this marginalisation is Avery Dulles' attention to Henry's views in *Models of Revelation*, op. cit., pp. 37–41, 47, 65, 76, 212, 250–2, 259–60.
4. For an investigation of the hermeneutical range in evangelicalism, see the author's *The Christian Story*, vol. 2, op. cit., pp. 60–5.
5. See the writer's definitions and discussions in 'Evangelical, Evangelicalism', in Alan Richardson and John Bowden (eds), *A New Dictionary of Christian Theology* (London: SCM Press, 1983), pp. 191–2, and *Ecumenical Faith in Evangelical Perspective*, op. cit. For an insightful current commentary on evangelicalism, see Alister McGrath, *Evangelicalism and the Future of Christianity* (Downer's Grove, IL: InterVarsity Press, 1995).
6. Background to this section is the writer's chapter, 'Carl Henry', in

Martin E. Marty and Dean G. Peerman (eds), *Handbook of Christian Theologians*, enlarged edn (Nashville: Abingdon Press, 1984), pp. 583–607.

7. Carl Henry, *God, Revelation and Authority: God Who Speaks and Shows*, vol. 4 (Waco, TX: Word Books, 1979), p. 136.

8. Ibid., p. 129.

9. For a discussion of Henry's view of inerrancy, see *The Christian Story*, vol. 2, op. cit, pp. 66–8.

10. Ibid., pp. 130–1.

11. Henry, op. cit., p. 129.

12. Ibid., p. 133.

13. Ibid., p. 162. Henry's views have their forebears in 'the Princeton school' of Charles Hodge and B .B. Warfield. See Charles Hodge, *Systematic Theology*, vol. 1 (New York: Charles Scribner and Co., 1872), pp. 153–81, and Benjamin B. Warfield, *The Inspiration and Authority of the Bible* (Philadelphia: Presbyterian and Reformed Pub. Co., 1948), passim.

14. Ibid., p. 133.

15. Ibid., p. 145.

16. For an elaboration of these distinctions, see *The Christian Story*, vol. 2, op. cit., pp. 69–75.

17. Ibid., pp. 137–8

18. Ibid., pp. 141, 152, 233.

19. Ibid., p. 207.

20. Ibid., p. 220.

21. The former construing inerrancy as an influence carried forwards from the inspired autographs but not coextensive with copies, and the latter as the actual continuance of the weight of inspiration in subsequent approved editions and translations. See the writer's *The Christian Story*, vol. 2, op. cit., pp. 62–9.

22. Henry, *GRA*, 4 op. cit., pp. 402–3.

23. Ibid., pp. 403–4.

24. *Webster's Collegiate Dictionary*, 5th edn, p. 796.

25. Henry, *GRA*, 4 op. cit., p. 197ff.

26. Ibid., pp. 118–19.

27. Ibid., pp. 148, 84, 200.

28. As, for example, in *God, Revelation and Authority*, vol. 6 (Waco, TX: 1983), in which Henry argues for significance in the sequence of the days in the Genesis accounts, while rejecting 'young earth' theories.

29. Henry, *GRA*, 4 op. cit., p. 12.

30. Ibid., p. 129.

31. Ibid., pp. 278–9, 282.

32. Ibid., p. 614.

33. Ibid., p. 468.

34. For a survey of alternatives, see *The Christian Story*, vol. 2, op. cit., pp. 133–56.

35. H. D. McDonald observes that some of those most concerned to redefine revelation as acts of God cannot avoid acknowledging the

revelatory significance of the document on which they rely for the understanding of those acts. So 'Brunner, "the written record is part of the revelation, it is not the whole", *Revelation and Reason*, p. 12. "Holy Scripture therefore does not only speak of revelation, it is itself revelation", op. cit., p. 21. Dodd, "The Church . . . offers the Bible . . . as the authoritative record of divine revelation in history", *The Bible Today*, p. 15. "The church offers this book as the revelation of God", p. 12.' McDonald, *Theories of Revelation*, op. cit., p. 283.

36. Henry, *GRA*, 4 op. cit., pp. 368–84.

37. See Josef Rupert Geiselmann, 'Scripture, Tradition, and the Church: An Ecumenical Problem', in Daniel J. Callahan et al. (eds), *Christianity Divided: Protestant and Roman Catholic Theological Issues* (New York: Sheed and Ward, 1961), pp. 39–72. For a critique of Geiselmann, drawing on the thought of Joseph Ratzinger, see Francis Schussler Fiorenza, 'Systematic Theology: Tasks and Methods', in Fiorenza and John Galvin (eds), *Systematic Theology: Roman Catholic Perspectives*, vol. 1 (Minneapolis: Fortress Press, 1991), pp. 71–2.

38. On Max Black and others of this mind, see Andrew Ortony (ed.), *Metaphor and Thought* (Cambridge: Cambridge University Press, 1979); and Clifford Geertz, *The Interpretation of Cultures* (New York: Basic Books, 1973).

39. Austin Farrer, *The Glass of Vision* (London: Dacre Press, 1948, 1954, 1966).

40. Ibid., pp. 42–4.

41. John Bunyan, *The Pilgrim's Progress*, Harvard Classics, vol. 15, ed. Charles Eliot (New York: P. F. Collier & Son, 1909), pp. 7–8.

42. Of special value: Janet Soskice, *Metaphor and Religious Language* (Oxford: Clarendon Press, 1985); Swinburne, *Revelation: From Metaphor to Analogy*, op. cit.; Anthony C. Thiselton, *New Horizons in Hermeneutics* (Grand Rapids: Zondervan, 1992); Avery Dulles, *Models of Revelation*, op. cit.; and Kevin J. Vanhoozer, *Biblical Narrative in the Philosophy of Paul Ricoeur: A Study in Hermeneutics and Theology* (Cambridge: Cambridge University Press, 1990).

43. Hans Frei's great gift lies here, as in the *Identity of Jesus Christ: The Hermeneutical Bases of Dogmatic Theology* (Philadelphia: Fortress Press, 1976).

44. Bruce D. Marshall, 'What is Truth?', *Pro Ecclesia* 4:4 (Fall 1995), 409.

45. Vanhoozer, *Biblical Narrative in the Philosophy of Paul Ricoeur*, op. cit., p. 248. For Vanhoozer's own related constructive proposals, see his essay, 'God's Mighty Speech Acts: Toward a Doctrine of Scripture', in D. F. Wright (ed.), *A Pathway into the Holy Scripture* (Grand Rapids: Eerdmans, 1994), pp. 143–82.

46. For his critique of narrative theology, see Carl F. H. Henry, *Gods of This Age or . . . God of the Ages?* (Nashville: Broadman and Holman, 1994), pp. 257–76.

47. Wilbur Urban's distinction in *Language and Reality* (New York: Macmillan, 1939), p. 443ff. See also Urban's essays, 'A Critique of Professor Tillich's Theory of Religious Symbol', *Journal of Liberal Religion* 2

(Summer 1940), 34–6, and 'Symbolism as a Theological Principle', *Journal of Religion* 19 (January 1939), 1–31.

48. 'Proposition, 5a', *The American Heritage Dictionary of the English Language* (Boston: American Heritage Pub. Co. and Houghton Mifflin Co., 1973), p. 1,049.

49. John Baillie, *The Idea of Revelation in Recent Thought* (New York: Columbia University Press, 1956), p. 38.

50. See Barth, *CD* I/1, p. 116.

51. So Phyllis Tribble on the former in *Texts of Terror* (Philadelphia: Fortress Press, 1985); and on the latter, Walter Brueggemann, *Texts Under Negotiation: The Bible and Postmodern Imagination* (Minneapolis: Augsburg/Fortress, 1993), who wants to make certain that the angularity of specific stories is not smoothed out to fit the overarching Story.

52. As reflected in his conversation with mainline theologies in his various works, his participation for years in the pluralistic American Theological Society, and his presidency of that body in 1982.

53. For an investigation of these temptations in the movement of the Religious Right, see the author's *The Religious Right and Christian Faith* (Grand Rapids: Eerdmans, 1982), especially pp. 45–52, 81–97.

54. Carl Henry, *God, Revelation and Authority*, vol. 3 (Waco, TX: Word, 1979), pp. 126–8, 223–4.

55. For such, see the writer's entry on 'Atonement' in Donald K. McKim (ed.), *Encyclopedia of the Reformed Faith* (Louisville: Westminster/John Knox, 1992), pp. 13–16.

56. For evangelical criticism of Henry that seeks to hold the 'personal' together with the 'propositional', see Stanley J. Grenz, *Revisioning Evangelical Theology: A Fresh Agenda for the 21st Century* (Downers Grove, IL: InterVarsity Press, 1993), pp. 65–72.

57. Henry fairly describes the writer's views in his account of narrative theology, and rightly sees that our differences lie at the point of the christological interpretation of Scripture. *Gods of this Age or . . . God of the Ages?*, op. cit., pp. 259, 272–5.

58. Swinburne, *Revelation: From Metaphor to Analogy*, op. cit., p. 101. In the same work, see Swinburne's discussion of 'inspiration', pp. 175–6, 196–202.

59. Henry, *GRA*, 4 op. cit., pp. 467–8.

60. Brevard S. Childs, *Biblical Theology of the Old and New Testaments: Theological Reflection on the Christian Bible* (Minneapolis: Fortress Press, 1992), p. 724.

61. Efforts are current in a diverse group of evangelical theologians, historians and biblical scholars to reclaim this lost chapter, as in the writings of Alister McGrath, John Stott, James Packer, Robert Webber, Anthony Thiselton, N. T. Wright, Mark Noll, Clark Pinnock, Stanley Grenz and Roger Olson.

PART III

Revelation as Reception

7

THE CHURCH:
ECCLESIAL ILLUMINATION

Does revelation 'continue'? No, if that means addition to, or supersession of, the defining act of Light in Jesus Christ (as in the claims of Sun Myung Moon of the Unification Church) or addition to, or supersession of, the inspired biblical testimony to the reconciling deeds of election and incarnation (as in the golden plates of Mormon teaching). What then of Pilgrim John Robinson's counsel to attend to God's 'ever new light and truth'? He speaks here not of new revelation, but of new *illumination* – fresh *light* shed on the unsurpassable deeds and disclosures in the narrative, and thus 'new light and truth *from God's holy Word*'.

The final phase of the revelation occupies the last three chapters of the Story: church, salvation and consummation – the illumination 'for us', 'for me', and 'for all'. We begin with *ecclesial illumination*, drawing on the Luke–Acts and the pentecostal beginnings of the church.

In Luke's accounts, we move from Easter to Ascension, from dawn to meridian, from the risen to the ruling Christ. The light/knowledge imagery is striking throughout. An empty tomb is found on 'the first day of the week, at early dawn' (Luke 24:1), and with it the sign of its Presence on the road when disciples testify of 'our hearts burning with us . . . while he was opening the scriptures to us' (Luke 24:32), and in a room when a table is spread and 'their eyes were opened and they recognised him' (Luke 24:31). Then this new Light that opens eyes rises as 'he was lifted up, and a cloud took him out of sight' (Acts 1:9).

The ascent of Christ is followed by the descent of the Spirit. From the Light above, the Sun of God, comes Fire on the earth:

> When the day of Pentecost had come, they were all together in one place. And suddenly from heaven there came a sound like the rush of a violent wind, and it filled the entire house where they were sitting. Divided tongues, as of fire, appeared among them, and a tongue rested on each of them. All of them were filled with the Holy Spirit and began to speak in other languages, as the Spirit gave them ability... In our own language we hear them speaking about God's deeds of power. (Acts 2:1–4, 11)

The pentecostal birth of the church is marked by eyes opened and tongues unleashed. By the power of the Holy Spirit, God has come not to shatter a tower of Babel, confusing knowledge and speech, but to give clarity of mind and tongue. So the Spirit enlightens the apostolic community, enabling it to know and to tell the Story. The *knowing* of the newly-birthed church is inseparable from its being. Thus the apostle gives a trustworthy account of 'God's deeds of power', locating their origins in the 'foreknowledge' of the Godhead and tracking the drama through the covenant with Israel to the coming and reign of Christ (Acts 2:22–36). This enlightening work of the Holy Spirit is a gift of understanding of the drama of reconciliation, from its origins in the purposes of God through 'prophetic testimony' in Israel to its turning point in Jesus Christ, and its sequel, the coming of the church, salvation and consummation – the overarching Story. As noted in Chapter 6, on Scripture, the church pentecostal – the apostolic communities proximate to the incarnate Word – is given a special light to tell the Story, the in-Spiriting of the record of deeds of God.

The light given to the privileged apostolic seers continues in *post*-apostolic gifts of understanding of the Story given to 'everyone who calls upon the name of the Lord', *ecclesial illumination*:

> In the last days it will be, God declares, that I will pour out my Spirit upon all flesh, and your sons and your daughters shall prophesy, and your young men shall see visions, and your old men dream dreams. Even upon my slaves, both men and women, in those days I will pour out my Spirit; and they shall prophesy ...Then everyone who calls upon the name of the Lord shall be saved. (Acts 2:17–18, 21)

The future-orientation of this portion of the homily points to a continuing light given to the newly-born community. Men and women, young and old, generations yet to come, will be empowered by the Holy Spirit to see visions and to prophesy. Not new 'revelation' that supersedes the defining deed of God in Christ, but an 'illumination' in which a deeper sight into ('insight') the Story is given. So John Robinson's counsel.

'Illumination', narratively considered, has its personal and eschatological aspects as well as its ecclesial locus, and so its chapters on salvation (the saving light that comes to persons: 'the eyes of your heart enlightened', Eph. 1:18) and consummation ('the Lord's great and glorious day', Acts 2:20). To these we shall subsequently turn. In the narrative, however, the chapter on the church is the occasion for the first appearance of the illuminative work of the Holy Spirit.

In the third *phase* of God's self-disclosure, we encounter one more of the century's major theologians, Karl Rahner, our conversation partner on the topic of the illumination of the church.

KARL RAHNER

Karl Rahner is considered by many to be the major voice of Roman Catholic theology in the twentieth century. Writing about him in *A Handbook of Christian Theologians*, Anne Carr says that

> his vision captured the minds and hearts of theologians and lay people alike, making Rahner something of a twentieth-century Aquinas in the universities, seminaries, and parish meeting rooms of the Catholic world as well as a spokesman for contemporary Catholic thought in the ecumenical community.[1]

While Rahner is remembered for his innovative thinking in areas that run from fundamental theology through Christology to missiology and eschatology, our focus here will be on his ecclesiological views, ones that reflect the mainstream of Roman Catholic teaching as it develops historically up to and through the second Vatican Council. Karl Rahner sets forth an understanding of the place of the church in the narrative of revelation fully consonant with official Roman Catholic teaching. Our resource is the key volume, *Foundations of Christian Faith*.

Rahner develops an encompassing view of divine disclosure, a 'elevated transcendentality' that puts all human beings in touch with

God's purposes. We shall give attention to this wider religious episte-mology. However, within that universal revelation there is a history of 'reflexive' and 'thematised' unveiling in which propositions about God are ventured both by individuals and communities of believers. Where these assertions conform to the real order of things, however mixed they may be with error, there is what Rahner calls *categorical* revelation. It comes to sharper focus in the revelatory history of Israel, and to unsurpassable climax in Jesus Christ.

In discussing access to categorical revelation in its purest form, Rahner's thought moves between two poles, ones focal for our inquiry:

1. In Jesus, God's communication to man in grace and at the same time its categorical self-interpretation in the corporeal, tangible and social dimension have reached their climax, have become revelation in an absolute sense. But this means that the event of Christ becomes for us the only tangible caesura in the universal history of salvation and revelation . . . [The] teaching authority of the Pope, and of the whole episcopate with the Pope, is not an authority through which we receive a new revelation from God.[2]

2. From this perspective, such structures (for example, a monarchial and episcopal constitution and a permanent Petrine office) can be understood as having origins in Jesus and *iuris divini*, at least if they are found in the apostolic period. For during this period the public history of revelation was not yet closed, as for example, the formation of the normative scriptures of the New Testament shows.[3]

Rahner seeks to be faithful to the emphasis of the second Vatican council on the definitive disclosure of God in Jesus Christ, and to the uniquely inspired, 'infallible' and in a certain sense 'inerrant' witness of Scripture to this revelatory event. At the same time, he argues for the privileged role of the church's teaching office in interpreting the mean-ing of that disclosure. Does the functional role of authority assigned to the magisterium undercut the formal assertion of the primacy of christological revelation and the singularity of biblical inspiration? The greatness of Rahner is related to his effort to honour this polarity in the Roman Catholic tradition and thus be open to ecumenical dialogue, especially with his chosen conversation partner in the West, 'Evangelical Christianity'. We place him at this juncture in our narrative of revelation because of what Avery Dulles calls the 'ecclesiocentric' character of his thought.[4] Thus 'illumination' plays a decisive role in his understanding of revelation. We want to learn from Rahner about the significance of the ecclesial point in the revelatory pilgrimage, but to relate it clearly to the priorities of *action* and *inspiration*.

UNIVERSAL REVELATION

Rahner begins his analysis of revelation in narrative fashion with broad epistemic graces. The 'natural revelation' of the Roman Catholic tradition is reconceived with the aid of a philosophical anthropology influenced by such disparate figures as Maurice Blondel, Yves Congar and Martin Heidegger. The resulting view of human nature holds that every person is oriented to the 'absolute mystery' by a grace that makes one aware of and open to 'the infinity of reality'. This 'experience of transcendence' is a gift of God's self-communication, placing before each human being the option to say Yes or No to the divine invitation. We must

> return again and again to its sources ... to the transcendental experience of our orientation toward the absolute mystery, and to the existentiell practice of accepting this orientation freely.[5]

When pressed to describe in ordinary terms this transcendentality, Rahner points to occasions

- where a responsibility in freedom is still accepted and borne where it has no apparent offer of success and advantage,
- where a man experiences and accepts his ultimate freedom which no earthly compulsions can take away from him,
- where the leap into the darkness of death is accepted as the beginning of everlasting promise,
- where the fragmentary experience of love, beauty, and joy is experienced and accepted purely and simply as the promise of love, beauty and joy, without their being understood in ultimate cynical skepticism as a cheap form of consolation for some final deception . . .,
- where one lets oneself go unconditionally and experiences this capitulation as true victory . . .
- where a man entrusts all this knowledge and all his questions to the silent and all-inclusive mystery which is loved more than all our individual knowledge which makes us such small people,
- where we rehearse our own deaths in everyday life, and try to live

185

in such a way as we would like to die, peaceful and composed ...

- there is God and his liberating grace. There we find what Christians call the Holy Spirit of God ... There is the mysticism of everyday life, the discovery of God in all things ...[6]

In this universal work of the Spirit, both truth and life, revelation and salvation, are offered to us. While *soteriological* assertions are associated with the experience – as indicated by Rahner's famous phrase, 'anonymous Christianity' – for our purposes, it is the *epistemological* claims that come to the fore. Human beings that may have no 'categorical' knowledge of Christ still have access through their common humanity to transcendental knowledge of God, indeed, enough that can assure their salvation if a right response is made. That response is an 'implicit' faith, one which 'justifies' by the grace given and received.

Throughout this work, allusion has been made to the covenant with Noah as a biblical touchstone for the doctrines of common grace and general revelation. In these reflections on a universally elevated transcendentality, Rahner takes up these themes, interpreting in fresh ways the traditional Roman Catholic teaching on natural grace, natural law and natural theology.

SPECIAL REVELATION

The *Dogmatic Constitution on Divine Revelation* of the second Vatican Council sets the stage for Rahner's thought on the particularity of revelation. In its opening paragraphs, it strikes a strong christological note. What is given definitively in Christ is anticipated in the earlier covenant with Israel, for

> At his own good time [God] called Abraham to make him into a great nation (cf. Gen. 12:2); after the patriarchs, he taught the nation, through Moses and the prophets, to acknowledge him as the only living and true God, the prudent Father and the just Judge, and to expect the promised Saviour.[7]

'Incarnation' is the decisive event of disclosure in the history of God according to the *Constitution*. The 'secrets of God'[8] are revealed in the Person of Christ. Thus the 'election' of Israel, God's special relationship to the chosen people, is part of the unique revelatory action of God.

Vatican II sets its references to *Heilsgeschichte* in the context of God's universal revelatory activity, alluding to the 'perennial testimony to himself in created things' and 'the natural light of human reason reflecting on created things (cf. Rom. 1:20)'.[9]

The particularities of revelation – the election of Israel and the incarnation of the Word – are acts of God whose meaning is transmitted to us through appointed media.

> For this purpose, Christ the Lord . . . commissioned the apostles to preach the Gospel to all – formerly promised through the prophets, and now fulfilled and orally proclaimed by himself – as the source of all saving truth and moral discipline . . . in what they had preached, did, and instituted, they handed on what they had received from Christ in his words, his way of life and his works, or what they had learned at the Holy Spirit's suggestions. This was also done by the apostles and the apostolic men who, inspired by the same Holy Spirit, wrote down the news of salvation.[10]

Thus the link to us for the 'transmission of divine revelation' is the 'apostles and apostolic men' who first proclaimed the Good News of the redemptive work of God, then made provision for its trustworthy preservation in written accounts. These documents have special revelatory weight, as

> our holy Mother the Church holds the complete books of the Old and the New Testaments, with all their parts, to be sacred and canonical. For, written under the Holy Spirit's inspiration . . . they are authored by God and have been handed on to the Church as such.[11]

At the Church's inception, therefore, the Holy Spirit released into its life powers to discern the meaning of the revelatory events and fixed the understandings in sacred texts 'firmly, faithfully and without error'.[12] While the unique inspiration of Scripture here asserted seems to entail 'inerrancy', the *Constitution* hastens to add that 'In Holy Scripture God spoke to men in a human way',[13] reminding the faithful of the issues of literary genre and the earlier official approval of the responsible use of critical scholarship. Also, an 'infallibilist' turn is given by the addition of the phrase 'for our salvation's sake', suggesting that Scripture's authority is focused on matters of faith and morals.[14]

While Scripture is accorded a unique status by virtue of its divine authorship/inspiration, its revelatory authority has to do with its reliable witness to 'God's Word' or 'the Gospel'. A companion to Scripture, 'Tradition', which itself 'issues from the apostles', also gives faithful testimony to the Gospel, for 'God, who spoke in the past, unceasingly talks to the bride of his beloved Son'.[15] The medium through which this continuing Word speaks, and by which Tradition is faithfully transmitted, is made up of the successors to the apostles, 'the bishops, to whom "they handed on their own teaching responsibilities"'.[16] Indeed, the 'living magisterium' of bishops in apostolic succession is the final arbiter of the meaning of the Gospel proclaimed in *both* Scripture and Tradition.

> The task of providing an authentic interpretation of God's Word in Scripture or Tradition has been entrusted only to the Church's living magisterium, whose authority is wielded in the name of Jesus Christ.[17]

While interpretive authority is lodged, finally, in the magisterium, the latter itself is always accountable to 'God's Word', never the source of new revelation.

In the carefully-crafted sentences of the Constitution, the second Vatican Council declined to endorse the popular but unofficial catechetical tradition that divided the transmission of revelation into two sources: Scripture which discloses one part of the divine truth, and Tradition which reveals the other part (the immaculate conception and the bodily assumption of Mary, for example). Rather, it stressed the unity of Scripture and Tradition, allowing for the possibility of holding that *all* of the divine revelation is available fully in both Scripture and Tradition, providing thereby a warrant for scrutinising any new doctrinal proposals by Scripture, or interpreting dogmatic deposits in the same biblical light. However, the clear statement of the accountability of biblical interpretation to magisterial authority tells another story, one to which we shall return in our assessment of Karl Rahner's understanding of revelation.

CATEGORICAL REVELATION

Rahner expounds his doctrine of revelation within lines laid down by the second Vatican Council as well as by earlier magisterial statements, employing distinctive terminology and occasional neologisms. A key term is the earlier-cited 'categorical' revelation. This 'reflexive' appropriation constitutes the 'thematising' of the primordial experience of grace. As it pertains to this present discussion of particular revelation, 'categorical' refers to the definitive disclosure of the reflexive and thematised knowledge of God. Rahner's exposition follows essentially the outlines of the *Dogmatic Constitution*. Jesus Christ is the central disclosure, the culmination of all that has come before, either in particular or universal revelation history, and unsurpassable by all that comes after. Human history

> reaches the God-Man, the absolute objectification of its transcendental understanding of God. In this objectification, namely, in Jesus Christ, the God who communicates himself and the man who accepts God's self-communication become irrevocably one, and the history of revelation and salvation of the whole human race reaches its goal . . . Not until the full and unsurpassable event of the historical self-objectification of God's self-communication to the world in Jesus Christ do we have an event which, as an eschatological event, fundamentally and absolutely precludes any historical corruption or any distorted interpretation in the further history of categorical revelation . . .[18]

The Incarnation is the locus of final revelation. Put in comparable terms:

> It has pleased God in his goodness and wisdom to reveal himself, and to make known the secret hidden in his will (cf. Eph. 1:9); through Christ, the Word made flesh, and in the Holy Spirit men have access to the Father . . . To see him is to see the Father (cf. John 14:9). Thus, by all his presence and self-manifestation, by his words and his works, by his symbolic actions and his miracles, and especially by his death and glorious resurrection from the dead, he – the Spirit of truth being finally sent – brings revelation to perfection by fulfilling it, and confirms it with the divine witness: God is among us to free us from the darkness of sin and death, and to raise us up to eternal life (*Dogmatic Constitution*) . . . In Jesus, God's communication to man in grace and at the same time its categorical self-interpretation in the corporeal, tangible and social dimension have reached their climax, have become revelation in an absolute sense. But this means that the event of Christ becomes for us the only really tangible caesura in the universal history of salvation and revelation, and it enables us to distinguish a particular and official history of revelation within the universal history of revelation before Christ (Karl Rahner).[19]

'The Old Testament history of revelation' is anticipatory of the fulfilled disclosure in Christ. Israel's election plays a role in revelation history, although Rahner's comments on it are muted. Here,

Nothing really happened in the realm of the categorical which does not also happen in the history of every other people. What makes this history a history of revelation is rather the interpretation of this history as the event of a dialogical partnership with God, and as a prospective tendency towards an open future.[20]

For Christians, the proximity to Christ and its place as the prehistory of Christ give Israel its revelatory significance.

How is the definitive revelation in Jesus Christ passed on to us? It comes through the church. Consonant with his belief in the status and role of reason, Rahner finds support for the magisterial doctrine of the church on the basis of the 'social nature' of human beings – the self as a 'being of interpersonal communication'.[21] The church, dogmatically established yet rationally defensible, is the transmitter of historic revelation, an 'ecclesiocentric' view of the narrative, or a doctrine of 'social inspiration'.[22] Conscious of 'Evangelical Christians' (continental Churches of the Reformation), contemporary biblical scholarship and the ecumenical movement, Rahner argues that few Christian traditions would deny the inseparability of Christ and the church, whatever differences might exist on where 'the church' is to be found, or however scholars might disagree on the church's founding by Jesus as in the disputed Petrine passage (Matt. 16:18–19). Touching the issue of revelation, the intimacy of Christ and church means that 'the original church's consciousness of the faith'[23] is the definitive carrying-forwards of the unsurpassable revelation in Jesus Christ. Thus the apostolic community – one that continues into the early decades of the second century – is connected to Christ and thus is the locus of normative teaching about Christian faith.

> Wherever ecclesial Christianity is found, it is convinced that it had its origins in Christ . . . If continuity and identity are to be maintained within an entity which exists historically, then it is inevitable that in an earlier phase of this historical entity free decisions are made which form an irreversible norm for future epochs.[24]

Within this defining period, the Holy Scripture emerges. It appears as the 'objectification' of the apostolic consciousness of faith.

> Everything which belongs to the original apostolic kerygma has been written down in scripture . . . For Catholic Christians too, tradition and the teaching office's understanding have their material source and their *norma non normata* only in Holy Scripture.[25]

Thus Scripture, including its constituting as canon, is a 'moment' in the norm-bearing period of the church's early life:

> The church objectifies its faith and its life in written documents, and it recognizes these objectifications as so pure and successful that they are able to hand on the apostolic church as a norm for future ages.[26]

The singularity of Scripture is finally grounded in its epistemological privilege as both 'inspired' and 'inerrant'.

> God is the *auctor* (author) of the Old and New Testaments as scripture . . . From the doctrine that Holy Scripture is inspired theology and the official doctrine of the church derive the thesis that scripture is inerrant.[27]

The divine authoring of Scripture does not preclude its literary composition by human beings. Such finitude warrants the use of critical scholarship, the results of which are to be taken into account in assessing its meaning. So too the concept of inerrancy requires interpretation, with errorlessness having to do with the Scripture's housing of teaching '*for the sake of our salvation*', as interpreted by '*analogia scriptura*', a hermeneutic that scrutinises the text in the light of a 'hierarchy of truths'.[28]

Who, finally, has the authority to employ these principles of interpretation authoritatively? And why are they so authorised? Rahner begins and ends his discussion of the transmission of revelation with this question, giving far more attention to it than the issue of Scripture's status. The grounds for his contention go back to Rahner's 'ecclesiocentric' approach. In the key period of juncture between Christ and the Church, concurrent with the 'moment' of scriptural objectification, there appears in the church and its definitive consciousness an institutional structure belonging to the essence of Christianity: the apostolic teaching office. The magisterium took rise in the normative apostolic age and continues to the present. Its validity as chief interpreter of the faith is established by these origins and the promise of the Spirit's guardianship of its faithfulness. The Holy Spirit guaranteed then, and guarantees now, the trustworthiness of teaching within the universal church.

> From this perspective such structures (for example, a monarchical and episcopal constitution and a permanent Petrine office) can be understood as having their origins in Jesus and as *ius divini*, at

least if they are found in the apostolic period. For during this period the public history of revelation was not yet closed, as for example, the formation of the normative scriptures of the New Testament shows. These structures can be understood this way even if they cannot be traced back to a specific, unambiguous identifiable saying of Jesus which founds them.[29]

While the teaching office guards the doctrine of the church and functions as arbiter of scriptural interpretation, it is bound to the original consciousness of the church and thus to its objectification in Scripture:

Insofar as the church's teaching office in later ages continues to be bound permanently to the original church's consciousness of the faith which is the constitutive beginning of the church as a whole, and insofar as that consciousness has been objectified in an authentic and pure way in Holy Scripture, the teaching office does not stand above scripture. Rather it only has the task of giving witness to the truth of scripture, of maintaining this truth in a vital way, and of always interpreting it anew in historically changing horizons of understanding as the one truth that always remains the same.[30]

Rahner seems to take the Vatican Council's view on the normativity of Scripture to its furthest point, suggesting that all doctrine must be legitimated by Scripture:

The second Vatican Council refused to make tradition a second source for us today which exists by itself alongside scripture, a source which testifies to individual material contents of faith which have no foundation at all in scripture.[31]

Not to be forgotten, however, is the interpreting 'who' that holds the hermeneutical key to Scripture: the teaching office of the Roman Catholic Church. Why? The answer is that its authority is grounded in Jesus Christ:

We must recognize a really Christological reason for this teaching authority of the church . . . Jesus Christ himself is the absolute, irreversible, and invincible climax of salvation history . . . Jesus Christ is the fact that makes it manifest that God's self-communication is present in the world as the truth of ultimate love, that God's loving truth and his true love are not only offered

> to man and his history, but also that they have really triumphed in
> this history and can no longer be abolished by man's rejection . . .
> Now the church of Christ is the ongoing presence and tangibility
> of this ultimate and victorious word of God in Jesus Christ . . .
> The controversial theological question between the Evangelical
> and Catholic understanding of the church cannot really be
> whether or not the church of Jesus Christ can lose the truth but
> rather it can ultimately be only the question *how* in the concrete
> God triumphs in the church in his victorious presence and in his
> communication of the truth . . .[32]

Thus we return to the christological warrant from which we began.
The faithful transmission of divine revelation depends on the trustworthiness of the church's witness through the magisterial authority
rooted in apostolic continuity because Jesus Christ by the power of
Spirit so guarantees it.

The stature of our twentieth-century interlocutors is related to the
comprehensiveness and catholicity of their thought. As Barth, Tillich
and Henry each make some formal place in their doctrine of revelation for the varied chapters of the narrative, so too does Karl Rahner.
Following the same trajectory as the *Dogmatic Constitution on Divine
Revelation*, we traced Rahner's references from a universally disclosive
transcendentality (the covenant with Noah) to the particular deed of
revelation in Jesus Christ to the chapter of the church where the
graces of both inspiration and illumination make their appearance.
And in Rahner is found the same eschatological reserve about the
revelation received, and this an acknowledgement that we yet await
'God's full self-communication'.[33] Thus revelation is inseparable from
the 'drama . . . a drama which has already reached its irreversible
climax in Christ'.[34]

CONTRIBUTIONS

Evangelical teachability means the willingness to listen to Roman
Catholic concerns about the ahistorical and individualistic temptations
of the Protestant tradition. The individual believer cannot overleap the
centuries to make simple contact with the purity of biblical times. The
church plays a crucial role in any interpretation of Scripture, both
descriptively and normatively. Further, self-criticism on these issues of
authority and interpretation press us deeper into matters of revelation.

How does Rahner's doctrine of revelation contribute to an ecumenical understand of our knowledge of God?

The church is the Body of Christ. The community brought to be at Pentecost was born and lives by the Spirit of the Son. This people, then and now, is inextricably related to Jesus Christ as a Body to its Head. Epistemologically stated, the Word enfleshed is inseparable from Word communicated to us. As such, a continuity exists between Incarnation and its ecclesial derivatives, apostolic inspiration and post-apostolic illumination. Rahner's concept of the 'objectification' of the Word in Scripture within the matrix of the Christian community bears witness to the former – apostolic inspiration, and his conjunction of the Word with the interpretive gifts given to the church, including its institutional underside, testifies to the latter – ecclesial illumination. The disputed point to which we shall return is not *whether* there is a continuity along the line of Christ, Bible and church – Incarnation, inspiration and illumination – but, as Rahner says, *how* that linkage is understood and *who* constitutes the hermeneutical community.

Rahner's contribution, and that of the Roman Catholic tradition, represents a corrective to Protestant understandings of revelation that weaken or sever the connection between Christ and the church. The promise of Christ to be with his people means a trustworthy epistemic 'presence' of Christ in the church. It entails as well the ministerial role of the church ecumenical in discerning the meaning of the magisterial Word written, in contrast to individualist and ahistorical readings of Scripture. With his acknowledgement of the primacy of Scripture, Rahner gives impetus, therefore, to an 'evangelical catholic' under-standing of the role of the church in the narrative of revelation.

Such an evangelical catholic reading of the role of the church includes an affirmation of the Spirit's work of illumination in the tradition of church universal. As early as the baptismal 'rules of faith', and subsequently in the ecumenical creeds, the Christian community recognised the need to 'encapsulate the central claims of the faith in as precise a way as possible'.[35] Hence the importance of

> a short guide by the same author [the Holy Spirit] . . . the Church's creeds and other traditions of public teaching of items treated as central to the Gospel message.[36]

Tradition as 'guide' within the church as 'resource' to identifying the gospel 'substance' of the biblical 'source' is an aspect of the structure of authority and interpretation integral to the doctrine of revelation here set forth.[37] While 'tradition' in this ecumenical framework includes more than the creeds and other early 'public teaching' in the church, that subsequent development stands in continuity with them. Here the 'evangelical' heritage needs to honour the contribution of Rahner and the broad 'catholic' heritage.

Rahner's contribution also includes a testimony to the place of other chapters in the narrative of revelation. He relates the ecclesial presence of the Spirit to a description of a wide-ranging 'drama' of disclosure, one that includes a common grace of preservation, the defining particularity of Jesus Christ, the inspiration of Scripture and the eschatological fulfilment of God's self-communication. Here is a compelling 'Catholic' story of the Holy Spirit's epistemic work needed in the development of an ecumenical doctrine of revelation.

Evidence of how compelling is the Catholic witness to the *church* chapter is its attraction to those who become aware of the reductionist temptations of their own alternative readings of the Story. While the Catholic ethos in its larger sense (Roman, Eastern Orthodox, Anglo-Catholic) draws adherents from other traditions for a variety of reasons, the stewardship of the Story in continuing *ecclesial* forms – creedal, dogmatic, liturgical and ministerial – appears to secure the Story against the winds of modernity and postmodernity. Hence the migration of some evangelicals to Rome, Constantinople and Canterbury, and the appeal to some 'ecumenicals' of these ecclesial solidities in the face of concern about the cultural captivity of mainline Protestantism. However, a 'catholic' reading of the Story alone, exclusive of 'evangelical' and 'ecumenical' contributions, entails its own shortcomings, as now discussed in the conversation with Karl Rahner.

PROBLEMS

We begin our examination of the problems attendant to Rahner's insights with the question: *How* in the narrative of revelation do we understand the intimate relationship between Christ and the church, the 'Word enfleshed' and the 'Word proclaimed'? We return to issues met in the previous section on the relation of Incarnation to inspiration, now in the form of the relation of Incarnation to ecclesial illumination.

A dialectical understanding of the revelatory relation of Christ to the church, like that of Christ's relation to Scripture, will find a place for a No as well as a Yes: Yes, the Word discloses itself unfailingly in the church. No, not inerrantly so. Yes, Christ is epistemically present in the church, No, not unbrokenly so. To say the 'Yes' without the 'No' is to conclude that 'the church of Christ is the ongoing presence and tangibility of the ultimate and victorious word of God in Jesus Christ'.[38] So stated, the same undialectical identification that Carl Henry makes between Christ and the Scripture reappears in Karl Rahner's view of the relation between Christ and the church. The radical singularity and primacy of the Word incarnate do not permit of fusion with subsequent chapters in the narrative of revelation.

When discontinuity as well as continuity between Christ and the church is asserted, Christ is understood to be free to speak *to* the church and even *against* the church, rather than speaking only *as* the church. The church is not the '*one* Word', but is other than, and thus always accountable to, that Word. The line between the Word incarnate and the words ecclesial cannot be blurred.

How does Christ the Word incarnate speak the one Word? Through the 'Word written': 'Jesus Christ, *as attested by Holy Scripture*, is the one Word whom we have to hear' (Barmen). That Word is spoken, 'now and then', through Scripture in the church as God chooses to do so by the power of the Spirit (Barth), but is also 'always and everywhere' accountable to the Bible by its gift of *inspiration* (Henry), albeit always under the norm of Christ (Barth). The priority in authority is Christ, Scripture and church. The revelatory underpinnings of these priorities have to do with the narrative of incarnation, inspiration and illumination. Jesus Christ as the *norma normans et non normata* (the norm which governs but is not governed) derives from the defining act of incarnation, the Word enfleshed. The primacy of Scripture's witness derives from its inspiration, the Word written. The ministerial role of the church in interpreting magisterial Scripture derives from the grace of illumination, the 'Word proclaimed'.

Rahner's 'ecclesiocentric' view of revelation, while acknowledging Scripture's unique inspiration, lodges it in a deeper trajectory that moves from Christ to the church. Thus God

> is the inspirer and author of scripture, although the inspiration of scripture is 'only' a moment within God's primordial authorship of the church.[39]

'Primordial authorship of the church' with Scripture as a moment within it does not do justice to the singularity of, and the accountability to, 'the one Word . . . attested by Holy Scripture'.

The problem of a christological–cum–ecclesial continuity, unbroken by the foregoing distinctions, is further deepened when particularised, as Rahner does in the teaching office of the Roman Catholic Church, the 'monarchical and episcopal constitution and the permanent Petrine office . . . having their origins in Jesus and *ius divini*'.[40] A case can be made for an episcopal teaching office within the Body of Christ, as in the World Council of Churches' ground-breaking consensus document, *Baptism, Eucharist and Ministry*. Yet, whatever form the pastoral office takes, it enjoys a ministerial not magisterial status, accountable to the self-testimony of the Word in Scripture as read from within the whole people of God. No equation can be made of an office within the Church with the authority of Jesus Christ. Narratively conceived, the chapter on Christ is distinguishable (although not inseparable) from the chapter on the church.

That ecclesial illumination is different from biblical inspiration, and subsidiary to it, can be argued from the text of the *Constitution on Revelation*, with its specific reference to Scripture as 'God's own speech written under the influx of the divine Spirit'.[41] Further, the canonisation process in the church of the early centuries which lifts the written Word above it, making itself accountable to it, is an embodiment of the distinction between the two moments of revelation, and the precedence of one over the other. The Spirit's gift of illumination enabled it to recognise the Scripture's inspiration. Rahner himself acknowledges the priorities here when he says 'the teaching office does not stand above scripture'.[42] However, in the *structure* of his doctrine of revelation, the formal continuity between Christ and the magisterium, and its functional one as arbiter of Scripture's meaning, dissolves the distinction and its priorities. Again, in a narrative of revelation, the integrity of the phases of revelation and their special status must be respected.

What of the place of the magisterium vis-à-vis the whole Body of Christ? The Holy Spirit gives life to the many parts of the Body. All the organs are required for its proper functioning. The manifold gifts and the call to interrelationship apply to epistemology as well as ecclesiology. The priesthood of all believers means the epistemological privilege of *the whole people of God*.

The epistemological priesthood of all believers is a historic Protestant teaching. However, its development and interpretation were associated too often with cultural ideologies of individualism, assuming thereby a solitary encounter and authoritative interpretation of the text by the believer. Subsequently, a more self-critical awareness of the pre-judgments which we bring to our reading of Bible challenged this individualism. So also has a deepened grasp of the Scripture's own teaching of the crucial role of the Christian community. The hermeneutical priesthood of all believers is a *corporate* reality. The Spirit's work of illumination goes on through the manifold of the Body's parts.

But who can encompass the church in its entirety? Only the *eschaton* will realise that vision. Paul's reminder of our epistemological limitations comes in the middle of his discourse on the Body of Christ, and its need for the interrelationship of its parts (1 Cor. 12–14). Epistemology and ecclesiology are so linked. Short of the final vision, illumination is given to the church in precisely the way the gift-ministries within the Body are called to relate to one another. First, they are to discern the variety within the Body and acknowledge their validity. Second, they are to enter into living relationship with one another. And the way of engagement is the vulnerability of Agape. Knowledge of the Gospel given to us in the Scripture is appropriated by us to the extent that we are open to the gifts of understanding brought by the various charisms within the totality of the Christian community. Paul did not claim the clarity, nor demand the entirety, of the End. For those *in via*, both salvation and revelation are *simul iustus et peccator*, a pilgrimage towards the promised life together – and *light* together – of the church triumphant.

The institutional underside of the journey in and towards openness entails *fora of conversation*. The process of listening and speaking and the Yes and No that go with it require institutional contexts for the exchange of perspectives. Where the epistemological priesthood of all believers has taken hold in the church, such places of mutual learning have emerged. They occur in many and varied forms. A prominent one is the congregation. In the free church tradition, the local church becomes the hermeneutical community, on the grounds that the Holy Spirit is distributed to all the members gathered in covenant. In its most extreme expression, the understanding of faith is formed by the testimony and exchange of the charisms *only* within the congregation, with no relationship to any partner-in-the-faith beyond it (including a transcongregational teaching ministry). In others, it is a community within the congregation – 'base community', 'house church', 'class meeting', 'woman church' etc. – that is the epistemologically privileged locus. Elsewhere in the church's history, the place of epistemological access has been one or another supracongregational forum, including the one discussed earlier as the magisterium of bishops in apostolic succession. Thus, even in traditions which explicitly reject 'democracy' as an epistemological medium, some element of collegial give-and-take is included. And that distribution appears to be increasing as decision-making is more and more dispersed in the Roman Catholic Church itself through parish councils, the role of national bishops-in-conversation etc. The twentieth-century vision of an ecumenical movement that gathers the gifts of conversation from every part of the Body of Christ is as critical in epistemology as it is in ecclesiology. The fullness of the truth is linked to the wholeness of the church. Where the universal priesthood has been reduced to the teaching office of the Roman Catholic Church, the catholicity and freedom of God's revelatory grace are restricted. Thus Rahner's *how* question cannot be separated from the *who* issue.

For all the stated differences between Reformation and Roman traditions, note must be taken of an interesting convergence suggested by the Roman Catholic teaching concerning the *sensus fidelium*. The teaching on the 'sense of the faithful' holds that while the magisterium sets forth official doctrine, in doing so it gives voice to a matrix of belief lodged in the common piety of the faithful. To the extent that the whole people of God at worship and work constitute the arena of ecclesial illumination, similarities exist with the Reformation witness to the epistemological priesthood of all believers. Both counsel attention to ranges of the church's life far beyond a delimited teaching office. If doctrine is finally traceable in Roman Catholic theology to the living faith of the whole church, then the *functional* magisterium *is* the *laos*.

Whether it be called the *sensus fidelium* or the priesthood of all believers, a *process* for discerning and articulating grassroots faith in its catholicity has yet to be found. The World Council of Churches' Faith and Order venture in seeking a fuller range of ecclesial traditions in the conversation on doctrine is a model of this quest for Corinthian inclusivity, as in the articulation and reception processes of *Baptism, Eucharist and Ministry* and *Confessing the Apostolic Faith Today*. So too the prominent bilateral dialogues alluded to earlier.

Is there a connection between Rahner's ecclesiocentric and magisterial view of revelation and his anthropology? In both ecclesiology and anthropology, soteric and noetic grace does its work: *finitum capax infiniti*. Grace so infused enables us to trust the possibilities of both human nature and the church's nature. We meet again in another context the 'Catholic' and 'Evangelical' differences on 'how far the fall'. The ecumenical orientation of this work here asserts the need for the continuing witness of the Reformation within the catholicity of the Church, and thus an evangelical catholic construal of this chapter of the Story.

The thought of Karl Rahner is a contribution to understanding the place of the church in the narrative of revelation. His insights are a corrective to theories that obscure the Spirit's ecclesial work of illumination. Yet ecumenical exchange requires a No as well as a Yes when other aspects of the revelatory journey do not receive their full due. Thus the importance of the mutual corrigibilities and complementarities of the four formative figures in the twentieth century-conversation on the doctrine of revelation.

NOTES

1. Anne E. Carr, 'Karl Rahner', in Dean G. Peerman and Martin E. Marty (eds), *A Handbook of Christian Theologians*, enlarged edn (Nashville: Abingdon Press, 1984), p. 520.
2. Rahner, *Foundations of Christian Faith*, op. cit., pp. 174–5, 381.
3. Ibid., p. 331.
4. Avery Dulles, 'Recent Protestant and Catholic Views', in Donald McKim (ed.), *The Authoritative Word* (Grand Rapids: Eerdmans, 1983), p. 345.
5. Rahner, *Foundations of Christian Faith*, op. cit., p. 54.
6. Karl Rahner, *The Spirit in the Church*, trans. John Griffiths, W. J. O'Hara, Charles Henkey and Richard Strachan (New York: The Seabury Press, 1979), pp. 21–2.
7. *The Dogmatic Constitution on Divine Revelation of Vatican Council II*, commentary and translation by George H. Tavard (London: Darton, Longman and Todd, 1966), p. 59. For catechetical commentary on the citations to follow, see *Catechism of the Catholic Church*, op. cit., pp. 19–38.
8. *The Dogmatic Constitution on Divine Revelation*, op. cit., p. 59.
9. Ibid., pp. 59, 60.
10. Ibid., p. 64.
11. Ibid., p. 72.
12. Ibid.
13. Ibid., p. 73.
14. Cf. *The Christian Story*, op. cit., pp. 69–74.
15. *The Dogmatic Constitution on Divine Revelation*, p. 66.
16. Ibid., p. 65.
17. Ibid., p. 67.
18. Rahner, *Foundations of Christian Faith*, op. cit., pp. 169, 157.
19. *Dogmatic Constitution*, op. cit., pp. 58, 59–60 and Rahner, *Foundations of Christian Faith*, op. cit., p. 175.
20. Ibid., p. 167.
21. Ibid., p. 322.
22. So described by Robert Gnuse in *The Authority of the Bible: Theories of Inspiration, Revelation and the Canon of Scripture* (New York: Paulist Press, 1985), pp. 54–5.
23. Rahner, *Foundations of Christian Faith*, op. cit., pp. 377.

24. Ibid., pp. 328–9, 330.
25. Ibid., p. 364.
26. Ibid., p. 373.
27. Ibid., pp. 374, 375.
28. Ibid., pp. 375, 376, 377.
29. Ibid., p. 331.
30. Ibid., p. 377.
31. Ibid., pp. 377–8.
32. Ibid., pp. 379–80.
33. Ibid., p. 445.
34. Ibid., p. 446.
35. Swinburne, *Revelation: From Metaphor to Analogy*, p. 193.
36. Ibid., p. 177.
37. See pp. 24, 25 for the diagrams on authority and revelation.
38. Rahner, *Foundations of Christian Faith*, op. cit., pp. 380.
39. Ibid., p. 375.
40. Ibid., p. 331.
41. *Constitution*, op. cit., p. 66.
42. Rahner, *Foundations of Christian Faith*, op. cit., p. 377.

8

SALVATION:
PERSONAL ILLUMINATION

—⁓⁓⁓ᴀᴀᴀᴀᴀ◎ᴀᴀᴀᴀ⁓⁓⁓—

> For by grace you have been saved through faith, and this is not
> your own doing; it is the gift of God – not the result of works, so
> that no-one may boast. For we are what he has made us, created
> in Christ Jesus for good works, which God prepared beforehand
> to be our way of life. (Eph. 2:8–10)

The saving Work of Christ as proclaimed and transmitted in the Body
of Christ is received by grace alone through faith alone. The chapter
on salvation in the story of reconciliation has to do with the Holy
Spirit's work of *pardon* and *power*. In the traditional language of Christian
theology, we have come to the doctrine of 'subjective soteriology', the
'application of the benefits of Christ' to believers.[1] As pardon, grace
comes *pro nobis*, as the declaration to sinners of 'justification'. As power,
grace comes *in nobis*, as growth in 'sanctification'. As sin persists in the
believer short of the final Reign of God, the need for pardon comes
at every stage of power.

In this chapter, as elsewhere, the narratives of reconciliation and
revelation are intertwined, made vivid by the proximity of one to the
other in the Ephesians letter:

> I pray that the God of our Lord Jesus Christ, the Father of glory,
> may give you a spirit of wisdom and revelation as you come to
> know him, so that with the eyes of your heart enlightened, you

may know what is the hope to which he has called you, what are the riches of his glorious inheritance among the saints, and what is the immeasurable greatness of his power for us who believe, according to the working of his great power ... (Eph. 1:17–19)

The graced *faith* that receives the declaration of pardon ranges *notitia* alongside *assensus* and *fiducia*, a knowledge of the mind – 'wisdom ... revelation' conjoined to the assent of the will and trust of the heart. The graced *love* that marks the growth in good works brings with it also a deepened knowledge of the truth.

Knowledge of God so given to the believer is the gift of 'illumination'. As Francis Martin points out,

> words related to the root *phos* are also used of the activity of God in the believer, presenting the act of revelation in history and conferring the light that allows one to participate in the act consciously and with understanding. As we have seen, Paul attributes 'the enlightenment' (*phōtismos*), which is the knowledge of the glory of God on the face of Jesus Christ, to an act of God that resembles the creation of light at the beginning (2 Cor. 4:6).[2]

Thus the journey of light/revelation which we have been tracing moves from creation to Christ to the believer's restored vision, 'so that with the eyes of your heart enlightened' *insight* – sight into the purposes of God – is given. And it is given by the power of God, the Holy Spirit, for

> when you had heard the word of truth, the gospel of your salvation, and had believed him, were marked with the seal of the promised Holy Spirit ... (Eph. 1:13)

The light shed here, as from the beginning of the story to its end, is the gift of that enlightening Spirit. In intention and preservation, in election and incarnation, in the fiery distribution at Pentecost to the church and now to the individual believer, the Holy Spirit is our trustworthy Counsellor. John Calvin comments on this continuity that reaches to this point in the illumined heart:

> For as God alone can properly bear witness to his own words, so these words will not obtain full credit in the hearts of men, until they are sealed by the inward testimony of the Spirit. The same Spirit, therefore, who spoke by the mouth of the prophets must penetrate our hearts, in order to convince us that they faithfully delivered the message with which they were divinely entrusted.[3]

The soteric life of birth and growth have as their companions the light given justification and its power granted in sanctification. Inextricable from the birth of faith in the soul of the believer is the initial enlightenment when the Word of pardon strikes home and the missionary hope of Paul comes true that we too 'may turn from darkness to light and from the power of Satan to God' (Acts 26:18).

The turn from night to light in saving faith that begins the Christian's pilgrimage with Christ continues as a 'walk in the light as he himself is in the light' (1 John 1:7). Sanctifying disclosure on the personal journey, like that in the life of the church, takes two forms. One is the making alive, ever and again, of the Word addressed to us, the response to Paul's entreaty:

> 'Sleeper, awake!
> Rise from the dead
> and Christ will shine on you'
> (Eph. 5:14)

Markus Barth comments:

> Knowledge of God is never a handed-down possession to be treated like some second-hand acquisition. It is always new. Neither does it concern a part (of us) only, such as (one's) brain or feelings. Rather, knowledge of God is that 'holding fast the bond of peace . . . with all lowliness and meekness, with patience, forebearing one another in love', to which Ephesians 4:2f. exhorts . . . God's revelation, the Gospel of salvation, calls and enables (us) to 'awake . . . and stand up from the dead'.[4]

Underscored here is the ever-fresh actualising of the Word which the sovereign God chooses to speak to us. Dead letter becomes living Word by the power of the Holy Spirit.

A second form of illumination as personal appropriation is in the tradition of the pilgrim John Robinson, who called his compatriots to cross boundaries, to attend to the 'ever-new light and truth that breaks forth from God's holy Word'. Here, old formulations are rendered corrigible and new territory illuminated, fresh insights into the Gospel given by the light of the ongoing Spirit. Growth in understanding of the Gospel is, like the development of church doctrine, a journey along the trajectory of the narrative, correcting mis-steps, enlarging vistas and extending the pilgrimage into new contexts. The seeing of unseen members in the Body of Christ, the hearing of new voices and the incorporation of the wisdom into the Body – women, dramatically so in our time – is part of such new growth.

> Reading biblical texts opens these horizons of promise. . . . The de-centering of the self which is brought into play by the message of the cross . . . may not 'fit' with my own initial criteria of relevance and life-world of social interests. But daily encounter with biblical texts, especially as vehicles of address from God, may transform these horizons in accordance with the creativity of divine promise.[5]

GIFTS GIVEN AND CLAIMS MADE

In the history of both piety and theology, constituencies within the church universal have been drawn to this chapter in the narrative. As noted, the interiority accent in evangelicalism is a case in point. Other very diverse developments outside the streams of pietism and revivalism also give pride of place to the Word *pro me*, as in existentialist emphases on the 'decision of faith'. In a more classical form, the tradition of *lectio divina* stresses the nourishment of the soul as the heart of biblical reading. In current hermeneutical theories that stress the participatory nature of biblical texts – in their extreme form of 'reader response' hermeneutics – the evocative comes to the fore.[6] Barth sums up the importance of the living Word this way:

> The Holy Spirit is simply but most distinctly the renewing power of the breath of His mouth which as such is the breath of the sovereign God and victorious truth. It is the power in which His Word, God's Word, the Word of truth, is not only in Him, but where and when He wills goes out also to us men, not returning to Him empty but with the booty or increase of our faith and knowledge and obedience . . .[7]

In the narrative of *reconciliation*, these witnesses to 'the booty or increase of our faith' have not let us forget that God comes to us as persons in a way commensurate with who God is and what God has done.

> Like is only understood by like . . . *quicquid cognoscitur per modum cognoscentis cognoscitur* . . .[8]

The passionate suffering and joyfully triumphant God of Calvary and Easter invites us into a relationship coordinate with that being and doing. Personal salvation is received by believers in decisions fraught with 'fear and trembling' and issuing in personal 'peace, joy . . .'. In the narrative of *revelation*, the knowledge of God comes with the same act of personal involvement, a gift of the 'internal testimony of the Holy Spirit'. Indeed, the conviction of sin and assurance of pardon *are* the noetic work of the Spirit inextricable from soteric graces. So too growth in the Christian life is coterminous with advance in personal Christian knowledge. Witnesses from evangelical to existential that give testimony to the interiority of both reconciliation and revelation are ministries among us.

But, as in other chapters of the story, temptations to foreshorten the story are ever at hand. 'Born-again' evangelical piety regularly succumbs to reductionism and is a showcase of the allurements of interiority. Thus the preoccupation with '*my* story' can obscure the other chapters of the Great Story. Pietist and revivalist traditions, stressing the centrality of personal decision, are tempted to reduce the revelatory narrative to the moment of conversion. The gospel songs that employ the imagery of 'story' are telling in this regard; so Fanny Crosby's 'This is my story, this is my song', James Rowe's 'The story telling, His praises swelling, for grace is satisfying me', and numerous hymns that speak of Jesus as 'wounded for me', lifting 'me' and loving 'even me'.[9] Even as such hymnody makes creative use of the narrative imagery and holds up the importance of the Good News *for me*, it invites the believer into a self-absorption that obscures the rest of the Grand Narrative of both reconciliation and revelation. In particular, the knowledge of God brought to be in the experience of new birth becomes the point to which testimony of who God is and what God does returns ever and again. But the understanding of God as the Giver of enriching soteric and noetic experiences – therapeutic, 'enthusiastic' and even financial – needs to be held accountable to the biblical Grand Narrative. The sharpest critics of the narcissistic temptations and tendencies associated with evangelical interiority have been evangelical thinkers such as David Wells, Alister McGrath, Mark Noll, Os Guinness and Richard Lints.[10]

The 'objectivity' of the Word of God in Christ enfleshed is a refrain integral to the theology of Karl Barth. Hans Frei, carrying forwards Barth's stress on the objectivity of the Word, notes the dangers of subjectivity in the evangelical tradition:

> In evangelical piety [the] relation is reversed; the atoning death of Jesus is indeed real in its own right and both necessary and

efficacious for the redemption of the sinner. Nonetheless, though real in his own right, the atoning Redeemer is at the same time a figure or type of the Christian's journey; for this is the narrative framework, the meaningful pattern with which alone the occurrence of the cross finds its applicative sense. What is real, and what therefore the Christian really lives, is his own pilgrimage, and to its pattern he looks for the assurance that he is really living it.[11]

Frei echoes Barth's call for the objectivity of revelation explored in Chapter 4 of this work. Yet we cannot forget the reductionist dangers here. In the light of the earlier effort in ecumenical complementarity, it is interesting that the Lutheran eye of Wolfhart Pannenberg sees that Barth, while opposing 'Schleiermacher's basing of dogmatics on faith' and arguing that 'human self-certainty is to be understood in terms of the certainty of God and not vice versa', on the other hand

> also spoke of the risk involved in counting on the reality of the Word of God; and he granted that logically this risk has the form of a regular begging of the question (*petitio principii*). Nevertheless, in this process does not the risk serve as the point of departure for counting on the reality of the Word of God? This surely means, however, that in fact Barth was again basing dogmatics on faith as risk if not on faith as experience. In the *Church Dogmatics* he said expressly that dogmatics 'demands Christian faith' and is itself an 'act of faith'. Does this mean that Barth had readopted the Schleiermacher-oriented thesis that theology is based on faith notwithstanding his criticism of this thesis in 1927?[12]

Anthony Thiselton's survey of hermeneutical options details the subjectivist assumptions of reader-response and 'socio-pragmatic' theories, noting that in these theories

> the text can never transform us and correct us '*from outside*'. There can be no prophetic address 'from beyond' . . . In the case of many biblical texts, theological truth-claims constitute more than triggers to set self-discovery in motion (even if they are not less than this). If such concepts as 'grace' or 'revelation' have any currency, texts of this kind speak not *from the self* but from *beyond the self*.[13]

Learnings come from the *lectio divina* tradition on how to conjoin the *pro me* of this chapter to the larger narrative of revelation, especially the phases of inspiration and ecclesial illumination. Thiselton describes them this way:

If 'spiritual reading', then, is undertaken with a particular reference to the boundaries of canon or of a stable Christian tradition of interpretation, we arrive at an example of . . . *lectio divina* . . . The non-cognitive feeling-related dimensions of symbol may operate productively and healingly because a community has already established an interpretive tradition which embodies cognitive hermeneutical judgments.[14]

While Thiselton's comments are made as a corrective to current 'productive', 'affective' and infinitely polyvalent readings of Scripture, they also serve as a reminder that the doctrine of revelation cannot be reduced to the illuminatory moment of initial conversion or ongoing occasions of personal convincement. Soteric illumination is a stage on a long journey of disclosure.

H. RICHARD NIEBUHR

The struggle to avoid the reductionist temptations attendant to this chapter of the revelatory narrative can be seen in the writings of H. Richard Niebuhr, especially so in his much-referenced work, *The Meaning of Revelation*.[15] Influenced by both the existentialisms and historicisms of the day, and shaped by the Reformed accent on the divine sovereignty,[16] Niebuhr's early 'confessional theology' struck a strong *pro me* note:

> When we speak of revelation we mean that moment when we are given a new faith, to cleave to and to betray, and a new standard, to follow and deny.[17]

For Christians, this personal moment, returning ever and again in a continuing revelation, is inextricable from a historical one, our 'Rosetta stone':

> The special occasion to which we appeal in the Christian church is called Jesus Christ . . . Revelation means this intelligible event which makes all other events intelligible . . . that special occasion which provides us with an image by means of which all the occasions of personal and common life become intelligible.[18]

Embedded as we are in history, 'being finite souls with finite minds in finite bodies',[19] we can make no universal truth-claims for this particularity of self-illumination, historical Referent or communal construal, but rather can only testify confessionally, not as a statement of what all men ought to do but as statement of what we have found it necessary to do in the Christian community on the basis of the faith which is our starting point . . . We can speak of revelation only in connection with our own history without affirming or denying its reality in the history of other communities into whose inner life we cannot penetrate without abandoning ourselves and our community. . . Such theology can attempt to state the grammar, not of a universal religious language, but of a particular language, in order that those who use it may be kept in communication with each other and with the realities to which the language refers.[20]

How is this view not a revelatory relativism in which truth is understood to be only truth 'for me', or, in its historically and culturally-informed version, only truth 'for us'? In the framework of the narrative of revelation, how is it not a reduction of the whole story to this chapter, one in which the subjective appropriation event or process excludes the revelatory objectivities of the covenants with Noah and Israel, the incarnation, biblical inspiration and ecclesial illumination? Some conclude that H. Richard Niebuhr's view of revelation so succumbs. Commenting on Niebuhr's comparison of revelation to a 'luminous sentence' in a 'difficult book' – the 'special occasion' of Jesus Christ by which we interpret all of life – William Placher says:

> To me Niebuhr's account makes the distinctions seem too subjective. If last evening's sunset helped you to see a kind of order in all things, and the intricacy of the spider's web in the corner of the barn did the same for me, then each could be, on his account, 'revelatory' for one of us.[21]

Critics of a 'Yale theology' with its lineage traceable to Niebuhr raise similar questions, whether it be biblical scholar Brevard Childs questioning the adequacy of an 'intratextual' interpretation of Scripture devoid of propositional truth-claims, or theologian Julian Hartt pressing narrative theologians and ethicists to speak of ontological truth 'for all' as well as ecclesial truth 'for us'.[22]

On the face of it, the combination of Niebuhr's stress on personal and participatory illumination, his realism about cultural rootedness, his Reformed sobriety about the divine transcendence that warns of our idolatries and calls us to *semper reformanda*, appears to invite the solipsisms – personal or social – which critics charge, and to which some forms of narrative theology do succumb. *The Meaning of Revelation* can be read as Placher reads it. However, Niebuhr appeared to be aware of these problems, explicitly criticising Kierkegaard's individualism, proposing instead a 'social existentialism' integrating both the presence of the Christian community and the weal of the human community in any 'leap of faith', while at the same time flagging the dangers of a 'social solipsism'.[23] Niebuhr's later *Christ and Culture* gives evidence of movement beyond an epistemological agnosticism. In this work, Niebuhr speaks of our cognitive limitations as a matter of fragmentary knowing rather than non-knowing, as such. The identification of five types of Christ–culture/church–world encounter means that each can

> make their confessions and decisions both with confidence and with the humility which accepts completion and correction and even conflict from and with others who stand in the same relation to the Absolute. They will then in their fragmentary knowledge be able to state with conviction what they have seen and heard, the truth for them; but they will not contend that it is the whole truth and nothing but the truth; they will not become dogmatists unwilling to seek out what other men have seen and heard of that same object they have fragmentarily known. Every man looking upon the same Jesus Christ in faith will make his statement of what Christ is to him; but he will not confound his relative statement with the absolute Christ. Maurice had a principle, gained from J. S. Mill, that commends itself to us. He affirmed that men were generally right in what they affirmed and wrong in what they denied.[24]

Niebuhr's typology is an effort to identify the mutually enriching and correcting perspectives in the Christian community on the critical Christ–culture issues. It is commonplace to observe that he had his own preference, type five, 'Christ transforming culture'. While he counsels against claims of comprehensiveness, in fact, he describes the fifth type as an effort to include the insights of the others, thus making a 'fuller truth' claim.[25]

In these later comments, we meet an ecumenical impulse. The doctrine of revelation cannot be reduced to historical camps and fragmentary perspectives. A conversation among them, including a typological inquiry, explores their contributions and limitations, a mutual corrigibility disclosing that they are 'generally right in what they affirmed and wrong in what they denied'. In our narrative framework, a fuller doctrine of revelation emerges as we traverse the path of the story of the divine disclosure. Fuller, but not fullest.

Niebuhr's 'radical monotheism', viewed narratively, tilts the divine sovereignty forwards. What we are given to know of God along the Already time line awaits the Not Yet.

NOTES

1. Salvation now – the present saving work of the Holy Spirit redeems powers as well as persons, and thus entails more than 'subjective soteriology'. Saving grace reaches towards the institutions of history and the processes of nature, as well as to and into believers (see *The Christian Story*, 3rd edn, op.cit., pp. 195–203). The reception phase of biblical disclosure in the narrative of revelation, however, requires a receiver, and hence illumination short of the *eschaton* has to do with believers and believing communities.

2. Francis Martin, *The Feminist Question: Feminist Theology in the Light of Christian Tradition* (Grand Rapids: Eerdmans, 1994), p. 23. On 'the inward illumination of the Spirit', see the Westminster Confession, I, 5, 6 and XIV, 1.

3. John Calvin, *Institutes of the Christian Religion*, vol. 1 (Grand Rapids: Eerdmans, 1957), Book 1, Chapter VII, p. 72.

4. Markus Barth, *The Broken Wall: A Study of the Epistle to the Ephesians* (Valley Forge: Judson Press, 1959), p. 86.

5. Thiselton, *New Horizons in Hermeneutics*, op. cit., p. 618.

6. Anthony Thiselton's map of these and other current hermeneutical theories, *New Horizons in Hermeneutics*, is unsurpassed. See especially the chapter 'The Hermeneneutics of Pastoral Theology', pp. 556–96, for a critical appropriation of existentialist, reader-response and *lecta divina* proposals.

7. Barth, IV/3/1, op. cit., p. 421.

8. Søren Kierkegaard, *Concluding Unscientific Postscript*, op. cit., p. 52.

9. For the discussion of the strengths and weaknesses of gospel song narrative and evangelical foci, see the writer's *Evangelical Faith in Ecumenical Perspective*, op. cit., pp. 123–46.

10. Wells, *No Place for Truth*, op. cit.; McGrath, *Evangelicalism and the Future of Christianity*, op. cit.; Richard Lints, *The Fabric of Theology: A Prolegomenon to Evangelical Theology* (Grand Rapids: Eerdmans, 1993); Os Guinness, *The American Hour: A Time of Reckoning and the Once and Future Role of Faith* (New York: Free Press, 1993); Mark Noll, *The Scandal of the Evangelical Mind* (Grand Rapids: Eerdmans, 1994).

11. Hans Frei, *The Eclipse of Biblical Narrative* (New Haven: Yale University Press, 1974), p. 142.

12. Wolfhart Pannenberg, *Systematic Theology*, vol. 1, trans. Geoffrey W. Bromiley (Grand Rapids: Eerdmans, 1991), p. 44.

13. Thiselton, *New Horizons in Hermeneutics*, op. cit., p. 531.

14. Thiselton, op. cit., p. 579.

15. H. Richard Niebuhr, *The Meaning of Revelation* (New York: Macmillan, 1941).

16. Nurture in the Evangelical Synod of North America that brought together both Reformed and Lutheran traditions was a shaping factor in the theologies of both Niebuhr brothers. On the Reformed influences, see Malcolm Reid, 'H. Richard Niebuhr', in David Wells (ed.), *Reformed Theology in America* (Grand Rapids: Eerdmans, 1985), pp. 280–98, and in the same volume, Gabriel Fackre, 'Reinhold Niebuhr', ibid., pp. 263–79.

17. *The Meaning of Revelation*, op. cit., p. 154.

18. Ibid., pp. 93, 109.

19. Ibid., p. 84.

20. Ibid., pp. 84, 82, 18.

21. William C. Placher, 'The Acts of God: What Do We Mean by Revelation?', *The Christian Century* 113:10 (20–27 March 1996), 340.

22. See Brevard Childs, 'The Canonical Approach and the New Yale Theology', in his *The New Testament as Canon: An Introduction* (London: SCM Press, 1984), p. 541–6; and Julian Hartt, 'Theological Investments in Story: Some Comments on Recent Developments and Some Proposals' and 'Reply to Crites and Hauerwas', in Stanley Hauerwas and L. Gregory Jones (eds), *Why Narrative? Readings in Narrative Theology* (Grand Rapids: Eerdmans, 1989), pp. 279–92, 311–19.

23. On the former, see H. Richard Niebuhr, *Christ and Culture* (New York: Harper and Bros, 1951), pp. 241–9; and on the latter, see *The Meaning of Revelation*, op. cit., p. 17f.

24. Niebuhr, *Christ and Culture*, op. cit., p. 238.

25. Ibid., p. 43.

9

CONSUMMATION: ESCHATOLOGICAL ILLUMINATION

————ᴡᴡᴡ◉ᴡᴡᴡ————

The last chapter of the Christian story is the consummation of the divine purposes, the final reconciliation when God is 'all and in all' (Eph. 4:6). To go from grace to glory in the narrative of reconciliation is also to move from 'insight' to 'sight' – the 'face to face' of the narrative of revelation when we 'know fully, even as [we] have been fully known' (1 Cor. 13:12).

The biblical book with the name of the doctrine under consideration, 'Revelation', is a critical source of Christian judgments about this finale. As befits insight short of the Not Yet, including that of inspired Scripture, the End is seen 'through a glass darkly' (1 Cor. 12:12 KJV). What will be *transparent* on the Great Day is now still *translucent*. But the stained-glass windows of the book of Revelation do let in the final light, distributing it in the shapes and colours of the Spirit's own artistry. We look to these penultimate portrayals for light on the fulfilment of both reconciliation and revelation.

RECONCILIATION

A fuller account of the Christian vision of the End would take us to four great 'last things', the creedal summary of the eschatological refrains of Scripture: the resurrection of the dead, the return of Christ, the last judgment and everlasting life.[1] As the focus of this chapter is on the finale of revelation, only the last 'stained-glass window' will be under scrutiny: 'everlasting life' in its rich and diverse expression in the book of Revelation. So we return to the visions of Chapter 1 with the divine intention for creation, the hope of Things to Come now assured by the deeds done in the narrative of reconciliation.

The coming of final *reconciliation* means the overcoming of all the alienations brought by the fall, and thus peace with God and in all creation – the life together of nature, human nature and supernature.

NATURE

'Then I saw a new heaven and a new earth' (Rev. 21:1). Nature is made new. The raging seas are 'no more' (Rev. 21:1), and from the throne of God flows 'the river of the water of life' (Rev. 22:1). The 'tree of life' grows at the riverside, rich 'with its twelve kinds of fruits' (Rev. 22:2). Nature shares in the redemption of history as the minerals of the earth find their home in the City of God – jasper, sapphire, onyx, agate, emerald, pure gold (Rev. 21:19–21), and 'the leaves of the tree are for the healing of the nations' (Rev. 22:2).

As nature is healed within itself, so is its rift with its Creator. It joins with all of its restored partners in creation in the praise of God:

> Then I heard every creature in heaven and on earth and under the earth and in the sea, and all that is in them, singing, 'To the one seated on the throne and to the Lamb be blessing and honour and glory and might forever and ever!' And the four living creatures said, 'Amen! . . .' (Rev. 5:13–14)

The reconciliation of nature envisaged in Revelation is anticipated throughout Scripture, as in the witness of the Isaianic corpus that speaks of the time when 'the wolf shall live with the lamb, the leopard lie down with the kid' (Isaiah 11:6). And again, 'Instead of the thorn shall come up the cypress; instead of the brier shall come up the myrtle' (Isaiah 55:13) – nature reconciled with nature; when 'the nursing child shall play over the hole of the asp, and the weaned child shall put its hand on the adder's den' (Isaiah 11:8) – nature reconciled with human nature; 'the mountains and the hills before you shall burst into song, and all the trees of the field shall clap their hands' (Isaiah 55:12) – nature reconciled to God. In the End, nature will no longer groan in travail (Rom. 8:22), but be born anew.

HUMAN NATURE

Reconciliation of sinners to God, won in Christ and received *in via* by grace through faith, reaches its home in everlasting life *together*, when God

> will dwell with them as their God; they will be his peoples, and God himself will be with them; he will wipe away every tear from their eyes. Death will be no more; mourning and crying and pain will be no more; for the first things have passed away. (Rev. 21:3–4)

With tears so wiped away, the move from grace to glory means that the 'pure in heart . . . shall see God' (Matt 5:8).

As in the Sermon on the Mount, and Paul's Corinthian visual imagery (partial to full), and elsewhere from 'faith to sight', the portrayal in the book of Revelation of the final reconciliation of human beings – with God, with one another and with all creation – is couched in the language of sight, thus merging eternal 'life' with eternal 'light'. The tradition of 'visio Dei' continues this fusion. Thus the final reconciliation of, and revelation to, persons will be treated together, reserved for the succeeding section on the latter subject.

SUPERNATURE

In the End, the angels too gather with their partners in creation before their Creator and Redeemer, falling 'on their faces before the throne . . . singing "Amen! Blessing and glory and wisdom and thanksgiving and honour and power and might be to our God forever and ever! Amen"' (Rev. 7:11–12). The Powers and Principalities of this world are brought into the throne room of reconciliation. Here they do the bidding of God, as the messengers they are called to be, now at the consummation, calling out to the world, 'Come gather for the great supper of God!' (Rev. 19:17).

REVELATION

All the foregoing are clues to the *content* of the consummated narrative of revelation, given now in the translucencies of Scripture's final vision. The doctrine of revelation that we are tracing has to do with the *way* of the Holy Spirit's work in communicating that substance. As revelation is disclosure *pro nobis*, we return to the light imagery used

215

in Scripture to describe our human participation in both reconciliation and revelation. When the final Day comes, the Light of God will
shine: 'And there will be no more night; they need no light of lamp or
sun, for the Lord will be their light' (Rev. 22:5). Things only dimly
seen by the earthly eye of faith will come clear in the heavenly radiance anticipated in apocalyptic vision:

> At once I was in the spirit, and there in heaven stood a throne,
> with one seated on the throne! And the one seated there looks
> like jasper and carnelian and around the throne is a rainbow that
> looks like emerald . . . Then I saw . . . Then I saw . . . Then I
> looked . . . Then I saw . . . (Rev. 4:2–3; 5:1, 6, 11)

Thus the rainbow sign reappears, before in promise, now in fulfilment.

So the unveiling to the eye of eschatological sight of . . . God. The
promise is kept that 'the pure in heart . . . will see God' (Matt. 5:8).
Revelatory consummation means that 'his servants will worship him;
they will see his face' (Rev. 22:3). Seeing 'face to face' (1 Cor. 13:12)
is the longed-for *visio Dei*. The transparency of the Persons to one
another in the triune Life takes derivative form in this eschatological
meeting. Whatever else the 'I–Thou' relation means on the human
plane pales by comparison to this vision of God.

Seeing the Light enables the worshipper to see *by* the Light. The
God of the ultimate Future is the God whose Kingdom has come.
The seer discerns the fulfilment of the world's life together brought to
be out of the purposes of the Divine Life Together:

> the holy city Jerusalem coming down out of heaven from God.
> It has the glory of God and a radiance like a rare jewel, like jasper
> clear as crystal. (Rev. 21:10–11)

Again the promise fulfilled: the breaking of swords into ploughshares
and spears into pruning hooks has come to be and is seen to come to
be, a seeing of the former enemy as friend, of the unseen victim as
brother and sister in the new commonwealth of God:

> The nations will walk by its light, and the kings of the earth will
> bring their glory into it. Its gates will never be shut by day – and
> there will be no night there. People will bring into it the glory
> and the honour of the nations. (Rev. 21:24–6)

The whole cosmos – 'angels' and 'elders' . . . 'every creature in
heaven and on earth and under the earth and in the sea, and all that is
in them' – *see* the Light, and *see in* the Light the One on the throne,

singing, 'To the one on the throne and to the Lamb be blessing and honour and glory and might forever and ever!' (Rev. 5:11, 13)

ESCHATOLOGICAL ADVOCACIES

As each previous chapter in the narrative is the occasion for a doctrine of revelation conceived essentially in its terms, so, too, this last chapter has its advocates. For some, the final glory itself is the *only* locus of 'the knowledge of God'.

> Knowledge of God as a kind of seeing may well describe that eschatological moment when 'we know even as we are known', but, Paul's talk of obscure sight and partial knowing notwithstanding, our current situation would better be described by non-ocular images.[2]

Ronald Thiemann presses the distinction between faith and sight, arguing that short of the consummation there is no 'knowing as seeing'. He associates standard claims to the knowledge of God in the narrative of revelation this side of the End with that inordinate claim. Ocular images have given expression to, and thus fortified, these traditional notions of revelation now difficult to maintain 'under the changed cultural and intellectual conditions of modernity'.[3] What is required is the preservation of the biblical assertion of God's 'prevenience', but cast in new revelatory terms.

Thiemann makes a case for reconceiving revelation as 'narrated promise'. Scripture and historic Christian faith have to do with narratives that disclose 'God's identity'. In that depiction, centred on the resurrection of Jesus from the dead, God makes promises that have yet to be fulfilled. We are therefore *in via* and cannot know the outcome, living by faith not sight.

> Ordinarily a doctrine of revelation is understood as an investigation of God's knowability. That definition encourages a conception of the doctrine as an inquiry into the conditions of the possibility that God can be known, i.e., as a foundational transcendental inquiry. In order to guard against this view but to maintain some continuity with a traditional understanding of revelation I suggest the following alternate formulation. *A doctrine of revelation is an account of God's identifiability* . . . The Christian claim to revelation asserts that God is identifiable 1) within the narrative as Yahweh who raised Jesus from the dead, 2) through the narrative

as the God of promise who in addressing his promise to the reader is recognizable as *pro nobis* and *extra nos*, and 3) beyond the narrative as the one who, faithful to his promises, will fulfill his pledge to those whom he loves.[4]

This reintepretation of the doctrine of revelation, therefore, makes no claim to *knowing*, choosing instead to speak of 'faith' and 'hope' based on the trustworthiness of the God identified in the narrative and the arguable coherence of the 'web of belief', a view that does not assert

> a claim either to God's epistemological priority or to God's temporal priority to Christian faith . . . It seeks rather to establish that God's reality (and thus his 'ontological priority') is implied by a set of concrete Christian beliefs concerning God's identity. Revelation in this view is not simply a temporally prior event to which faith is a response. Revelation is the continuing reality of God's active presence among his people. Since it is a reality 'not seen' and not fully experienced, it must be expressed by a confession of faith, i.e., an 'assurance of things hoped for, a conviction of things not seen' . . . But that is nothing more than to say that the God identified in the biblical narrative is trustworthy, i.e., that those to whom he issues his promises trust him and wait in the expectant hope of fulfillment . . . The justifiabilty of one's faith and hope in the trustworthiness of a promiser is never fully confirmed (or disconfirmed) until the promiser actually fulfills (or fails to fulfill) his/her promises. Until the moment of fulfillment the recipient must justify faith and hope on the basis of a judgment concerning the character of the promiser . . . Consequently we live in a situation in which there can be no indubitable foundation for knowledge and thus in which both belief and refusal to believe can appear to be justified.[5]

While Thiemann represents with clarity the focus on the last revelatory chapter, and does so from within a narrative framework kindred in some respects to this work,[6] the major twentieth-century theologians of 'hope' and 'the future', Jürgen Moltmann and Wolfhart Pannenberg, strike similar notes on the eschatology of revelation. Pannenberg has spent a lifetime exploring the doctrine of revelation within an eschatological framework, although his focus has been on 'revelation as history'. His qualification of knowledge-claims short of the End is parallel in some respects to that of Thiemann, but also different with respect to the present role of a universal rationality.

> As the revelation of God in his historical action moves toward the still outstanding future of the consummation of history, its claim to reveal the one God who is the world's Creator, Reconciler and Redeemer is open to future verification in history, which is yet incomplete, and which is still exposed, therefore to the question of its truth . . . Personal assurance of faith always needs confirmation by experience and reflection . . . In this regard we should not think it strange if epistemologically the statements of dogmatics and the theses of the Christian doctrine it presents are given the status of hypotheses . . . Dogmatics may not presuppose the divine truth which the Christian doctrinal tradition claims. Theology . . . must treat it as an open question and not decide it in advance . . . Even the question of God's reality, of his existence in view of his debatability in the world as atheistic criticism in particular articulates it, can find a final answer only in the event of eschatological world renewal . . .[7]

Here too, revelation as indubitable disclosure awaits the End. However, in contrast to Thiemann, in the time between the times, the pre-eschatolgical revelatory claims of Christian faith and teaching are formally subject to either confirmation or disconfirmation by public standards of evidence and reason. While holding that there is 'no position-neutral point of view from which one can evaluate competing positions',[8] Thiemann does avoid charges of fideism by modest arguments for the plausibility of Christian assertions.

KNOWING IN PART AND IN FULL

A narrative of revelation that culminates in a chapter in which 'the city has no need of sun or moon to shine on it, for the glory of God is its light . . .' (Rev. 21:23) calls into question all premature closures. Eschatological views of revelation bear a critical witness to foreshortenings of the Story. Bracketing for a moment whether and to what degree public warrants for the Christian claims can be adduced short of the End, Thiemann's essay on revelation, and Pannenberg's sweeping eschatological rereading of the Christian doctrine, are necessary witnesses to this final phase of the revelation drama. In the narrative of revelation under consideration, they are right in what they affirm: revelation in its fullest sense is reserved for Last Things – when the Kingdom comes and God's will and way are done and seen by all.

Throughout this work, attention has been given to the role of ecclesial and related theological traditions in the shaping of perspectives on revelation – the Reformed perspective in Barth's view of the christological chapter, the Roman Catholic tradition in the chapter of the ecclesial illumination, the evangelical tradition in matters of inspiration. The eschatological accent as here articulated by Thiemann and Pannenberg may be related to a feature of their common Lutheran tradition.[9] The centrality of justification by a radical act of faith – faith as *the trust of the heart* – lived out in Martin Luther's paradigmatic encounter, and graphically expressed in Kierkegaard's figure of the believer as treading water over '70,000 fathoms',[10] is worlds away from forms of piety and theology that suggest a serene stroll with Jesus in the garden. Faith is a journey fraught with fear and trembling, all human securities taken away, with grace alone, faith alone, Christ alone the companions. On this journey we are never there until the End, always *simul iustus et peccator*.

Eschatological epistemologies like those of Thiemann and Pannenberg are not known for their Kierkegaardian *angst*, indeed, are notable for the subtlety and nuance of left-brain argument. However, both reflect the accent on faith short of its ultimate homecoming, and thus epistemologically understood as *trust* not 'sight', as the risk and insecurity of a revelatory Not Yet. For all the intimations and provisional validations, we wait 'in hope' for eschatological verification.

While not directly posing the issue as a Lutheran-Reformed controversy, it is interesting that both Thiemann and Pannenberg give major critical attention to prominent Reformed theologians. Thiemann contests Calvin's 'foundationalist' and Thomas Torrance's intuitive confidences, and Pannenberg questions Barth's 'subjectivist' certainties. These are natural targets, for classical Reformed teaching is quite definite about knowledge-claims being integral to faith. Thus the Heidelberg Catechism defines 'true faith' (Question 61) as 'a *certain knowledge* [my italics] by which I accept as true all that God has revealed to us [and] a wholehearted trust which the Holy Spirit creates in me through the gospel'.[11]

As the Lutheran *finitum capax infiniti* corrects the reductionist tendencies of the Reformed *finitum non capax infiniti* in Barth's reading of the christological chapter of the revelation narrative, so the Reformed accent on 'knowledge' must challenge any non-cognitive or eschatologically precognitive understandings of faith. In this respect, the Reformed premise joins a long tradition of classical theology which links *notitia* to *fiducia* and *assensus* as the ingredients of faith: the knowledge of the mind, the trust of the heart and the assent of the will.

Revelation, as true assertions about states of affairs, divine and human, is a gift of knowledge given to humans by the Holy Spirit. Short of the final chapter of the Story, it is knowledge *in part*: 'we know only in part' (1 Cor. 13:9). Its *fullness* awaits the Finale: 'when the complete comes, the partial will end' (1 Cor. 13:10). About this knowledge, in all its incompleteness, we can have certitude – 'assurance' – a claim which is of a different order from either 'hope' or 'hypotheses'. Thus there is a certain irony in Thiemann's citation of the confidence of the writer of the epistle to the Hebrews – the '*assurance* of things hoped for' – for the word used in the context of Chapter 11 means more than 'hope' as possibility and desire – the point of its juxtaposition to 'things hoped for'. It is a gift of trust in the 'word of God' and a faith by which 'we understand that the worlds were prepared by the word of God' (Hebrews 11:3). Pannenberg also appears to make assertions inconsistent with his major premise of Christian truth-claims as 'hypotheses' awaiting eschatological confirmation, by speaking of our adherence to them as 'provisionally made in human hearts by the convicting ministry of the Spirit of God'.[12] How, in Christian faith, is 'the Spirit of God' not 'the Spirit of Truth who comes from the Father' (John 15:26, also 14:17, 16:13)? Unless the Holy Spirit is thought to be other than the Author of truth (the source of a disconfirmable hypothesis), a conviction born of the third Person of the Trinity must be trustworthy knowledge. Cast in terms of the Reformed category earlier seen to have its own reductionist flaws, but here making its valid witness, conviction of truth this side of the End is a gift of 'sure and certain knowledge' given by 'the internal testimony of the Holy Spirit'.

The epistemological modesties counselled by both Thiemann and Pannenberg appear to be related as well to the weight given to culture in the understanding and formulation of Christian faith. Thiemann's project is based on the assumption that the crisis of revelation has occurred 'within a cultural context decisively marked by radical pluralism'.[13] Thus, faith's plausibility must be articulated in the range of current modern and postmodern premises, while at the same time not allowing them to adjudicate Christian assertions. Pannenberg, while acknowledging the Spirit's role in personal conviction and the finality of eschatological validation, wants to make the case for revelation before the bar of universal reason itself. Does culture, particular or universal, here exercise too quick a veto over Christian truth-claims? The covenant with Noah is the revelatory warrant for relating Christian faith to culture. Yet the christological centre of the Story makes us wary of control by its questions or its categories. While they are in the very different context of debates about religious pluralism, Mark Heim's comments on the cultural sources of John Hick's epistemology are germane to any sharp distinctions between faith and knowledge:

> Hick stresses the gap between subject and object in knowing which has marked Western philosophy. The Real is an instance of this general principle. Hick enthusiastically pursues Kant's move to sacrifice knowledge to make way for faith.[14]

The role of ecumenical correction of important but not to be inflated contributions to the narrative of revelation is not limited in eschatology to the Reformed–Lutheran exchange. Roman Catholic and evangelical testimony to the *presence* of the Future is also germane. While the temptation to collapse the Not Yet into the Now or the Then has plagued traditional Roman Catholic ecclesiology (the church as the Kingdom of God) and evangelical epistemology and soteriology (the Bible as the inerrant and univocal christological or eschatological Word, or the born-again experience as entry into the saint-and-no-sinner status of the Not Yet), both traditions make their witness to the *continuities* along the line of God's past and present deeds and disclosures towards the ultimate Future. Yes, *discontinuities* that preserve the integrity of the full Light of the final Day, and thus the critical role of defenders of this chapter of the Story. No, the Light of the Future is present in the rainbow sign of Noah, the pillar of fire that led Israel, the dawn of Easter morning, the lamp of Scripture given to prophet and apostle, the descending pentecostal flames that illuminate the church and the believer, as well as the meridian sun of the last Day. And it must be said that while Lutheran restraint about knowledge-claims is here to the fore, other Lutheran commitments do give grounds for asserting the epistemological presence of the Future, not the least of which is the Lutheran *finitum capax infiniti* earlier discussed. Why should not the *real Presence* of Christ in the eucharist have its counterpart in the *real presence* of the knowledge of God in the church and the believer? Subject to the broken conditions of sin and finitude, but in both cases the presence and power of a saving and knowing grace 'in, with and under' all the ambiguities of its media.[15] Indeed, in the *Small Catechism*, Luther ends the statement and exposition of each article of the Apostles' Creed with just that assurance: 'This is most certainly true'.[16]

CONCLUSION

The last chapter of the narrative of reconciliation is the final phase of the narrative of revelation. Here, *illumination* is entire, a Day with a cloudless sky, error and ignorance as well as sin having passed away. 'Then I will know fully, even as I have been fully known' (1 Cor. 13:12). The light- and sight-imagery of Scripture are themselves only broken metaphors of this ultimate radiance and disclosure.

We are in the debt of the stewards of this chapter of the Story, who remind us ever and again of the shortfall of all revelatory claims in this world. They are right in what they assert – the singular clarity of the eschatological 'eye of sight'. They are, however, wrong when they deny the cognitive trustworthiness of the 'eye of faith'. Opened by the power of the Holy Spirit all along the revelatory pilgrimage – from the common grace of preservation to the particular grace of Israel's election and the Word's incarnation and the appropriating grace of inspiration and illumination – the eye of faith is given the Light it needs to make its way to the final moment of truth. So the story of both reconciliation and revelation moves from *grace* to *glory*.

> My God! how wonderful Thou art, Thy majesty how bright! . . .
> How wonderful, how beautiful the sight of Thee must be,
> Thine endless wisdom, boundless pow'r, and awful purity! . . .
> My God, how wonderful Thou art,
> Thou everlasting Friend
> On Thee I stay my trusting heart,
> Till faith in vision end.[17]

NOTES

1. See *The Christian Story*, vol. 1, op. cit., pp. 210–48.
2. Thiemann, *Revelation and Theology*, op. cit., p. 153.
3. Ibid., p. 153.
4. Ibid., p. 153.
5. Ibid., pp. 80, 154, 155.
6. As when Thiemann speaks of the *macro*-narrative of God's prevenience, the 'relatively stable background belief within Christian practice' embedded in the eucharistic prayer that moves from creation to consummation. Ibid., pp. 99–103.
7. Wolfhart Pannenberg, *Systematic Theology*, vol. 1, trans. Geoffrey W. Bromiley (Grand Rapids: Eerdmans, 1991), pp. 257, 56, 447.
8. Thiemann, *Revelation and Theology*, op. cit., p. 155.
9. For other evidence of the relation of eschatology to the Lutheran

tradition, see Ted Peters, *God – The World's Future: Systematic Theology for a Post-Modern Era* (Minneapolis: Fortress Press, 1992).

10. Kierkegaard, *Concluding Unscientific Postscript*, op. cit., p. 204.

11. *The Heidelberg Catechism*, trans. Allen O. Miller and Eugene Osterhaven (New York: United Church Press, 1962), p. 27.

12. Pannenberg, *Systematic Theology*, vol. 1, op. cit. p. 56.

13. Thiemann, *Revelation and Theology*, op. cit., p. 5.

14. S. Mark Heim, *Salvations: Truth and Difference in Religion* (Maryknoll, NY: Orbis Books, 1995), p. 24.

15. Is the 'evangelical catholic' voice within Lutheranism – one that stresses the continuities between Christ and the church catholic, including the importance of apostolic ordination, teaching office and received dogma – the assertion of the *finitum capax infiniti* aspect of the Lutheran heritage against the tendency within the same tradition to accent the ambiguities of the *simul iustus et peccator* that find their way from subjective soteriology into epistemology, and thus imperil Christian identity? See especially the writings of Robert Jenson, most recently *Unbaptized God: The Basic Flaw in Ecumenical Theology* (Minneapolis: Fortress, 1992) in which the Roman Catholic Church itself is seen to depart from its own premises, needing the 'drastic Christology intended by both Alexandria and original Lutheranism' (ibid., p. 131).

16. M. Reu, *An Explanation of Dr. Martin Luther's Small Catechism* (Columbus, OH: Wartburg Press, 1947), pp. 89, 101, 118.

17. Frederick William Faber, 'My God! How Wonderful Thou Art', verses 1, 3, 7.

Epilogue

GOD:
THE REVEALER REVEALED

—˄˄˄ʀʀ℗ʀʀ˄˄˄—

Only when the story is over and the book put down do we know what the writer wants us to know about its characters. Their identity is depicted in their doing, fully disclosed when the narrative has run its course. In a narrative interpretation of revelation, the doctrine of God belongs, therefore, at the End. Who God is is disclosed in what God does. In Christian faith, the being of God is known from the divine economy, the immanent Trinity inseparable from the economic Trinity. Hence this Epilogue at the close of the economy of revelation.

In a full-scale work in narrative systematics, the Epilogue would strive to identify the attributes of God manifest in the economy of reconciliation: the 'formal qualities' of transcendence and immanence, eternity, aseity, subjectivity, all-sufficiency (omnipotence, omniscience, omnipresence), and the 'material qualities' of holiness and love, right-eousness and compassion. And most of all, in the Christian story, the doctrine of God will deal with the inner nature of God – the divine triunity – that expresses itself in the attributes. To return to earlier def-initions and distinctions, the nature and attributes of Deity are the *who* and *what* of the matter. As this volume is a prolegomenon to detailed systematic inquiry about the doctrines of Christian faith – the standard *loci* or, as we have described them here, the *chapters* in an overarching Story – the *why* and *where* have been to the fore, theological *method*, rather than the theological *content* of the doctrines. Thus the Epilogue must confine itself to the prolegomenal status of this inquiry and speak only of a final *that*, not the detailed *who* and *what* fitting for full-scale investigation of the locus on the doctrine of God. Another volume in this series is designed for that purpose.

What is appropriate for this Epilogue, however, is a summary comment on the doctrine of revelation. Viewed from the vantage point of the journey traversed, the Christian doctrine of revelation affirms that the triune God by a common grace gives sustaining glimpses of the divine purpose, and by anticipatory action in Israel and definitive incarnation in Jesus Christ discloses who God is and what God wills, as communicated to us by inspired Scripture appropriated by an illumined church and believer, and revealed in its full glory at the End.

The reader of this work will remember that we began with a Prologue on the doctrine of Trinity. And, throughout the telling of the revelatory tale, assumptions and references have been made to christological and other doctrinal content integral to the narrative of reconciliation. So the hermeneutical circularity of Christian theology: attention to any one locus will lead to, and presuppose, aspects of all the others. This locus on revelation and authority required those kinds of tangents and premises, suggestive but not exhaustive. In the case of the doctrine of God that meant a trinitarian prologue in the 'order of being' to launch the narrative in the order of doing and knowing. Of such is the asymmetry in theological work in this world.

The Epilogue is also the occasion for the prayerful word of eschatological reserve appropriate to any Christian doctrine of revelation. For all the grace of revelation given, short of the final light of Day, we both exult and confess with Paul:

> O depth of the riches and wisdom and knowledge of God! How unsearchable are his judgments and how inscrutable his ways!
>
> 'For who has known the mind of the Lord?
> Or who has been his counsellor?'
>
> ... For from him and through him and to him are all things. To him be the glory forever. Amen. (Romans 11:33–4, 36)

INDEX